What to Read

Also by Mickey Pearlman

AUTHOR

Listen to Their Voices: 20 Interviews with Women Who Write

COAUTHOR

A Voice of One's Own: Conversations with America's Writing
Women (with Katherine Usher Henderson)

Tillie Olsen (with Abby H. P. Werlock)

EDITOR

American Women Writing Fiction: Memory,
Identity, Family, Space

Mother Puzzles: Daughters and Mothers in
Contemporary American Literature

The Anna Book: Searching for Anna in Literary History

Canadian Women Writing Fiction

Between Friends: Writing Women Celebrate Friendship

A Place Called Home: Twenty Writing Women Remember

A Few Thousand Words About Love

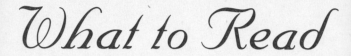

What to Read

The Essential Guide

for Reading Group Members

and Other Book Lovers

Revised and Updated

MICKEY PEARLMAN, PH.D.

HarperPerennial

A Division of HarperCollins*Publishers*

HarperCollins books may be purchased for educational,
business, or sales promotional use. For information please
write: Special Markets Department, HarperCollins Publishers, Inc., 10 East 53rd Street, New York, NY 10022.

FIRST EDITION

Designed by Elina D. Nudelman

Library of Congress Cataloging-in-Publication Data

Pearlman, Mickey
    What to read / Mickey Pearlman.—Rev. ed., 1st ed.
      p.   cm.
    "The essential guide for reading group members and
other book lovers."
    ISBN 0-06-095313-6
    1. Best books—United States—Bibliography.
2. Group reading—United States.   I. Title.
Z1035.9.P4   1999   98-53037
015.73'073—dc21

03 ❖/ RRD 10 9 8 7 6 5 4

This edition of *What to Read* is for:

Mia Pearlman, superreader and best friend, and for the grown-up children of my Thanksgiving family:

Ted and Betsy Pearlman, Jill and Gary Heiman, Bill Glaser (M's F), Gayle Shomer, Rafi and Simone Laufer, Brooke and Adam Hirschfelder, Rob Mank, Sophie Schlondorff, Mandy Wilson, Roger Norum, Suresh Bashet, Josh and Michael Rayfield, Jessica, Lenny, and Eric Appleman, and for my grandnieces, Carli Marisa and Paige Eliza Heiman.

And in memory of Jamie O'Hagan, the wonderful son of my friends Christine and Patrick O'Hagan.

Contents

Acknowledgments

Continued and sincere thanks to all who were cited in the first edition of *What to Read*. I am grateful for your expertise in various subject areas and for your willingness to share it.

I would like to acknowledge particularly the continued technical support of the B.L.s (Beloved Librarians) in my small-town but extremely professional library. They know their stuff, and watching them access information quickly and efficiently from seemingly complicated systems continues to thrill this person from a generation that evolved from fetal matter before computers, E-mail, fax machines, and the Internet. They are: Marie Brady, Brian Cazanave, Gloria Hand, Michele Lynam, Loretta Martinotti, Rob Pawson, Sharon Rahim, Peggy Wylie, *and particularly Sherri Kendrick and Michele ("with one l") Skowronski*, the resource librarians. As with the first edition, they made the interlibrary loan system scream for mercy, and, on my behalf, showed none. And, yes, I now understand Option, Full, and How to Access by Subject.

Thanks too for the emotional support of my friends at the Split Rock Arts Program in Minnesota: Phyllis Campbell, Andy Gilats, Vivian Oja, and Carole Schweiger; to the "Duluth 9," my students in a course on "The Art of the Interview" ("Write It Down!"), and the "Duluth 10," who were part of a week on "Publishing the Non-fiction Book" ("Suck It Up and Get Over It"). I appreciate the constant, important, sustaining encouragement of the members of both my New Jersey and New York City book clubs, my friends at the Porch Table in Boston, and Michelle Woodruff and Nina Smiley at Mohonk Mountain House, where I run the November weekend called "A Celebration of Readers and Their Favorite Books." I love my E-mail and actually know how to use it, thanks to my son, Ted, and I rely on my E-mail writer/editor buddies: Dennis McFarland, Brian Hall, Katharine Weber, Reagan Arthur, Carol Houck Smith, Angela Davis-Gardner, Linda Pritchett, Sandy Benítez, Jim Kondrick, Sylvia Watanabe, Margot Livesey, Abby Werlock, Martha Coventry, Christine O'Hagan, Lois Lowry, and many others to reestablish normalcy and promote mental health whenever possible.

Thanks too to my extraordinarily patient agent, Vicky Bijur, to the many people in bookstores across the country (especially Bibelot in Baltimore and Flo Wetzel at Barnes & Noble in Edgewater, New Jersey) who have helped me sell it, and to all the many readers who have sent suggestions and compliments. Every writer works in an empty room and these letters have filled it up with joy.

A Note to the Reader

For the last several years I have often been on the road, either talking and listening to writing women—from Jane Smiley and Joyce Carol Oates to Sandy Benítez and Sylvia Watanabe—or speaking at bookstores about the two collections of interviews, *A Voice of One's Own* and *Listen to Their Voices,* for which these conversations were designed. (Of course, as anyone who has been on the road knows, you can only eat so many unidentifiable "flat breaded things," deal with time in a sardine can [formerly known as an airplane], sit for hours in a noisy zoo [formerly known as an airport], or function, in unfamiliar places, without the comfort of established relationships.) That's probably why I also recently edited two collections of memoirs, not coincidentally called *A Place Called Home* and *A Few Thousand Words About Love.*

As I related in the first edition of *What to Read,* a peculiar phenomenon emerged from these visits to bookstores and from my engagements as a speaker or writer-in-residence at various colleges. Each time I mentioned that I had been running a "book club" for several years, and that I had an extensive reading list on computer disk, some shy student or book buyer would approach the lectern and ask quietly if I would mind printing out my reading list so their well-established or newly forming reading group could use it.

This is what writers call a book idea waiting to happen, and what grew from those conversations five years ago was the first edition of *What to Read*. You are holding the second edition in your hands now, with additions and revisions to each of the original thirty-three lists, and the addition of many new ones, including "What An Adventure!," "Watch Your Mouth" (about food), "Keep It Short" (collections of short stories), etc., for essentially a total of forty-two lists. As in the first edition, I have tried hard to be inclusive—paying some attention, for example, to ethnicity, i.e., "Mi Vida Latina"; to religion, "A Jewish View"; and to race: "African-American Images," "An Asian Ethos," and "Native American Ideas." (But of course all works by writers of Asian, African, or Native American heritage, or of the Jewish faith, are *not* listed only on those lists—*nor should they be*.) "Gay Writes," a list where writing men and women address the issue of sexuality in fiction and non-fiction, exists to serve a large and growing audience for books by gay men and lesbians, but it should go without saying that people of all sexual persuasions exist on every list.

Geography seemed important to me in 1994, since many writers are inspired by place and community, and "Go West," "Southern Comfort," and "New York Stories" spoke to that phenomenon. This subject still compells me, so I have added "My Kind of Place," where setting prevails almost as a character. In spite of ubiquitous shopping centers, all of which seem to look alike and underscore the idea of *sameness*, and all those cloned and usually odious fast-food restaurants, anyone who travels a lot—even at the end of this century—is struck finally by the reality of regional *differences* in food, angle of vision, energy levels, and spiritual bent. Trust me on this one; I've had lutefisk in Minnesota, étoufée in New Orleans, bean sprouts on everything but the ice cream in Colorado, and salmonburgers in the Pacific Northwest. We have not yet, thankfully, been completely homogenized in food or in philosophy. And I am not just whistling "Dixie" on this one.

I have tried to be mindful of those preferences shared by readers, like the thousands of mystery novel devotees. Some excellent books appear on the two revised lists (by men and by women) called "It's a Mystery to *Me,*" the two updated lists called "One to Beam Up, Mr. Scott," compiled for the prospective or already enthusiastic science fiction reader, and on the revamped "War Is Hell . . . Continued."

Since a book of lists inevitably reflects the taste and interests of the writer, and since I seem to be outliving many of the trees I have loved (they are wood pulp), I've expanded the list called "Save the Planet," largely books about the physical environment in the United States.

There are no lists on "How to Succeed in Business Even While Trying Very Hard," which interests me not at all, but "Be a Sport" (for the armchair or actual athletes among us) does reflect one of my own long-standing enthusiasms. I admit that for me the word "sports" always means baseball, so in this edition I have indulged myself and included a list called (of course) "Who's on First?" Since I never tire of fairy tales, and myths, and nursery stories, I have retained "Fairy Tales for Grown-ups," combined the former list called "la, la, la, It's Magic" with "Questioning the Miraculous," and added an entirely new list called "More Fairy Tale Time"—sojourns into the magical and mythical. Although I have not developed any interest in devising lists on fashion, self-help, or technology, I and many people I know have been touched by what seems on some days to be an avalanche of cancer cases, and too many subsequent trips to the oncologist and the radiologist. My way of dealing with all this sadness was to include a new list called "Think About Health" to accompany "The Impact of Illness," which has been revised and updated. (Dealing with so much illness probably also inspired the new lists called "Life Is (Definitely Not) a Bowl of

Cherries" and "Ain't Love Grand?; Pass the Aspirins.") If you wish to pursue books on health and/or illness and you are *not* familiar with these valuable references, ask your librarian to introduce you to *Books in Print*, *Forthcoming Books in Print*, and *Paperback Books in Print*. While you are at it, get acquainted with *Book Review Index* and *Book Review Digest*, which will help you create better discussions at book club meetings.

Since I hope *What to Read* will also serve the parents, aunts, and godfathers who are buying books for children, I've enlarged the list now called "Stop Kidding Around" and described classics and newer books on two lists, one for younger and one for older children. There are now so many good books in print for these age groups that children's departments (17,000 choices in a Nashua, New Hampshire, Barnes & Noble alone) threaten to overtake the entire establishment, and many chains have separate stores. (And by the way, children's reading clubs are starting to appear in after-school programs and in bookstores across the country, and recent surveys report that sales of children's books have more than doubled in the last few years.) All book lovers hope these efforts will help children in our MTV/Nintendo/Internet world become good readers, and that they will lighten the burden on teachers—who are now responsible for everything from breakfast and nutrition, AIDS and sex education, to gun control and weapon removal on the playground. (They could use the help.)

As the editor of three collections of memoirs, I would of course urge any book club to read widely in this area and to this end two lists called "Let's Talk About *Me*" now exist: one about the lives of women, one evoking the experiences of men. Biographies of writers are described in "The Writer's Life" (an entirely new list). Many of these writers seem obsessed by failed family relationships, and problems with sexuality and obsessions of varying kinds. More family issues emerge in "Family Feuds," so many, in fact, that a new list, "My Family, Myself," was necessary. What seems to be everyone's fascination is explored further in "Mothers and Daughters," and on an accompanying list, "Fathers, Sons, and Brothers." Both could have been tripled in length had there been space to do it.

I hope you will keep this guide in your briefcase or book bag when you visit your local library or bookstore, and that you will use it when your book club is deciding what to read. And remember what Isaac Asimov said: "Thinking is the activity I love best, and writing to me is simply thinking through my fingers." Reading saves those thoughts, and cradles them in the safety of your own welcoming hands.

Mickey Pearlman, Ph.D.

Introduction

So you thought that patchwork quilts, block parties, doubleheaders, Monday Night football, Thanksgiving dinners, Rose Bowl parades, and rodeos were American phenomena. And so they are. But add to this list one of America's best and most productive creations—the reading group.

Book or reading clubs have been going strong since some tired white women finally sat down in Charlestown, Massachusetts, around 1813 to read nonfiction. According to Pat Neblett, author of *Circles of Sisterhood: A Book Discussion Guide for Women of Color,* "the first known black women's discussion group [was] the Female and Literary Society, founded in Philadelphia in 1831." (The first black male group, the Reading Room Society, was founded in 1828.) But reading clubs really got going when in 1878 the Chautauqua Literary and Scientific Circle, part of the Baptist-affiliated cultural center in western New York State, was organized to send out books—*A Short History of the English People*, *Fourteen Weeks in Human Physiology*, *Merivale's General History of Rome*, *Cyrus the Great and Alexander the Great,* and *Walks and Talks in the Geological Field*—to readers, who were often isolated on farms and in rural places. According to Willam Zinsser in *American Places*, those members (over

8,400 people in the Chautauqua Circle's first year) would read together in small, hometown discussion groups, and those who completed the four-year course would descend on Chautauqua for a summer graduation ceremony. "Within a decade enrollment had reached 100,000, and by 1914 the program had enlisted half a million members in 12,000 circles in every state and had graduated almost 49,000." Most circles formed in towns of 3,500 people or fewer, mainly in Pennsylvania, Ohio, New York, Iowa, and Illinois, but, says Zinsser, "lively groups also sprang up in big cities such as New York, Brooklyn, Philadelphia and Chicago." Sometimes the members (most of whom were women) met "in a Methodist, Presbyterian, Baptist or Episcopalian church; denominational ties were encouraged. . . . They were hungry for the education they hadn't been able to obtain, and some of the most poignant mementos in the club's archives are letters from farm wives, explaining that they had been too busy with their chores to finish the assignment on time."

The Great Books Foundation, a concept promoted by Robert Maynard Hutchins and Mortimer Adler, both of the University of Chicago, was launched in 1947. They published inexpensive editions of selected books—Plato, Rousseau, Shakespeare, Gibbon, for example—and trained leaders in a method called "shared inquiry" (ask but never answer interpretive questions), and encouraged the establishment of book clubs, many of which still exist.

Now reading groups are everywhere, and you certainly don't have to be a Protestant to join one! And you are most definitely not limited to the so-called Great Books. In fact, you don't even have to leave the house to join the largest book club in history—fifteen to twenty million people turn on Oprah Winfrey's TV book club each month; she is responsible for several new writer millionaires (but, Oprah, why *no* calls to this phone!), and the publishing community prays daily at her shrine. No one has made reading and book clubs into "the thing to do" like Oprah. (And long may she live.)

But as for non-TV book clubs with actual people in the room, if you want to read Victorian novels, African-American writers, women, American literature, mysteries, biography, Booker Prize winners, or anything else, it's easy to find a group that suits your taste. Check at your local neighborhood library, where most groups read a healthy mix of classic and contemporary, fiction and nonfiction, U.S. and foreign authors. In Elmhurst, Illinois, for instance, they issue bookmarks listing the selections, dates of the meeting, the phone number, and the name of the room in which they meet. (These book clubs have become so popular that my little local library in my mostly working-class small town has THREE of them, one meeting in the morning and two that meet in the evening.) However, said Betsy Levins, in her Elmhurst library, *the choice of the book is entirely up to the librarian* [my emphasis] leading the discussions." Why does this phrase tend to make me a little nervous? Because I still remember what ensued when the southern librarian of my childhood caught me—in the long ago 1950s—reading novels in the Adult Section. (Librarian to my mother: "What's this child doing, reading Faulkner?" Mother to librarian: "She's up to the F's.")

And the enthusiasm for reading groups is not limited to libraries. Book Passage in Corte Madera, California, one of the best bookstores in the country and one deeply committed to reading groups, runs four book clubs of twenty-four members each, for ten-week sessions. And because the interest in reading groups transcends cultural backgrounds, Book Passage now offers sessions in Spanish. At another great independent bookstore, The Tattered Cover in Denver, Virginia Valentine, their book club expert, consults with approximately three hundred book groups each year. The same phenomenon repeats itself on a smaller scale at Brookline Booksmith, near Boston, at Bibelot in Baltimore, and at Village Bookshop in Omaha, Nebraska, where the manager says she has 850 book club members on her mailing list.

In the South, near the North Carolina triangle of Raleigh, Durham, and Chapel Hill, Quail Ridge Books discounts books for more than twenty reading groups, and Davis-Kidd Booksellers in Knoxville holds "Match-Making Evenings." Similar events are arranged in Lexington, Kentucky, at Joseph Beth Bookstore. In the North, Philadelphia's Borders Book Shop has a packed reading group and all the Barnes & Noble superstores in New York City fill groups on women's studies, mysteries, fiction, and African-American writers as soon as the sign-up lists are posted.

Bookstores like the famed Politics and Prose in downtown Washington, D.C., sponsor public reading clubs every month except August with groups of twelve to thirty-five readers who concentrate on fiction by authors abroad, often published by small presses. (They discuss the choices, but Carla Cohen, the owner, has the final say. This store discounts books for at least 100 active book clubs and they have 250 book clubs on their list.) Chapters, another wonderful independent Washington, D.C., bookstore, runs a poetry group that discusses new collections; their meetings usually coincide with visits of poets to the store. In Winnetka, Illinois, the owner Roberta Rubin has been running "Wednesday Mornings at The Book Stall at Chestnut Court" since 1985. Here, book discussion leaders, adult education experts, writers, and Ph.D. candidates lead discussions on everything from Tolstoy's *The Death of Ivan Ilyich* to Scott Turow's *The Burden of Proof*. Like most stores, they have a "hardcore group of twenty or so and then new people each time." In Taos, New Mexico, the Moby Dickens Bookshop even draws readers for its "Who Did It? A Grammatically Correct Mystery Book Club." Does all this sound as if book discussion groups bring in business and that bookstores are crazy about them? You bet.

Other reading groups evolve from professional affiliations, like the club in Raleigh, North Carolina, consisting mostly of faculty and medical school employees at Wake Forest Medical School. Or, as an example, if you have a special interest like Jungian analysis, you can E-mail (listproc@csf.colorado.edu) the C. G. Jung people, and you will be notified each time the author of a book on Jung will be available, on-line, for an electronic book club meeting.

Many groups are mixed by gender, age, and education, or share a heritage, like the club at New York City's Rodelph Sholem Synogogue where several pairs of married couples used to argue several years ago. I was one of their guest leaders and taught a so-called woman's book (their translation: a novel *by a woman*), which was scheduled, unfortunately, for the day after a Pro-Choice March on Washington with which certain members were uncomfortable. I'm happy to say that my wounds have healed nicely and that I did not require reconstructive surgery. Some groups, like "Monday Night Readers" of Columbia, Maryland, are restricted to women, but of varying races and/or religions. (If you can get into the Happy Bookers in Rhode Island, you get soup with each session: 3-ingredient black bean with *Angela's Ashes,* potato-leek with *Stones from the River*, green bean with *Wild Swans.* I leave it to the psychiatrists to figure out the connections.) All have members who note that their taste in literature has evolved along with their careers, and many believe that their intensified sense of their own potential is related in still unexplained ways to their reading experience.

Clearly we are in a time when our perpetual need to connect with each other is being played out, at least in part, by membership in a book club. Many people are choosing to trade in the scramble for riches, exemplified by the last several decades, for an experience that is, instead, enriching. Reading groups are here to stay. My own mother, who had been a member of the "Books in Brief Book Club of Miami, Florida" for thirty years—when she died at eighty-six—would be pleased.

How to Organize

READING GROUPS, EAST TO WEST

If you are thinking of organizing a book club, here's how some other clubs did it and what they think works. Specific hints are italicized.

BIG APPLE BOOK WOMEN

In one New York City book club, all members (*including the teacher, who is paid and is as much a member as a leader*) come with credentials: one runs a folk art museum, another works at the Metropolitan Museum, one is an urban planner, another is a writer, and they all have great language skills. *They choose their members not by how many books they have read, but by WHAT they read, and they invite them to sit in for a meeting before they are asked to join.*

The group has twenty members and invites novelists once or twice a year to discuss their new books. They know that the desire of publishers to court reading groups is now so great that, *if you call the publicity department of any major publisher, or access Bookwire (on the Internet) and check the book tour schedules of authors,* you can probably get one of your favorite writers to come to your book club meeting. Local writers will usually come, free of charge, if you are reading *their* new or backlist books and if you set up a book sale.

NEW JERSEY BOOK LOVERS

My own reading group, "The Bones-in-a-Baggie Book Club," is still flourishing after more than nine years. (About the name: Well, during one particularly memorable discussion, a member did tell this v-e-r-y l-o-n-g story about a friend whose husband was cremated, but when they sent the ashes north . . .)

This group—a lower-school principal, a cellist, several psychiatric social workers, two lawyers, a former hand model, many experienced learning specialists, a physician, *and* an emergency room nurse—is committed to and more than prepared to read challenging books, *whether they "like" them or not*. The group's consensus is that since they've lived through Ishiguro's *The Unconsoled*, they can read anything. And much to their surprise, Anne Fadiman's nonfiction book *The Spirit Catches You and You Fall Down* elicited a long and meaningful discussion about immigration issues, Western versus Eastern medicine, and what it means to assimilate. The group (which includes an Orthodox Jew and a member whose aunt is a nun) meet in my apartment for eight sessions each year; the last one, presummer, is a dinner meeting.

THE MAINE EVENT

The Wayne-Winthrop Women's Reading Group *provides a handout that lists the date, place, time, and a short synopsis of the book to be discussed* although "we don't have to call anyone—they remember on their own."

This group grew out of a reading series called "The Journey Inward: Women's Autobiographies." "We enjoyed each other's company so much that we thought we would try to conduct the group without the benefit of a leader," said the organizer, but we soon realized that "there were decisions to make: *how often and where to meet, what to read, and how to obtain the books.*" So, "*every two or three months we plan ahead for the next several meetings*, and we *do* have *a self-appointed leader/facilitator who types up the meeting schedule, arranges for an occasional* speaker, and *orders the books in advance from a local book-seller or remainder catalog."* (*Edward Hamilton or Daedalus are two*; the addresses are available in any library.) "Twenty women looking for the same book from a small-town library or from interlibrary loan would overload our system, so our *librarian supports us by having one available copy of our monthly selection.* Our local *independent bookstore has offered us a 15 percent discount* on our orders and usually stocks a copy or two of the books we read. The *leader/facilitator prefaces each discussion with a brief biography of the author and a summary of the work."* (For such background information, refer to *Contemporary Literary Criticism* and *Contemporary Authors* (known as *CA*), and the *Dictionary of Literary Biography* (usually called the *DLB*). This group consists of women from their mid-twenties to mid-seventies, including retirees who "read more and longer books than some of our younger members, who have jobs and children." *Most groups profit from this age mix.* "We have found that meeting once a month from 7:00 to 9:00 P.M. works well for us all; it allows us to read something other than the chosen book, to take care of our families, and to pursue other pleasures."

AFRICAN-AMERICAN READERS IN DETROIT

Attorney-at-law Nora Hudson says that her "Woman's Cultural Club/Literary Circle" "grew out of a need to alleviate the stress and strain of being working wives or single parents, and the core group consisted of women who were old college friends." Because "we all belonged to too many formal organizations with bylaws, officers, dues, and rules or regulations—which added stress—we decided that this club would have none. We just agreed to meet, and members volunteered to be in charge of monthly meetings."

For the sake of order they have now decided *to prepare a six-month schedule of monthly coordinators and a book list.* (Such planning is both necessary and inevitable if a reading club is to work.) *The coordinator is responsible for choosing the author, investigating his or her oeuvre, no-*

tifying the group members of the date of the meeting (usually scheduled for the third or fourth Sunday of the month from 3:00 to 6:00 P.M. because most members attend church on Sunday mornings on a regular basis), *and selecting the location.*

PHOENIX RISING: DENVER

"The Phoenix Book Club" is named after the first book they read, *I Knew a Phoenix*, by May Sarton. Their membership is limited to twelve, with four women in each age group: fifties, sixties, and seventies. The youngest member is forty-nine. The books, mostly fiction, are *picked by the group in August at a retreat in the mountains; each member makes a list of three suggestions and then the group votes.*

CALIFORNIA READING

Carol Benet, Ph.D., the reigning reading group queen of northern California, leads a group of eighteen men and women who read only works by Jewish writers. (The members are not necessarily Jewish.) It grew out of the Bronfman Seminars, sponsored by the University of California about ten years ago. (This idea can easily be duplicated with Irish writers, African writers, Catholic writers, etc. See "Other Lands, Other Voices.")

Their aim is to read the most representative books of the Jewish experience—in each decade from the 1890s to the present—and then to relax, after five months of discussion, with a potluck at a member's home. Benet suggests that you *take a year to read National Book Award or Booker Prize winners, or Nobel laureates*. If you live in an area where writers lived, or about which they wrote, *visit the sites described in the novels*. (She takes one of her groups to John's Grill, where the action in Dashiell Hammett's *Maltese Falcon* takes place.)
    Also:

1: Think *seriously* about hiring a good high school English teacher or an underpaid college professor to lead your group.

They are trained to not only provide answers but to supply the right questions. If you do not hire a teacher or leader, choose one person to arbitrate disagreements and conflicts during the discussion.

2: If you are looking for members, put an ad in your alumni, church, or synagogue bulletin.

3: Ask your local INDEPENDENT bookstore/health club/supermarket/coffeehouse to let you post a notice.

4: If you are a member, contact the American Association of University Women or the National Council of Jewish Women or 100 Black Women, etc., or call the 800 number for the Great Books Foundation.

5: Schedule a half hour for socializing and then go on to discuss the book. Don't confuse these two activities.

6: Try to establish at the outset that you expect all members to attend *all* sessions, except for emergencies, business trips, and family obligations that cannot be postponed. A reading group (like any other organization) creates its own dynamic, which is seriously disturbed when the configuration (in this case, people) changes.

HAVE FUN. THERE IS NO MIDTERM OR TERM PAPER, AND THERE WILL BE *NO* POP QUIZZES!

How to Read
A Short Course

Here are my two best pieces of advice:

1: BAN at the outset any discussion that focuses on "Did you like the book?" This is not a popularity contest, and any worthwhile piece of fiction or nonfiction, no matter how beloved or detested, teaches the reader something. *The real issue is what to read.* And a book club discussion that starts with this question goes nowhere.

2: If you are reading good fiction by talented writers, try not to concentrate on *plot*. It represents the least important aspect of a developed work. Use Rosellen Brown's novel *Before and After* as an example: A married couple with two children live in New Hampshire. (There is some role reversal since the mother is a medical doctor and the father is a sculptor.) Inexplicably, their son kills a neighborhood girl. They agonize, the father slightly more sympathetic and supportive than the mother, and at the end of the novel they move to Houston.

Of course this is light years from what Brown is writing about. But to understand what she is saying you should:

3: Think about the *title* and decide whether Brown is really writing about the *nature of time* and about *memory*.

4: Look up and think about the *names*. The father, Ben, has a son's name. (Ben in Hebrew means "son of.") The son, Jacob, has a patriarch's name, a father's name. Why?

Names like Anne (the ultimate mother, since she is the mother of Mary, Jesus's mother), and Hannah (Hebrew for Anna) are *always* important even if we do not know whether the writer chose them consciously or unconsciously. And before you write to me: it doesn't matter if they did it consciously or *un*consciously. (See *The Anna Book*, edited by Mickey Pearlman.)

For instance, James Joyce (in *The Dead*) and Lois Lowry (in *The Giver,* where the character is a special boy child!) name an important character Gabriel. Why? Gabriel is the archangel who announces the birth of Christ.

Most groceries have inexpensive books of names near the checkout counter, but I suggest that you purchase a more expensive version that lists derivations and common meanings for each name. Believe me, all the writers own books of names and no one uses a name like Gabriel because they can't think of the name Harry.

5: Invest in an inexpensive set of *Guides to the New and Old Testaments*. Are you reading about miracles, about a daughter-in-law who won't leave her mother-in-law, or a boy baby placed in a container, and then in a body of water, and found by a kind adoptive mother? (Every culture I can think of has the Moses story—even the landlocked ones.) Hemingway's Old Man is in the sea for forty days; Jesus wandered in the wilderness and Moses walked in the desert—for how long? (Pay attention to numbers.) Similarly, in Oscar Hijuelos's novel *Mr. Ives' Christmas*, he is writing a father/son story about rebirth, redemption, forgiveness, etc. What is the relationship of Christmas to those ideas?

6: Buy a copy of Edith Hamilton's *Mythology* or a similar book. Reading about a long journey with many obstacles? Do I hear Odysseus calling? Or any of the other heroes, in every culture, who are on a long journey, a quest? (Perhaps you want to reread Richard Ford's *Independence Day* again with this in mind?) Does someone seem blind, literally or metaphorically, to reality? Is this an Oedipus story? King Lear? Or any of the other characters dominated by eye (seeing, sight) problems? Or is the writer subtly alluding to a long-suffering Job or any one of many mythic or biblical archetypal characters? As we used to say at the City College of New York: "You could look it up." And you will have a better book club discussion for having done so.

7: Pay closer attention to *setting*. Does the story start in the fog? *Hamlet*? *Bleak House*? The woods and/or the forest? In the water? What does water symbolize in your culture, in your religion, in the culture and religion of the character? *This is a chance to think beyond your own religious or cultural context.*

8: Look up words like *parable*, *allegory*, *bildungsroman*, *deus ex machina*, *fin de siècle*, *irony*, *carpe diem*, *utopia/dystopia*, *weltschmerz,* and *Sturm und Drang*. See *A Glossary of Literary Terms*, edited by M. H. Abrams; you may as well start at the top.

9: Ask the B.L. (Beloved Librarian) to introduce you to the three best prepublication review journals: *Publishers Weekly*, *Kirkus Reviews*, and *Booklist*. All neighborhood libraries get these publications, but they are usually not displayed in the public areas. These journals run reviews approximately three months before the publication of the book. Learn how to access the *New York Times* daily and Sunday reviews for many books published in the last few years. (Make friends with the word "on-line.")

10: Here's *How to Read*:

DON'T BE AFRAID.
AND S-T-R-E-T-C-H.

When to Read

You want to join a book club that meets in a beautiful living room, with cushy sofas, soft lighting (to hide the pressures of the work week), lots of delicious cappuccino and nondiet cookies, and perhaps the proverbial fireplace, filled with crackling logs. (Unless, of course, it's August and you are in Texas.) But you get the idea.

Failing that, there are still plenty of good places to read together that you may not have envisioned.

1: How about a book club at the *office*? Can you set aside one lunch hour, once a month? This kind of book club will probably draw from a more diverse population and cross more borders of ethnicity, race, age, and economics than would the one in your living room, usually drawn from a more homogeneous sample. And that, to quote you-know-who, is "a good thing."

2: Are you in a group that is going on tour, to a ranch, on a cruise? A cellist friend just left for Japan with three books, one for each week of her orchestra's tour. She didn't have to look for book club members; one was in the first violins, another was in the brass section, and so on. And this provided a relief from talking about music and performances and orchestra gossip for three weeks straight!

3: Are you going "down the shore" (as we say in New Jersey), or to the lake, or the mountains, or on a dig, or to an extended summer program at a university? Ask the people who are sharing that experience with you to help choose the books, organize a reading group, and make that summer experience count.

4: How about a family reunion? Some of them last for more than a few days, and if you have a book club you can fight with your family over what someone *else* said (in this case, wrote). And I have conveniently included two lists on family and one each on brothers, sons, and fathers, and mothers and daughters.

Don't forget: Book clubs can be portable!

Where to Read
ON-LINE AND BY E-MAIL

Okay, you've looked and you've searched and you can't find ten like-minded people with whom to form a reading group; they all want to read science fiction and you want to explore the novels of Toni Morrison. Or, you are snowed in most of the time; you're not allowed to leave the house; you have too many children and they all play soccer; the dog ate your address book; you forgot how to make coffee; you already have two jobs, or any of the acceptable excuses (like illness or disability) for not organizing a book club in your living room. (Remember, I was a teacher for a l-o-n-g time.)

This is where E-mail book clubs and on-line book groups enter the picture. (And it's not always pretty!)

How to Organize an E-Mail Book Club (A Ten-Step Program)
You do not have to be on-line in order to form a group; you just need E-mail capacity (a modem) and a server (examples: Bell Atlantic, AOL, CompuServe, etc.). If you do not already have E-mail (And why don't you? Grown children of this generation do not write letters and they all move to some place you had never heard of at their age), call your local phone company; they will explain how you get a server.

E-mail book clubs allow you to choose your members from virtually everywhere, and one of the great benefits of living in and enduring the computer age is that you can now talk Jane Austen with people in Anchorage and San Antonio while you are happily ensconced in Duluth. Remember, though (as Angie Boynter of Baltimore explained to me), that many people prefer "face-to-face interaction and real-time responses" and that E-mail book clubs are not for everyone. Consider these issues:

1: Choose eight to ten members. More is unwieldy. But in my opinion, the more diversity—in age, geography, racial and ethnic background—the better. In this way you are truly taking advantage of the advantages of E-mail.

2: Encourage all participants to introduce themselves to the group by E-mail before the first meeting. This is a good time for members to mention the books they've been reading, the writers they enjoy reading, and the genres (short stories, anthologies, mysteries, etc.) they would like to explore. It would also be fun, and helpful, if everyone would disclose the titles of the last five books they have read.

3: Each member should select a book; go alphabetically by last name to avoid confusion.

4: Try to choose inexpensive and relatively short paperbacks or books that are easy to find in libraries.

5: Remember that most people like to read someone else's comments. But many people, including those who seem to be good candidates for an E-mail book club, are often insecure about their ability to write a coherent sentence. Make sure to emphasize that no one is grading these responses and that you are interested in insight, and not in semicolons and dangling participles. Make it clear that grammar and spelling don't count. (You can't know how difficult it is for a former English teacher to write these words! But can I at least say, hopefully, [incorrect in this context; it means "full of hope"] and for the last time: "alot" is NOT A WORD!)

Okay, deep breaths . . . I'm over it.

But, I can't stress this strongly enough—E-mail book clubs work best with people who like to write and who feel comfortable in front of a computer.

6: Schedule E-mail meetings five weeks apart on, for instance, the Thursday of the fifth week. If too much time elapses between selection and discussion, life takes over and you forget what (a) you planned to say and (b) the important details of the narrative.

7: Designate one person to be the facilitator each month. THAT SHOULD BE THE SAME PERSON WHO IS CHOOSING THIS MONTH'S BOOK. That way, everyone shares the responsibility and no one turns into The Boss.

8: Ask all the members to E-mail their comments on the book to the facilitator during the fifth week. The facilitator will then forward all of the responses to each member by the designated night. (In other words, you have four weeks to read each book; the fifth week is for exchanging and reading the comments on the book you have just read. By the designated night everyone should have read the book, read the E-mail, and be ready to go on to the next book, announced by the new facilitator on that evening.) There should be no obligation to comment on, argue with, or refute the opinions of another member.

9: Remember that some people ARE busier than others. Make it clear that each member can and should write only as much as they wish to write: three pages for one person; two lines for another.

10: Try to devise standard questions—not answerable by Yes or No—to facilitate discussion, i.e., "What is the author trying to say in this book?" (See "How to Read" for more suggestions.)

If the facilitator wishes to E-mail analyses of any given book to her members, she can look these up, among other places, on Amazon.com. (They carry the Booklist reviews.)

An E-mail book club does not have the interaction of an on-line club, or the intimacy of a more traditional book club, but it allows old friends and new acquaintances—all far from your living room—to participate in and enrich your intellectual life.

Go for it.

ON-LINE

On-line book clubs provide readers with a chance to talk about a designated book with participants around the world on a specific day. (For example, RuthAlice Anderson's club meets in cyberspace on the third Tuesday of each month at 10:00 P.M., EDT.) An on-line club mimics a nonelectronic conversation with the usual interactions, interjections, and interruptions, so it is far less static than any E-mail book club you can create on your own.

You can find out about the myriad on-line book clubs by using a search engine (Yahoo, BookWire, etc., and clicking on "book clubs." It will be apparent immediately—even to the beginner—that many on-line book clubs are sponsored by publishers (an example: "Ruth's Group," under the banner of Simon & Schuster's "SimonSays.") Many of these publishers' book clubs revolve around the work of one of their authors (Mary Higgins Clark, Clive Cussler, etc.).

Others, like the #CB on-line reading club, with more than one hundred members from Canada to India, function more like E-mail book clubs. Comments are left in chat rooms, or on electronic bulletin boards, that can be accessed when it is convenient for you. The "Online Reading Club"—thirty people in five countries—is similar. They read world literature (one selection every two weeks), and send their reviews in via E-mail. Of course, they send them in in German, French, and whatever, so you better hope you didn't throw out your third-year language primer or you are going to be in some deep you-know-what in this club.

Salon, one of a growing number of electronic magazines, has a group called "Salon Table Talk." They invite authors to participate, so you are able to discuss the book, hear the discussion, and talk to the writer. The week I listened in, Carol Shields was on-line.

Mystery, crime, and suspense fans have their own clubs and can discuss everything from radio mysteries to Nancy Drew and Sherlock Holmes. "The BookWire Index" lists other special groups run by the *Washington Post*; Western Carolina University (a club for kids); the Buffalo, New York, library system; and "Pasadena Bookstores," with even a web-based discussion of the erotic books of Anne Rice, written under her various pseudonyms. You too can remain anonymous by registering for this book club under a nickname (usually called a "nick") and by not including your E-mail address. (And that anonymity sounds like a good idea to me!) "The Lavender Salon Reader Online" provides a directory of gay and lesbian book clubs as well as book reviews of selected books.

The main thing to note is that all on-line book clubs make it easy to join. They explain how to download the discussion (when you wish to) and which software to purchase for chat room access. With on-line book clubs you are part of a world community, always in flux, but for whom reading books is as basic and as important as breathing.

My Family, Myself

An entirely new list of novels about everyone's favorite (?) subject. (See "Family Feuds.")

1. *Roommates: My Grandfather's Story*   **Max Apple**
Novelistic memoir of the memorable Herman (Rocky) Goodstein, who at ninety-three went to college with his grandson, Max Apple.

211 pp.; 1994

2. *Behind the Scenes at the Museum*   **Kate Atkinson**
I would nominate this as one of my favorite novels of the last five years. The first chapter about this decidedly dysfunctional English family (over several generations) is even narrated directly from the womb. Atkinson, to the surprise of the British literary world, beat out Salman Rushdie for the Whitbread Book of the Year Award. For once an awards committee got it right.

333 pp.; 1996

3. *The Book of Color*   Julia Blackburn
This is a strange but haunting book by an English writer whose family originally came from the island of Mauritius in the Indian Ocean. I can only say that it is about curses, race, mental affliction, and a truly dysfunctional family.

175 pp.; 1995

4. *The Invisible Circus*   Jennifer Egan
Vietnam, drugs, sex, and rock and roll, i.e., the 1960s, provide the tone for a novel set in 1978 about Phoebe O'Connor and her beloved older sister, Faith, who commits suicide in 1970 in Italy under mysterious circumstances. Beautiful language here, backed by the author's sensitivity and intelligence.

338 pp.; 1996

5. *Independence Day*   Richard Ford
Frank Bascombe, the hero of Ford's 1986 novel *The Sportswriter,* still living in Haddam, New Jersey, and now a Realtor associate, spends a weekend with his troubled son as they visit sports halls of fame in Springfield and Cooperstown.

451 pp.; 1995

6. *The Short History of a Prince*   Jane Hamilton
Her first novel, *The Book of Ruth*, was an *Oprah* book club selection. (Okay, the rest of us are NOT jealous!) The story of an ordinary young woman in a small-town, unexceptional family, it is a favorite of book clubs everywhere. Hamilton returns to the Midwest with the story of a young man's passion for dance and the ways in which a son's place in the family can change that family overnight.

320 pp.; 1998

7. *A Widow for One Year*   John Irving
All of Irving's novels deal with the themes of lost children and absent parents. His newest is about a mother, severely depressed by the accidental death of her two sons, who disappears for thirty-seven years.

537 pp.; 1998

8. *Native Speaker*   Chang-rae Lee
A first novel by a Korean American that transcends the usual "Who am I; where are my roots; what is an American" harangue. In this one Henry Park works as an ethnic intelligence spy for a private organization that is keeping tabs on a rising Korean-American politician, marries a white woman, loses a son, and reconciles with his family's past. A beautiful debut.

384 pp.; 1995

9. *Angela's Ashes*   Frank McCourt
It was hard for me to believe that any book could be as good as this one was touted to be. But it is. And if you are not an Irish American, or a Roman Catholic, and you luckily escaped the horrors of McCourt's childhood poverty, you will be no less mesmerized by this story of endurance and suffering. Note to fledgling writers: McCourt's language is what your teachers were talking about when they were trying to explain "voice."

364 pp.; 1996

10. *Purple America*   Rick Moody
Moody is a writer whom other writers read. Here a debilitated mother, a stepfather in the nuclear power industry, and a responsible son become part of a rumination about mortality.

298 pp.; 1997

11. *Black and Blue*   Anna Quindlen

What I like about Quindlen is that she knows how to TELL A
STORY, even when it is about the abuse of a wife by her husband, a
cop, and her escape—with the help of an underground organization—from this quite frequent occurrence. Although she won a
Pulitzer Prize for her *New York Times* columns, she is first of all (as
she says) a practicing Roman Catholic, a mother of three, and a res-
ident of the great state of New Jersey. And she has not forgotten that.

293 pp.; 1998

12. *Persian Brides*   Dorit Rabinyan

As the *New York Times* said, "We may still be astonished to encounter a culture in which ordinary girls' sexual intimacies are
known by every neighbor, mothers probe their sleeping daughters'
private parts to confirm the 'family honor,' and a girl's first men-
struation is announced from the rooftops." This Israeli playwright
has conjured up such a society in a Jewish community in turn-of-
the-century Persia.

236 pp.; 1998

13. *The God of Small Things*   Arundhati Roy

Complicated story of an Indian family, fraternal twins, the accidental death of their English cousin, Marxist politics, a wife-abus-
ing entomologist, and more. Winner of the Booker Prize in 1997.

336 pp.; 1997

14. *The Stone Diaries*   Carol Shields

I like Shields's work so much I'd read her grocery lists. This story
of a woman from childhood to marriage to motherhood to old age,
in Canada and the United States, deservedly won the Pulitzer Prize
for 1994. Some of us were not surprised. I liked *Larry's Party* too
but some of my book club members thought I had perhaps been to

one party too many, and stayed too late! I still think Shields is a marvelous writer.

361 pp.; 1994

15. *The Far Euphrates* **Aryeh Lev Stollman**

My book clubs loved it. If you know something about the Cabbala, the Sefirot, or mysticism, it will greatly enrich your reading of this novel. (This is another one of those times when you will appreciate your local resource librarian.) But, with apologies to Levy's rye bread, "you don't have to be Jewish to love [Stollman]."

206 pp.; 1997

16. *Loving Edith* **Mary Tannen**

Frankly, in many ways this book annoyed me since it suffers from the kitchen-sink style of including every idea that the author had while writing it and of repeating several of them several times. But it is a new twist on how an adopted child, now a young woman working as an intern on a New York magazine, finds herself, and her biological parents, all in a New York minute.

275 pp.; 1995

Family Feuds

1. *Shadow Play*   Charles Baxter

Life in Five Oaks, Michigan, where love and social responsibility collide. Beautifully written, almost melodic, with a clear moral vision (as is *First Light*, his first novel).

352 pp.; 1993

2. *Mystery Ride*   Robert Boswell

The mystery ride in this novel is marriage. (The title is from a Springsteen song.) Boswell returns here to his best material, dysfunctional families, found also in his memorable second novel, *Crooked Hearts*, set in Yuma, Arizona.

333 pp.; 1993

3. *The Runaway Soul*   Harold Brodkey

Set in 1930s St. Louis, the story of Wiley Silenowics, an adopted child who is raised in the St. Louis household of his cousins and their daughter, Nonie.

848 pp.; 1993

4. *Before and After*   **Rosellen Brown**
When a New Hampshire teenager kills his girlfriend, his parents are forced to examine their own moral truths as well as their relationship. A gripping, beautifully written novel.

354 pp.; 1992

5. *My Antonia*   **Willa Cather**
Turn-of-the-century farm life as lived by Slavic and Scandinavian immigrants on the open prairies of Nebraska and the finest work by one of America's greatest writers. Shimerda emerges from this novel as the most memorable American mother in twentieth-century literature.

372 pp.; 1919

6. *Mrs. Bridge*   **Evan Connell**
If you've seen the movie, you'll always picture Joanne Woodward in this sympathetic portrayal of a housewife and mother of three in Kansas City beween World Wars I and II. Of course, in the *movie*, Mr. Bridge was Paul Newman, so how bad could things have been?

254 pp.; 1959

7. *Ragtime*   **E. L. Doctorow**
The bestselling story of immigrant Jews on the Lower East Side of New York and their evolution into citizens with money and stature.

236 pp.; 1975

8. *Geek Love*   **Katherine Dunn**
Olympia Binewski, an albino hunchback dwarf, narrates this novel about her carnival family; will they breed specimens for their own freak show?

348 pp.; 1989

9. *Middlemarch*   George Eliot

Considered to be Eliot's masterpiece and one of the greatest books of the nineteenth century, this is life in a provincial English town. The players are Dorothea, a modern St. Teresa; Lyngate, prototype for today's fashionable liposuction doctor; Rosamond, representing triviality and egoism; and the doomed banker, Bulstrode. There is also Casaubon, the husband nobody wants but everyone will recognize. No one is educated without reading it. A must.

795 pp.; 1871–1872

10. *The Sound and the Fury*   William Faulkner

Difficult but compelling study of the Compsons, an old Southern family. This novel concentrates on that complex and subtle time of memory that meshes past and present, reality and illusion, the conscious and the subconscious. My personal choice for best American novel written in the first half of this century. Read the shorter *As I Lay Dying* too.

427 pp.; 1929

11. *The 14 Sisters of*   Oscar Hijuelos
Emilio Montez O'Brien

Author of the Pulitzer Prize–winning *The Mambo Kings Play Songs of Love* writes here about an Irish immigrant who travels to Cuba as a photographer during the Spanish-American War and meets the sensitive and poetic Mariela Montez. She bears him fourteen daughters, and, finally, a son, Emilio. A paean to the feminine from a male author.

484 pp.; 1993

12. *Natural History*   Maureen Howard

When a society tramp kills a soldier toward the end of World War II, Billy Bray, a detective, is called on to investigate the case.

The murder reveals an undertow of sex, crime, and moral confusion that sweeps Bray and his family into an uncertain future.

416 pp.; 1992

13. *Very Old Bones*   **William Kennedy**

By the author of *Ironweed*, this sixth novel is a fictionalized version of Kennedy's life as a writer. Albany is for him what Dublin was for Joyce.

292 pp.; 1992

14. *Passing On*   **Penelope Lively**

The Booker Prize winner in 1987 for *Moon Tiger* writes about the death of a difficult mother and follows the lives of her middle-aged son and daughter. Great for book clubs.

224 pp.; 1992

15. *The Member of the Wedding*   **Carson McCullers**

McCullers, who died young, was only twenty-three when she created a literary sensation with this novel about Frankie Addams, a twelve-year-old girl, and her family.

195 pp.; 1946

16. *At Weddings and Wakes*   **Alice McDermott**

The tender and captivating story of an Irish-American family in Brooklyn during the 1950s and 1960s, and their encounters with ordinary rituals and extraordinary emotions. I prefer it to *Charming Billy.*

213 pp.; 1992

17. *Long Day's Journey into Night*   **Eugene O'Neill**

A play that catalogs the ills of America's dysfunctional families: drug addiction, alcoholism, disaffected children, jealousy among siblings, bad marriages, etc. In the Tyrones we see the entire list.

176 pp.; 1956

18. *A Thousand Acres*   Jane Smiley
The Pulitzer Prize– and National Book Award–winning modern
version of King Lear and his daughters, this time on an Iowa farm,
but with the additional burden of incest. Also recommended are
the novellas *Ordinary Love* and *Good Will.*

371 pp.; 1991

19. *The Man Who Loved Children*   Christina Stead
This masterpiece by a third-generation Australian is about a father, six children, a stepchild, and a mother named Henny, who, as
Randall Jarrell wrote, is "one of those immortal beings in whom
the tragedy of existence is embodied."

491 pp.; 1940

20. *Saint Maybe*   Anne Tyler
Tyler is America's chief chronicler of domesticity and its discon-
tents, often in Baltimore. Here Ian Bedloe, seventeen, stumbles
into a storefront that houses the Church of the Second Chance, a
tiny popular sect that demands reparations from its members for
their sins.

337 pp.; 1991

21. *To the Lighthouse*   Virginia Woolf
The chief figure of modernism in England writes about the
Ramsay family, their artistic friend Lily Briscoe, and how the tri-
fling events of everyday existence define life. If you are interested in
symbols, this is your book!

310 pp.; 1927

Life Is (Definitely Not) a Bowl of Cherries

1. *If on a winter's night a traveler*   Italo Calvino

An unusual novel that is really ten novels, each with a different plot, style, ambience, and author. This would be a great choice for an adventurous book club.

260 pp.; 1979

2. *Paddy Clarke Ha Ha Ha*   Roddy Doyle

This Irish novel, which won the 1993 Booker Prize, is the story of an unforgettable ten-year-old boy in 1960s Dublin. I have to say that I found this book difficult to read and enormously challenging, but it is no doubt worth the effort.

282 pp.; 1993

3. *Tender Is the Night*   F. Scott Fitzgerald

Based in part on his wife, Zelda, and her experiences in various sanitoria. If you are interested in the lives of women, be prepared to be furious.

315 pp.; 1962

4. *Save Me the Waltz*   Zelda Fitzgerald

This is Zelda Fitzgerald's only novel, a parallel view (to *Tender Is the Night*) of their joint experiences. The Wharton scholar Abby Werlock suggests that you read this novel along with Wharton's short story "Miss Ella" and Faulkner's "Miss Ellie." In these stories "it's the men who are crazy but the women who suffer from their abnormal (male?) behavior."

255 pp.; 1932

5. *Bury Me Standing: The*   Isabel Fonseca
Gypsies and Their Journey

As the *Washington Post* said, this illuminating and alarming book is about the least understood people on earth. Fascinating.

322 pp.; 1995

6. *The Unconsoled*   Kazuo Ishiguro

Several critics have suggested that this novel (by the author of *The Remains of the Day*) should be listed under chaos theory. It details four days in the life of a celebrated pianist who arrives in an unnamed Central European town to give a concert; both his schedule and any sense he had of control over his own life are lost. I still think it's a great choice for book clubs even though the members of one of mine almost shot me.

535 pp.; 1995

7. *Diary of a Mad Housewife*   Sue Kaufman

Interesting to read this fictional account of a New York City woman's life in the 1960s and compare it to a woman's life in the 1990s. Times have changed.

311 pp.; 1967

8. *How Late It Was, How Late*   James Kelman

This much-lauded novel about Sammy, an ex-con in Glasgow, won the Booker Prize in Britain and caused a sensation. If you don't like four-letter words, it's not for you, but if you can get past this issue, the language is rich, if vernacular, and reflects both the character and the circumstances of his life.

374 pp.; 1995

9. *The Light of Falling Stars*   J. Robert Lennon

Winner of the Barnes & Noble Discover Great New Writers Award, this novel opens with a devastating plane crash that kills all but one passenger. Lennon understands grief, tragedy, and the ways in which lives often change instantly.

308 pp.; 1997

10. *Defiance*   Carole Maso

Maso, one of the writers on whom nothing is wasted, also has intelligence, emotional resources, and some great plot ideas. The author of *Ghost Dance* writes here about sex, class, gender, memory, and about Bernadette O'Brien, a physics professor at Harvard, now on death row for the sexual murder of two of her most promising male students. Not for a day at the beach.

264 pp.; 1998

11. *Breakfast on Pluto*   Patrick McCabe

The only Irish novel among the five finalists for the 1998 Booker Prize, McCabe's story opens as Mr. Patrick Pussy Braden, "our hero(ine)," resplendent in housecoat and head scarf, reclines in Kilburn and writes her story of life on the streets of London and Belfast for Dr. Terence, the elusive psychiatrist. Brilliant, gritty, violent, and tragic.

199 pp.; 1998

12. *Mother's Day*   **Robert Miner**

Very unusual and explicitly sexual story of a single father and the ways in which his life and his psyche are transformed by "motherhood."

250 pp.; 1978

13. *Butterfield 8*   **John O'Hara**

Based on the real story of twenty-five-year-old Starr Faithfull, drowned off Long Beach, New York, in 1931, which O'Hara transformed into the story of Gloria Wandrous, a prototypical New York party girl who emerges as Elizabeth Taylor in the movie version. For those obsessed with the Nicole Simpson story, here's a chance to see an early version of scandal, vice, and murder. Recently reisssued.

208 pp.; 1935

14. *Down and Out in*   **George Orwell**
    Paris and London

Orwell attempts to live as one of the disenfranchised and poor people of the world in the slums of Paris, in London's East End, and with hoboes and migrants as they travel throughout Europe. Part autobiography, part novel, and recommended by many readers.

213 pp.; 1933

15. *Benjamin's Crossing*   **Jay Parini**

I'm not usually crazy about biographical novels, but Walter Benjamin, a social critic, philanderer, philosopher, and leading intellectual in pre-Nazi Germany was such a complicated figure that Parini's book, covering only a few months in Benjamin's life, adds some clarity. A difficult read, but worth the effort.

308 pp.; 1997

16. *Gain*   **Richard Powers**
Two narratives here: the story of a small family soap-and-candle business that grows into a giant conglomerate, and the tale of forty-two-year-old Laura Bodey, a divorced real estate saleswoman with ovarian cancer. As the *New York Times* said, "the pointed association of business growth with a tumor growth, of a corporation's robust health with a woman's agonizing infirmity, is deliberate."

355 pp.; 1998

17. *Good Morning, Midnight*   **Jean Rhys**
Repeat after me: Rule One: Anger turned inward creates despair. Read this book. Also *Wide Sargasso Sea*.

189 pp.; 1970

18. *American Pastoral*   **Philip Roth**
Nathan Zuckerman again, this time telling the story of his high school classmate Swede Levov, a man blessed with good fortune until his teenage daughter, Merry, takes part in a 1968 terrorist bombing that kills a man and ruins her life and the lives of her parents. Roth won the National Book Award for this one.

423 pp.; 1997

19. *A Four-Sided Bed*   **Elizabeth Searle**
The story of Allie, J.J., Kin, and Bird, who badly need to hear the message that one character voices: "Ever heard of the straight and narrow? Get on it. Stay on it." A promising debut.

299 pp.; 1998

20. *Daughter of Earth*   **Agnes Smedley**
Dirt-hard proletarian feminist novel re-creates the story of a tireless political activist, in most ways Smedley herself, who emerged from poverty and a life as a tobacco stripper.

391 pp.; 1987

21. *A Late Divorce* A. B. Yehoshua

Yehoshua suffers a bit in this early novel from overidentification with Faulkner; not many writers can make those unending sentences work. But this novel still draws you in as you watch a family fall apart at holiday time.

354 pp.; 1984

Let's Talk About Me

MEMOIRS BY WOMEN

1. *The Bookmaker's Daughter*   Shirley Abbott

The emphasis here is on Abbott's father, a promising scholar and avid reader, who was also a bookie and bootlegger, and her childhood in Hot Springs, Arkansas.

256 pp.; 1991

2. *I Know Why the Caged Bird Sings*   Maya Angelou

In part one of a popular five-volume autobiography, Angelou recalls both life with her grandmother and racism in Arkansas. After she was raped by her mother's boyfriend when she was eight, she remained silent for five years. President Clinton chose his "fellow" Arkansan to read her poetry at his first inauguration.

281 pp.; 1969

3. *Spinster*   Sylvia Ashton-Warner

This book focuses on issues of educational theory and racial understanding that grew out of the author's unorthodox method of teaching Maori children to read by using a "key" vocabulary. She was widely criticized in her native New Zealand but the book sold well in the United States.

242 pp.; 1958

4. *Black Ice*   **Lorene Carey**

Life as a black student at the exclusive (and formerly all-white and all-male) St. Paul's School in Concord, New Hampshire.

256 pp.; 1991

5. *The Road from Coorain*   **Jill Ker Conway**

A favorite of reading groups, this is a memoir of an Australian who grew up to be an American college president. She continues with memories of life in Australia in *True North* as she leaves for Harvard and marriage to a war-scarred historian, eleven years of Canadian university life, and the presidency of Smith College. All smart and ambitious women will recognize part of their own stories here.

256 pp.; 1989

6. *Memoirs of a Dutiful Daughter*   **Simone de Beauvoir**

The autobiography of the fascinating woman who wrote *The Second Sex,* loved Sartre, and changed the way we all think about gender.

360 pp.; 1959

7. *An American Childhood*   **Annie Dillard**

This is the Pulitzer Prize–winning author's vivid, moving memoir of growing up in Pittsburgh in the 1950s.

255 pp.; 1987

8. *Autobiography of a Face*   Lucy Grealy
Attacked at nine by a bone cancer that literally ate her face,
Grealy had eighteen years of surgical reconstructions. She is a
miraculous survivor.

223 pp.; 1994

9. *A Romantic Education*   Patricia Hampl
An evocation of the author's Czech heritage that blends the personal and the historical.

344 pp.; 1981

10. *The Kiss*   Kathryn Harrison
OK, I've read all the reviews about how shocking and dirty this
book is. Give it a rest. Whether you like the book or not, this memoir is about abandonment, loneliness, the absence of family, and the
fear of being alone, and not about s-e-x. I'd ignore all the reviews
and make up your own mind.

207 pp.; 1997

11. *Lost in Translation*   Eva Hoffman
When Hoffman emigrated at thirteen from Poland to Vancouver, she lost her language, her culture, and her footing. This intellectual's version of the classic immigrant success story is the final
step in her re-anchoring.

288 pp.; 1988

12. *Fear of Fifty*   Erica Jong
I like Erica Jong, I like her poetry and her fiction, and I think she
has the best grasp of what it really means for a woman to get old(er)
in America.

325 pp.; 1994

13. *French Lessons*   Alice Kaplan

My agent, Vicky Bijur, loves this memoir about immersing one-self in another language. And believe me, she knows *what to read.*

221 pp.; 1993

14. *The Liars' Club*   Mary Karr

Much more than a memoir of a childhood in "the Texas Ring-worm Belt," where the cancer rate from oil refineries rivals Chernobyl's. As Karr reminds us, *Business Week* called her hometown one of the ten ugliest places on the planet. She also had to survive a "nervous" mother (married seven times) who was insensible half of the time from drugs and alcohol, and an emotionally constipated father. This book is so gripping (even if you think you have yourself OD'd on stories of dysfunctional families) that it is hard to believe it is Karr's first published work.

320 pp.; 1995

15. *The Woman Warrior*   Maxine Hong Kingston

Subtitled *Memoirs of a Girlhood Among Ghosts*, this won the National Book Critics Circle Award for nonfiction; it contains Kingston's autobiography, recounts the evolution of her Asian-American identity, and remains one of the most influential and widely read books by American women in the late twentieth century. A must.

209 pp.; 1977

16. *Road Song*   Natalie Kusz

In 1969, Kusz and her family packed up the car and headed for Alaska. They ended up a hundred miles from Fairbanks, with temperatures of sixty below. Then disaster struck.

258 pp.; 1990

17. *Secret Ceremonies*   Deborah Laake

A woman's memories of being raised a Mormon, the unhappy marriages that ensued, and her life now as a Jack, or lapsed, Mormon in Phoenix. Face it, we're all fascinated with secret church ceremonies.

240 pp.; 1993

18. *Memories of a Catholic Girlhood*   Mary McCarthy

Raised by relatives after both parents died in 1918, this book recounts the severe, rigid Catholicism that dominated her emotionally deprived childhood. In any case, she grew up to write *The Group* and much fiction and nonfiction.

245 pp.; 1957

19. *Angels and Aliens: A*   Mary Morris
California Journey

This new memoir by a writer with both heart and brains follows *Nothing to Declare: Memoirs of a Woman Traveling Alone* and *Wall to Wall: From Beijing to Berlin by Rail.*

250 pp.; 1999

20. *Silent Dancing: A Partial*   Judith Ortiz-Cofer
Remembrance of a Puerto Rican Childhood

Recipient of a PEN citation and a Pushcart Prize, Ortiz-Cofer talks about how females are conditioned and the price of that lesson.

168 pp.; 1990

21. *Johnny's Girl*   Kim Rich

Subtitled *A Daughter's Memoir of Growing Up in Alaska's Underworld*, Rich is a journalist whose father, Johnny Rich, Jr., was a well-known mobster in Anchorage. Her mother was a former stripper who died the year before her husband was murdered.

288 pp.; 1993

22. *The Hacienda: A Memoir*   Lisa St. Aubin de Teran

This British novelist/poet (a bride at sixteen) writes a harrowing memoir about the seven years she spent on a sugar plantation deep in the Venezuelan Andes with an aristocratic but mad husband (who announced on their wedding day that he "was a bank robber and a wanted man") and his crazy parents. She ends up as a benefactress of the plantation workers, whose children are plagued by a sickness called "La Mayera." My question is: Where were HER parents and how did she end up there in the first place?

342 pp.; 1998

23. *Journal of a Solitude*   May Sarton

Inner and outer worlds, daily life in New Hampshire, and the solace of silence.

208 pp.; 1973

24. *Dreaming*   Carolyn See

See is one of the most honest and daring writers I know, and this story of her family's marriages and alcoholism and money troubles is compelling in part because she doesn't turn out to be Polly Perfect—completely functional and a paragon of virtue. What a relief. Subtitled *Hard Luck and Good Times in America*, she's had plenty of both.

343 pp.; 1995

25. *Slow Motion: A True Story*   Dani Shapiro

Shapiro says, "It's a coming-of-age story partly about growing up in an Orthodox Jewish family and undergoing a fairly massive rebellion that involved a relationship with a much older, powerful, married man." Sound familiar?

245 pp.; 1998

26. *The Four of Us*   Elizabeth Swados

The gifted composer chronicles the ways in which her schizophrenic, self-destructive brother dominated her family. The book
is divided into four sections, each focusing on a different family
member.

243 pp.; 1991

MEMOIRS BY MEN

1. *Night: Night Life, Night Language,*   A. Alvarez
Sleep, and Dreams

Every book lover should own this volume. I refer to it all the
time, both as a reader and a teacher. I don't know if it will make you
less scared of the dark, but it is fascinating nevertheless. An untyp-
ical memoir.

290 pp.; 1995

2. *Days of Grace*   Arthur Ashe
and Arnold Rampersad

The recollections of the great tennis champion reflect the
courage needed for his triumph on the tennis court, his survival as
a black man in America, and his confrontation of death as a casualty
of AIDS, contracted through a defective blood transfusion during
heart surgery.

441 pp.; 1993

3. *Black Dog of Fate: A Memoir*   Peter Balakian

Balakian, an Armenian "Jersey boy," grew up in Tenafly in a close-
knit extended family that included his aunts, Nona and Anna, both
well known in New York's literary world. At its center was the un-
spoken knowledge of the Ottoman Turkish government's extermination of more than a million Armenians in 1915, in this century's
first genocide. This book is history, memoir, and poetry.

289 pp.; 1997

4. *To the Hoop: The Seasons of a Basketball Life*   **Ira Berkow**

The famed sports columnist for the *New York Times* played his first basketball game at age eight in Chicago. This is a lifetime's worth of games, sometimes with Oscar Robertson, Nancy Lieberman, and lesser knowns who have been known to show up at the courts for pickup games (shirts versus skins) at the New York University Medical Center's courts. I loved it.

295 pp.; 1997

5. *Be Sweet: A Conditional Love Story*   **Roy Blount, Jr.**

I'm beginning to think that everyone who grew up in the American South was told by some family member to "be sweet." Here Blount, a funny man with heart, deals with his memories of a difficult mother and a Georgia childhood.

320 pp.; 1998

6. *Coming Up Down Home*   **Cecil Brown**

Subtitled *A Memoir of a Southern Childhood*, and by the author of *The Life and Loves of Mr. Jiveass Nigger*, this engrossing memoir of childhood evokes the small farming village of Bolton, North Carolina.

256 pp.; 1993

7. *The Journals of John Cheever*   **John Cheever**

This is the writer's life from the late 1940s to his death from cancer in 1982, including his twenty-year battle with chronic alcoholism, his hidden homosexuality, and his many affairs with women other than his wife. Read his daughter Susan Cheever's memoir, *Home Before Dark,* too.

399 pp.; 1991

8. *Pack My Bag: A Self-Portrait*   **Henry Green**
Originally published in Britain, this is pretty much all that is known of a very enigmatic novelist, revered in some writerly circles, who lived from 1905 to 1973.

242 pp.; 1940

9. *Life Work*   **Donald Hall**
The very ill poet writes here what the *New York Times* calls "a brief, dense, painful and memorable book . . . a notable contribution to our strange new genre, autothanatography."

124 pp.; 1993

10. *Between Worlds*   **Leo Lionni**
Published when Lionni was eighty-seven years old, the story of this Renaissance man of graphic art, illustration, and design moves from his birth in Amsterdam, to Philadelphia, Genoa, Zurich, Milan, New York, and his studio in Tuscany. He knew Man Ray, de Kooning, Mondrian, and even Andy Warhol. Marvelous, with no pettiness or gossip.

295 pp.; 1997

11. *Unfinished Journey:*   **Yehudi Menuhin**
    Twenty Years Later
First published in 1976, Menuhin added four chapters to this edition. He debuted on the violin at seven, lived up to his child genius label, and speaks here of his friendships with Willa Cather and Marc Chagall.

393 pp.; 1996

12. *A Different Person*   **James Merrill**
Son of the man who gave his name to the world's largest brokerage firm, the famed poet discloses how he journeyed to Italy and,

with the help of a good psychiatrist, made peace with his homosexuality and began to write.

271 pp.; 1993

13. *Becoming a Man*   Paul Monette

Subtitled *Half a Life Story*, this National Book Award–winner chronicles Monette's struggle to finally accept his homosexuality.

288 pp.; 1992

14. *And When Did You*   Blake Morrison
Last See Your Father?

This memoir by the British poet of life with his complex, arrogant, and difficult Yorkshire physician father is full of stories worth reading.

219 pp.; 1995

15. *What Did I Do?*   Larry Rivers

Outrageous and uncensored portrait of the artist's often perverse life as part of the postwar New York art, jazz, and literary worlds in postwar New York.

512 pp.; 1993

16. *Hunger of Memory*   Richard Rodriguez

A Chicano essayist born in San Francisco, Rodriguez wrote this autobiographical account of his education and search for identity. His second book was *Mexico's Children*.

195 pp.; 1982

17. *Secret Life: An Autobiography*   Michael Ryan

Childhood sexual abuse, sexual obsession, alcoholism, and perversion are all hard to take. But I must admit that Ryan's blatant honesty and his fine writing style captured me. What a rocky road some people have to walk.

356 pp.; 1995

18. *Burning the Days*   **James Salter**
Salter moves from a Manhattan boyhood, to West Point, to service as a fighter pilot in the air force during the Korean War. An extraordinary account of one man's life and beautifully written.

365 pp.; 1997

19. *The Cliff Walk:*   **Don J. Snyder**
   A Memoir of a Job Lost and a Life Found
This assistant professor at Colgate expects to have a clear path to a tenured teaching job in the Ivies. But when his contract is not renewed and he endures ninety-nine rejection letters for another college teaching position, he finally gets a grip and embraces another kind of life. The *New York Times* review said it best: "By book's end, writer and reader have relearned the lessons that both academic and manual labor efficiently teach: (1) Do the work. (2) Think of others. (3) Life is unfair." Exactly.

265 pp.; 1997

20. *Up from Slavery*   **Booker T. Washington**
Freed from slavery at the age of eight, Washington managed by 1872 to gain entrance to Hampton Institute, from which he graduated in 1876. One of the founders of Tuskegee Institute, this extraordinary man had a profound influence upon the Americans of his day.

330 pp.; 1900

21. *Dancing with Strangers*   **Mel Watkins**
A former editor at the *New York Times Book Review* who is a black man tells a straight story without dumping guilt on himself or anyone else. Bravo.

320 pp.; 1998

22. *Will This Do? An Autobiography*   Auberon Waugh

It's hard to understand why anyone who could say this would have children: "I abhor their company because I can only regard children as defective adults, hate their physical ineptitude, find their jokes flat and monotonous." Evelyn Waugh also sent all six of his off to boarding school as soon as he could. Auberon, his son and the author of five novels, writes here about how he tried to live up to this parent's standards and about his own life as a writer.

288 pp.; 1998

23. *The Duke of Deception*   Geoffrey Wolff

Wolff recounts life with his father, a confidence man—"bright, quick, musical, charming, a wonderful storyteller" and "also a bullshit artist who doctored his bloodline and fabricated his *curriculum vitae*, becoming the man he felt he should have been rather than the man his history had made."

275 pp.; 1979

24. *This Boy's Life*   Tobias Wolff

Flannery O'Connor said that anybody who survived his childhood had enough to write about for the rest of his life. In Wolff's case, that includes the separation from his father and brother, wandering with his mother from Florida to Washington State, and life with a Dickensian stepfather.

288 pp.; 1989

25. *Black Boy*   Richard Wright

The years pass but this remains an unforgettable story of growing up in the Jim Crow South. Wright is one of America's most powerful writers.

528 pp.; 1945

The Writer's Life

Hundreds of biographies exist of dead and living writers. But this list—by no means complete—represents an attempt to know more about the writers whose lives intrigue and interest me. The list reflect's one person's taste and is not meant to either award or deny a critic's imprimateur on the writer's work.

1. *Dickens*   Peter Ackroyd
Over a thousand pages about the unique figure of Charles Dickens. More mystery and intrigue than you would imagine from reading *A Christmas Carol.*

1,195 pp.; 1991

2. *Anaïs Nin: A Biography*   Deirdre Bair
Bair says Nin has a place in the pantheon of "great minor writers." Nin was also, in my opinion, one of the most self-absorbed and insecure people on the planet. But no doubt she has a place in literary history. Read on.

654 pp.; 1995

3. *Life of Samuel Johnson*   James Boswell

Boswell (1740—95) collected every scrap of information—including journals and Johnson's voluminous writings—in order to respect Johnson's well-known insistence on accuracy and truth. These pages are filled with fascinating people, witty conversation (of the male variety), and it is altogether a joy to read. Don't hesitate.

435 pp.; 1791

4. *Writing Dangerously:*   Carol Brightman
Mary McCarthy and Her World

As Nancy Milford has written, this is the biography "of the pretty orphan from the West, the poor Catholic, ambitious Vassar girl who becomes the fatal woman of mid-century American letters." Includes the tale of her innumerable lovers and four husbands, including a tempestuous marriage to Edmund Wilson.

714 pp.; 1992

5. *Zola: A Life*   Frederick Brown

Émile Zola became the moral conscience of France during the Dreyfus affair in the late 1800s and Brown suggests that he may have been murdered for his goodness. He hated hypocrisy and he forced an entire country to face their own complicity and duplicity. He was, simply, a great man

888 pp.; 1995

6. *Talking at the Gates*   James Campbell

The black homosexual writer James Baldwin found life in these United States a trial. He lived in Paris for much of his life and this biographer, who knew him, combines the factual with the subjective.

288 pp.; 1991

7. *Charlotte Brontë: A Passionate Life*   Lyndall Gordon

The latest biography of the author of *Jane Eyre* addresses the dichotomy between her "timid, mouselike demeanor and her passionate, caustic prose" (*New York Times*). In the spirit of our dysfunctional time, Gordon also discusses in detail the physical and nervous breakdown that Brontë supposedly suffered in the winter of 1851–52.

418 pp.; 1995

8. *The Autobiography of Malcolm X as Told to Alex Haley*

The story of the civil rights leader, former Muslim, and failed small-time hood, and finally a believer in brotherhood, who is now an icon to many. There are millions of copies in print.

608 pp.; 1965

9. *Trollope: A Biography*   N. Jon Hall

Trollope wrote sixty long novels during his long life (most of them still eminently readable), and he was in all ways an outstanding personality. Hall does a great job with the life and the work.

581 pp.; 1991

10. *Inventing Mark Twain:*   Andrew Hoffman
The Lives of Samuel Langhorne Clemens

Hoffman suggests that Clemens grew to hate his own creation: Mark Twain. Certainly Clemens was a brooding man whose unhappy childhood, including the early deaths of his brother, sister, and father, was the source of his private demons. During his marriage to Olivia Langdon, both a son and daughter died young— Susy of spinal meningitis, and their son at nineteen months. Their daughter Jean, an epileptic, drowned in the bathtub. A complex and often sad life.

572 pp.; 1997

11. *George Eliot: Voice of a Century*   Frederick R. Karl

Eliot's ideas about women would not be warmly welcomed among the feminists of today, but her novels are almost beyond great and her life as a woman in the nineteenth century was anything but typical. Also *George Eliot: A Life* by Rosemary Ashton.

708 pp.; 1995

12. *Virginia Woolf*   Hermione Lee

Woolf has been assessed in various biographies, but I think Lee's is one of the best. Particularly good on the issue of Woolf's mental problems; maybe your book club would read it along with *Mrs. Dalloway.*

893 pp.; 1997

13. *Tom: The Unknown Tennessee Williams*   Lyle Leverich

My friend Christine O'Hagan tells me that the Irish always say "I'm sorry for your troubles." Whew—wait till they read this: paranoia, hypochondria, obsessive medicine dosing, a disturbed mother, a beloved sister who is lobotomized, and it goes on. It's amazing that Williams was able to write one decent play, but he greatly enriched the American theater world with many plays, almost all still performed regularly.

644 pp.; 1995

14. *D. H. Lawrence: The Story of a Marriage*   Brenda Maddox

The issue of whether Lawrence was homosexual haunts Maddox, but she points out that his fiction is also loaded with men who loved women. She does a good job, considering that it is hard to get too enthusiastic about a man who was a virulent racist, anti-Semite, and a misogynist of the first order. Her biography of Nora Joyce, wife of James, was published in 1988.

620 pp.; 1994

15. *Anne Sexton:*   Diane Wood Middlebrook
   A Biography

National Book Award for 1991. A definitive examination of the poet and her life that uses therapy session tapes to round out the picture. Even if you're not interested in poetry, you'll like this one.

448 pp.; 1991

16. *Salem Is My Dwelling*   Edwin Haviland Miller
   Place

Subtitled *A Life of Nathaniel Hawthorne*, Miller looks for the secrets in Hawthorne's life, but finds instead the essence of nineteenth-century America in Massachusetts.

596 pp.; 1991

17. *Keats*   Andrew Motion

Since Keats lived from only 1795 to 1821, died from tuberculosis, was thwarted in his love for Fanny Brawne, and was promptly forgotten for about thirty years after his death, it's amazing that there are at least four major biographies of this Romantic poet. This one concentrates on his political leanings as well as the sad details of a short life.

636 pp.; 1998

18. *Thomas Mann: A Life*   Donald Prater

His first novel, *Buddenbrooks* (1901), was an overnight sensation and from that point on, Mann, a German, struggled with his often-cited greatness. With six children and during fifty years of a faithful marriage, he held his clearly homosexual yearnings in check. Two sisters and two sons committed suicide, and the family's drug problems and sexual confusion emerged in his fiction. He won the Nobel Prize for Literature in 1929, five years after the publication of *The Magic Mountain*.

554 pp.; 1995

19. *Randall Jarrell:* **William H. Pritchard**
   A Literary Life

A very good critic describes the life and explains the work of a very unusual American poet.

338 pp.; 1990

20. *Anton Chekhov: A Life* **Donald Rayfield**

Chekhov is usually portrayed as a saint who also wrote the four greatest plays in Russian literature. Son of a freed Russian serf who was a tyrant, Chekhov became a doctor who treated plague victims, visited penal colonies, and died at forty-four, just three years after his marriage to a well-known actress. Rayfield spent five years examining the newly opened archives of the former USSR, and Chekhov now turns out to be less saintly and a hell of a lot more interesting. As the *New York Times* reports, "it is Chekhov's sex life that is the major surprise here."

674 pp.; 1998

21. *Emerson: The* **Robert D. Richardson, Jr.**
   Mind on Fire

A somewhat unctuous acquaintance once remarked, regarding my passion for trees, that I had "perhaps read too much Emerson." I only wish that I'd read more. Richardson shows how Emerson, according to the *New York Times*, "translated his personal difficulties into intellectual achievement."

671 pp.; 1995

22. *Balzac: A Life* **Graham Robb**

I knew very little about this French novelist, born in 1799 and reputed to be the greatest novelist of the nineteenth century. Balzac, Robb says, was a glutton, opium smoker, and "one of the best-dressed bankrupts in Paris," and was probably the inventor of the well-known cash-flow problem. He seemed to experience every-thing and to know everybody, and the two thousand characters in *The Human Comedy* reflect this. Excess at its best.

521 pp.; 1994

23. *Christina Stead: A Biography*   Hazel Rowley

Australian-born but truly a wanderer, Stead's work evokes this quality of restlessness and ephemerality. She had a difficult and strange life.

646 pp.; 1994

24. *The Life of Graham Greene,*   Norman Sherry
Volume 2: 1939–1955

Somehow I got the idea in graduate school that G.G. was a Catholic writer who produced realistic fiction. Now I find out that Greene, according to Sherry, found solace only in drink, drugs, sex, and war, and that he may have turned Kim Philby, his boss in British intelligence who defected to the Russians, into a double agent for the West.

562 pp.; 1989

25. *Genet: A Biography*   Edmund White

This biography of Jean Genet, one of France's most original and forceful novelists and playwrights (who was also a thief and a ped-erast), places Genet's personal and literary vision squarely in his ex-clusively homosexual experience. White is the author of *A Boy's Life*, which deals with his own homosexuality.

728 pp.; 1993

26. *Borges: A Life*   James Woodall

The late Argentine poet and essayist (born in 1899) supposedly had no life outside his work, lived with his widowed mother, married at sixty-eight, and divorced three years later. In 1986, a few weeks before he died, he married his ex-student, who was his secretary and traveling companion. An anti-Marxist and conservative, Borges is generally considered a twentieth-century master.

333 pp.; 1997

6

Ain't Love Grand?;
Pass the Aspirins

1. *Pride and Prejudice*   **Jane Austen**

Mr. and Mrs. Bennett, five daughters, the irresistible and autocratic Darcy, lots of love's complications, and multiple looks at marriage. No one has yet improved on this one, and they probably can't!

374 pp.; 1813

2. *As Max Saw It*   **Louis Begley**

Charlie and Max, two ex-classmates at Harvard, meet twenty years later at Lake Como. The complications begin when Max's life becomes increasingly intertwined with Charlie's, and with his adolescent companion, Toby. Disturbing and different.

146 pp.; 1994

3. *The Blue Afternoon*   **William Boyd**

In 1936 architect Kay Fischer is approached by an old man who claims to be her father and who insists that she accompany him to Lisbon as he searches for his great, lost love.

367 pp.; 1995

4. *Brief Lives*   **Anita Brookner**

Fay Langdon looks back on her relationships with her husband and lover. Brookner always writes poignantly about the sadness of an unfullfilled life, as in *Hotel du Lac*.

260 pp.; 1991

5. *The Awakening*   **Kate Chopin**

Rediscovered classic that lay dormant for eighty years, it is the story of the scandal caused by twenty-eight-year-old Edna Pontellier after she discovers passion for the first time.

341 pp.; 1964

6. *The North China Lover*   **Marguerite Duras**

Set in Vietnam, this revised version of *The Lover* is about a French girl obsessed with a Chinese man.

128 pp.; 1992

7. *The Antelope Wife*   **Louise Erdrich**

The suicide attempt by Richard Whiteheart Beads, a Native American, results in the asphyxiation of his eleven-year-old daughter in the back of his truck. Interwoven are the stories of his wife, the guilt over her affair, and the history of Bead's friend Klaus Shawano, and his ex-lover, Sweetheart Calico, the antelope wife. Powerful tale of love, loss, and survival.

240 pp.; 1998

8. *The Great Gatsby*   **F. Scott Fitzgerald**

The Jazz Age, bootleggers, and moral failure in the persons of Tom Buchanan, an overaged adolescent; Daisy (who wasn't one); Jordan Baker, a cheat; and Gatsby, a re-created man dominated by dishonesty and obsession. Pay attention to Dr. T. J. Eckleburg when you read this novel, one of the greatest written by any American in the twentieth century.

228 pp.; 1925

9. *Madame Bovary*   **Gustave Flaubert**

Emma, the bored wife of a *very* provincial French doctor who is also *very* boring, has been loved or detested by generations of readers. If you were stuck with good old Charles, would you have gotten in this much trouble? Good reasons for this classic to have lasted, and book clubs love it.

424 pp.; 1928

10. *Love in the Time*   **Gabriel García Márquez**
of Cholera

This story of unrequited love—fifty years, nine months, and four days' worth—is set in a country on the Caribbean coast of South America and ranges from the nineteenth century to the early decades of the twentieth. García Márquez won the Nobel in 1982.

348 pp.; 1988

11. *Fear of Flying*   **Erica Jong**

The unforgettable phrase, "the zipless fuck," comes (oops!) from this novel. *Don't miss it.*

340 pp.; 1973

12. *Foreign Affairs*   **Alison Lurie**

An American college professor, sensible Vinnie Miner, meets the unsuitable but irresistible Chuck Mumpson on the plane on her way to London for a sabbatical. Despite his green raincoat and other shortcomings, the inevitable attraction occurs. Winner of the 1984 Pulitzer Prize for fiction. Her newest, *The Last Resort*, is making a big splash.

425 pp.; 1984

13. *Enduring Love*   Ian McEwan

As the *New York Times* reported, this is a book about "one man's obsessive, unrequited love for another, and an exploration of the randomness of fate, the limits of reason and the many varieties of love that draw people together and drive them apart." McEwan is often known by readers as Ian Macabre principally because of *A Child in Time* (a toddler disappears in the supermarket), *Black Dogs* (vacationers are attacked by dogs), and *The Comfort of Strangers* (sadism in Venice). *Amsterdam* recently won the Booker Prize.

256 pp.; 1998

14. *Talking in Bed*   Antonya Nelson

If your book club wants to talk about marriage, longing, loss, and a woman who loves two men, this is the book. Deeply meditative and intelligent.

275 pp.; 1996

15. *The Bird Artist*   Howard Norman

A wonderfully weird novel set in Newfoundland in 1911. When Fabian Vas's mother starts sleeping with Botho August, the lighthouse keeper, during her husband's long absence, her bird artist son loses his bearings. Written in a spare, graceful style, this novel and *The Northern Lights* are both exceptional.

289 pp.; 1994

16. *I Lock My Door Upon Myself*   Joyce Carol Oates

Calla, a mysterious redheaded woman, falls in love with an itinerant water diviner after she has been married off at seventeen to a farmer more than twice her age. The novel was inspired by a painting by the Belgian artist Fernand Khnopff.

98 pp.; 1990

17. *Madness of a Seduced*   **Susan Fromberg Schaeffer**
Woman

Based on a true story, the woman here is driven to murder after she is abandoned by her lover. Good picture of turn-of-the-century Vermont.

578 pp.; 1983

18. *After Moondog*   **Jane Shapiro**

First novel about a marriage that begins in 1965. Joanne and William meet while talking to Moondog, the New York street character who wore a Viking helmet and stood on the corner of 54th Street and Sixth Avenue for many years. Shapiro has an invigorating writing style.

323 pp.; 1992

19. *Anna Karenina*   **Leo Tolstoy**

The archetypal story of the conflict between maternal and sexual love, in nineteenth-century Russia and everywhere else, and never surpassed in the telling by any writer.

855 pp.; 1900

20. *Brother of the More Famous Jack*   **Barbara Trapido**

Moving story of how a naive eighteen-year-old student falls in love with the Goldmans, her philosophy professor's family. British critics compared the voice to Jane Austen, the plot to *Brideshead Revisited*, and the heroine to Moll Flanders, all praise, which, in this case, is richly deserved. Trapido should be much better known in the United States. Also *Noah's Ark*, *Temples of Delight*, and *Traveling Hornplayer*.

218 pp.; 1982

21. *The Accidental Tourist*   Anne Tyler

Muriel Pritchett, an inventive survivor, falls into the life of Macon Leary and her eccentric, disorderly world becomes Macon's gentle reprieve.

355 pp.; 1985

22. *A Handful of Dust*   Evelyn Waugh

Satire of a certain stratum of English life where all the characters have money—but not much else. A marriage breaks up here from the wife's terminal boredom; the parasite she chooses next is worse than the husband.

308 pp.; 1932

23. *Ethan Frome*   Edith Wharton

Watch out for trees if you're on that final sleigh ride with the niece of your boring, angry wife; even unconsummated love affairs can be very dangerous! This is, simply, a *great*, almost existential, book about wasted lives.

260 pp.; 1911

24. *Written on the Body*   Jeanette Winterson

Fourth novel from this British writer, this one describing an erotic affair between the narrator, whose gender we do not know, and Louise, unhappily married to a workaholic cancer researcher. Also *The Passion*.

192 pp.; 1992

7

Watch Your Mouth!

A list for people who love to eat, to cook, to read about food, and who have never seen a menu that was not worth perusing. These are NOT, for the most part, recipe books, but books primarily about food.

1. *The Jane Austen Cookbook*   **M. Black and Deirdre Le Faye**

Food historian Maggie Black has adapted the eighteenth- and nineteenth-century recipes for the meals eaten by Austen and the characters in her fiction. A great idea!

128 pp.; 1995

2. *The Way to Cook*   **Julia Child**

While you're lying there reading—and not on your exercise bike or your treadmill—you may as well read about all the butter, sugar, and cholesterol you are no longer allowed to eat. Child is my hero since the day she said, "Life itself is the proper binge."

544 pp.; 1989

3. *Home Cooking* and   **Laurie Colwin**
   More Home Cooking

Colwin died suddenly several years ago at a young age, so there will be no more of her beautiful words about the joy of eating. Don't miss these.

191 pp.; 1988

4. *Becoming a Chef*   **Andrew Dornenburg**
                                        and Karen Page

Provides the first behind-the-scenes look into some of the most celebrated restaurant kitchens across the nation. A chef's is a complex life.

311 pp.; 1995

5. *Like Water for Chocolate*   **Laura Esquivel**

A novel with love, hope, sex, and recipes, all on a Mexican ranch.

241 pp.; 1992

6. *The Gastronomical Me*   **M. F. K. Fisher**

As much about this feisty, now-deceased writer's sense of self and independence as it is about food.

252 pp.; 1989

7. *Reef*   **Romesh Gunesekera**

A finalist for the Booker Prize, this novel by a young Sri Lankan writer is the story of Triton, a talented young chef so committed to pleasing his master's palate that he forgets that a revolution is brewing outside the kitchen door.

190 pp.; 1994

8. *Moosewood Cookbook*   **Mollie Katzen**

A lot of information about vegetarian meals with less oil, and fewer eggs and dairy products, from the great Ithaca restaurant maven. An antidote to Julia, grown-up, and almost as much fun. (In any case, your cardiologist prefers this one.)

227 pp.; 1977

9. *Nobody Knows the Truffles I've Seen*   George Lang

Hospitality is also a business, as in Lang's Four Seasons in Manhattan and his reopening of the famous Café des Artistes near Lincoln Center. But behind this success is a Nazi labor camp, the torture and murder of his Hungarian-born parents, and his escape to post–World War II New York. This is a man with an unending sense of wonder, energy, and pleasure.

416 pp.; 1998

10. *New York Eats (More)*   Ed Levine

It's probably clear by now to all but the moribund that I love New York. And one of its great gifts is the unending supply of every imaginable food from every imaginable corner of the planet. Levine is a celebrant, a man who can enjoy life, a guy who greets the sun—and he knows where to buy the best of anything you can put on a plate. Hooray!

382 pp.; 1997

11. *Under the Tuscan Sun*   Frances Mayes

Mayes loves her house, the food, and, as the subtitle suggests, she is *At Home in Italy*.

280 pp.; 1996

12. *A Year in Provence*   Peter Mayle

Not strictly about food, this immensely popular book is a month-by-month account of the frustrations that Mayle, his wife, and even their two large dogs encounter when they buy a two-century-old farmhouse in France. Of course there are plenty of stories about cooking and eating as the story moves along. Also *Toujours Provence*.

207 pp.; 1990

13. *Stand Facing the Stove*   Anne Mendelson

Subtitled *The Story of the Women Who Gave America The JOY OF COOKING*, this is an engaging biography of Irma Rombauer and her daughter, Marion Rombauer Becker. It's also a history and critique of cookbook and food writing. I love this title because the first time my children tried to teach me how to use my computer, they said, "Sit facing the screen!"

474 pp.; 1996

14. *Never Eat Your Heart Out*   Judith Moore

As Susan Cheever said in the *New York Times*, "the food Moore cooked while she was falling in love and reveling in adultery throbs and oozes, drips and swells with the juices of passion." I think I'll leave it at that.

328 pp.; 1997

15. *Rao's Cookbook*   Frank Pellegrino

Even most New Yorkers who know everything else don't know about Rao's, a 102-year-old restaurant in East Harlem. It has ten tables, seven of which are reserved each night for regulars like Woody Allen.

207 pp.; 1998

16. *Tender at the Bone:*   Ruth Reichl
Growing Up at the Table

Everybody has a story and some read like fairy tales. Reichl, now the restaurant critic of the *New York Times*, had a manic-depressive mother who created near-lethal casseroles, a distant father, a volunteer grandmother named Birdie, and a Guyanan college roommate. Forget the recipes; this wonderful book, about triumph over adversity, will speak even to the people who live on take-out food and frozen diet dinners.

282 pp.; 1998

17. *The Making of a Chef:*   Michael Ruhlman
Mastering Heat at the Culinary Institute of America

Ruhlman moves his photographer wife and baby daughter to a "one-bedroom garret above a garage in Tivoli, New York, a Hudson River Valley town with a one-to-one human-cow ratio" to chop and dice and sauté and sear his way through the eighty-one-week boot camp that is the Culinary Institute of America.

305 pp.; 1997

18. *Bruculinu, America*   Vincent Schiavelli

Remembrances of Sicilian-American Brooklyn (which these immigrants called broo-koo-LEE-noo), *Told in Stories and Recipes.* The neighborhood was so closely tied to its southern Italian roots, he writes, that "you imagined if you could ride the subway a little longer you'd be in Palermo." A treasure.

336 pp.; 1998

19. *Delia Smith's Winter*   Delia Smith
Collection: Comfort Food

British, and much better known there, this food queen's book is full of exquisite photos and recipes that a nonexpert can actually follow. (Or, like me, you can just gaze—and pretend you are doing the work.) Heartily recommended; I absolutely love this book.

254 pp.; 1995

20. *The Man Who Ate*   **Jeffrey Steingarten**
    Everything and Other Gastronomic Feats,
    Disputes, and Pleasurable Pursuits

Vogue's food critic; my kind of guy. He thinks that food is good for us, we should EAT it, and that we should enjoy every mouthful. May he live forever.

512 pp.; 1997

21. *Food in History*   **Reay Tannahill**

My daughter (the food maven) loves this book. In the most enjoyable of ways, Tannahill explains how food has shaped the development of society, how the cow became sacred, what cinnamon had to do with the discovery of America, and how pepper contributed to the fall of the Roman Empire. A remarkable job.

424 pp.; 1988

Think About Health

Only a sample of the many books on mental, spiritual, and physical health that are available. If you are interested in this subject, see "The Impact of Illness."

1. *Your Heart: An Owner's Manual* — American Heart Association

Cardiovascular disease is the number one killer in America for both men and women. Here is some practical advice that you can actually follow (while trying, for instance, to make a living, raise a family, have a life, etc.) about nutrition, exercise, and weight loss.

368 pp.; 1995

2. *The Women's Complete Healthbook* — American Medical Association

An easy-to-access reference guide with more than two hundred illustrations and charts. The thirty-nine chapters—on pregnancy, menopause, aging, fertility, etc.—are written by female physicians and experts in women's health. It's about time.

708 pp.; 1995

3. *Sex on the Brain: The Biological*   Deborah Blum
   Differences Between Men and Women

The *New York Times* noted that Blum remains "appropriately cautious and skeptical." But think what a good time your book club can have with this one!

352 pp.; 1997

4. *Our Bodies, Ourselves*   Boston Women's
   for the New Century   Health Collective

Revised, after fourteen years and four million copies, this edition includes information on breast cancer treatment options and holistic approaches and herbal remedies.

752 pp.; 1998

5. *The Gravest Show on Earth:*   Elinor Burkett
   America in the Age of AIDS

As Burkett says, "AIDS never got a chance to be simply a disease. It was too busy masquerading as a scourge from God, a comment on the nation's sexual practices, an opportunity for homophobes and heterophobes, even a shot at a Nobel Prize." She divulges the history of this plague in vigorous, straightforward prose and takes on the gay community, the drug companies, and the politicians.

399 pp.; 1995

6. *Finding Flow:*   Mihaly Csikszentmihalyi
   The Psychology of Engagement with Everyday Life

Maybe if more of us understood how "flow experiences," those fleeting "flashes of intense living," are evoked, we'd be able to live fully in the here and now, as Csikszentmihalyi suggests. He maintains that even trivial acts inevitably have an impact on the future.

181 pp.; 1997

7. *Bitter Pills, Inside the Hazardous*   **Stephen Fried**
   World of Legal Drugs

I've known several people who've had serious negative reactions to perfectly legal drugs. So I was particularly interested in Fried's research into Floxin, an antibiotic prescribed to his wife for a minor infection, which impaired her neurological capacities.

417 pp.; 1998

8. *The Coming Plague: Newly*   **Laurie Garrett**
   Emerging Diseases in a World Out of Balance

Garrett describes our fifty-year battle with microbes, from the savannas of eastern Bolivia to the poor sections of the South Bronx. TB, she reminds us, claims 3 million lives annually, malaria kills 105 million people, and by 1994, 16 million adults and 1 million children had been infected with the AIDS virus. There are also *E. coli* 0157.H7, toxic shock syndrome, hantavirus, etc., to worry about. Fortunately, she points to some solutions.

727 plus pp.; 1994

9. *Women of the Asylum:*   **Edited by Jeffrey L. Geller**
   Voices from Behind the Walls,   **and Maxine Harris**
   1840–1945

This collection traces changing perceptions—i.e., "brain strain," "hysteria"—of female sanity through twenty-six first-person narratives. The authors also discuss the treatments: cold baths, sedatives, lobotomies, clitoral cauterizations, and the ways in which "confinement" sometimes becomes security.

349 pp.; 1995

10. *Mind/Body Medicine:*   Edited by Daniel Goleman
    How to Use Your Mind for   and Joel Gurin
    Better Health

Has anyone mentioned in the last five minutes that s-t-r-e-s-s causes illness? The connection between mind and body is undeniable and this book gets to the specifics—how the immune system breaks down from hostility, how to use relaxation techniques, and how pets can improve both your mood and your health. Goleman points out in *Emotional Intelligence* that factors other than IQ contribute to a happy life.

482 pp.; 1993

11. *Living with Our Genes:*   Dean Hamer and
    Why They Matter   Peter Copeland
    More Than You Think

Hamer, a molecular geneticist whose cutting-edge discoveries of specific genes linked to behavioral traits—anxiety, homosexuality, et al.—says here that because of our individual DNAs we arrive more or less ready-made, but that it is also our nature to respond to nurture. Some good news about the link between aging and spirituality.

355 pp.; 1998

12. *An Unquiet Mind:*   Kay Redfield Jamison
    A Memoir of Moods and Madness

A professor of psychiatry at Johns Hopkins, Jamison is an expert on manic-depressive illness/bipolar disorder. Along with some 2.5 million Americans, she is also manic-depressive. Here she talks about her disease, descents into depression, resistance to lithium treatment, a suicide attempt, and bouts with mania. Since so many are suffering with these disorders, she should be commended for her bravery and for the reliable information offered here.

223 pp.; 1995

13. *Listening to Prozac*   **Peter D. Kramer**
Details many of the scientific and social reasons why America may be turning into a Prozac nation.

409 pp.; 1993

14. *How Healthy Is Your Family*   **Carol Krause**
Tree? A Complete Guide to Tracing
Your Family's Medical and Behavioral History
Your genetic stock is turning out to be of major importance in understanding your risk factors for heart disease, alcoholism, mental illness, and many other conditions. This book has good hints on finding the medical records and death certificates of relatives and suggestions for talking to those who are alive but reticent about family secrets.

167 pp.; 1993

15. *In the Country of Illness: Comfort*   **Robert Lipsyte**
and Advice for the Journey
Lipsyte, a well-known sportswriter, survived testicular cancer. But the heroes of this book are his former wife, Margie, with whom he sits as she dies of cancer, and his son Sam, who attends to his mother with gentleness. As one reviewer noted, "the last week of Margie's life was its own benediction." And like many of us, Lipsyte found out "that at his weakest and most vulnerable, he was indeed his best."

252 pp.; 1998

16. *Dr. Susan Love's Breast Book*   **Susan Love, M.D.,**
with Karen Lindsey
I've lost track of how many copies of Susan Love's book I have purchased; in my view, it is the most helpful thing you can do immediately when you hear that you or a friend has breast cancer. This volume covers everything—breast-feeding, breast cancer, mammo-

grams, hormone therapy, silicone implants, and information about the BRCA1 breast-cancer gene. All of us owe Dr. Love a tremendous debt.

627 pp.; 1995

17. *Examining Your Doctor:*   Timothy B. McCall, M.D.
A Patient's Guide to Avoiding Harmful Medical Care
As McCall says, "Most people passively follow the dictates of their doctors. People who wouldn't buy a toaster without consulting *Consumer Reports* become meek and deferential in the presence of a stethoscope and a long white coat." Many of his case histories cite doctors who are rushed, practice defensive medicine (that means they won't get sued for malpractice), or order unnecessary tests. Even if you don't need a doctor now, read this book.

384 pp.; 1996

18. *The Wisdom of the Body*   Sherwin B. Nuland, M.D.
Author of *How We Die*, here Nuland offers a picture of the universe within us—not just cells and tissue, but a portrait of how humans have transcended mere survival and made use of our unique biology. The chapter on his wife's first childbirth is unforgettable. Also an extremely helpful glossary of medical terms.

395 pp.; 1997

19. *How the Mind Works*   Steven Pinker
As *Discover* said, this is a guided tour of the inner recesses of your psyche, which looks less like the Freudian house of horrors than a house of mirrors.

660 pp.; 1997

20. *Winter Blues*   Norman E. Rosenthal, M.D.
I have a close friend with seasonal affective disorder and I have come to realize that this is no laughing matter.

325 pp.; 1993

21. *Successful Aging*   John W. Rowe, M.D., and Robert L. Kahn, M.D.

A *New York Times* writer said that this book, based on a study of men and women seventy and above . . . will fail to get the attention it deserves because "it isn't 'sexy' enough," meaning "the news is good. Most Americans are in reasonably good health, living independently and generally doing well. As the ancient Greeks noted, the goal is 'to die young, as late in life as possible.' "

265 pp.; 1998

22. *Little Girls in Pretty Boxes:*   Joan Ryan
The Making and Breaking of
Elite Gymnists and Figure Skaters

I don't want to ruin anyone's fun here, but behind all those darling gymnasts and elegant figure skaters is an American nightmare, according to Ryan, of "legal, even celebrated, child abuse, overbearing parents, obsessive coaches, anorexia, humiliation and pressure with a big, big P." According to Ryan, this mess needs to be cleaned up, even if we have to sacrifice a few medals along the way.

243 pp.; 1995

23. *The Quiet Room: A Journey Out*   Lori Schiller
of the Torment of Madness   and Amanda Benne

Schiller bravely chronicles her own battle—from her late teens to her thirties—with manic depression and schizophrenia. Then the drug Clozapine helped.

288 pp.; 1994

24. *To Dance with the Devil: The*   Karen Stabiner
New War on Breast Cancer

Anyone, male or female, who has had to sit in the waiting room while someone you love gets chemotherapy or radiation for breast cancer could probably attest to what the *New York Times* calls "a journalist's scary account of tumult in a cancer center, where treatments, careers and hopes are in constant, unmanageable flux."

512 pp.; 1997

25. *Curing Cancer: The Story*   Michael Waldholz
of the Men and Women Unlocking
the Secrets of Our Deadliest Illness

The deputy editor for health and science at the *Wall Street Journal* takes us through the minds and laboratories of cancer researchers. Why does a normal cell suddenly turn deadly? They don't know, but his reporting here is accessible, and comforting, even for those of us who have been through it with many friends.

320 pp.; 1997

26. *Spontaneous Healing: How*   Andrew Weil
to Discover and Enhance Your Body's
Natural Ability to Maintain and Heal Itself

Weil is an advocate of alternative and natural therapies—herbal medicine, mental imagery, acupuncture, diet, exercise, and—as your mother suggested—rest. His advice should be coupled with a healthy and legitimate respect for high-tech medicine when needed.

309 pp.; 1995

27. *Conquering Schizophrenia:*   Peter Wyden
A Father, His Son, and a Medical Breakthrough

Wyden had two sons: one is a U.S. senator, the other is a schizophrenic, the disease that *Nature* says is "arguably the worst disease affecting mankind . . . AIDS not excepted." Wyden's discussion of psychopharmacology was enlightening and energizing for me.

335 pp.; 1997

The Impact of Illness

1. *The Savage God* — A. Alvarez

Alvarez was the first writer on the subject of depression and suicide who moved me deeply. Read this book together with William Styron's chronicle of his own descent into mental illness.

299 pp.; 1972

2. *Anatomy of an Illness* — Norman Cousins

The book grew from an article published in 1976 in the *New England Journal of Medicine* about the partnership beween a physician and a patient in battling illness, and the holistic idea that the human mind and body are a single entity. Cousins was the editor of the *Saturday Review* for more than thirty years.

160 pp.; 1979

3. *The Broken Cord* — Michael Dorris

Fetal alcohol syndrome, an incurable but preventable birth defect, is what often happens when pregnant women drink. Should be required reading for every potential parent in America, not just those from the late author's own Native American culture.

300 pp.; 1989

4. *An Autobiography*   Janet Frame

Gathered together here are *To the Is-land*, *Angel at My Table,* and *Envoy from Mirror City*. New Zealand's greatest novelist was misdiagnosed as schizophrenic and spent eight years in and out of mental hospitals. She was saved from brain surgery not by a doctor's epiphany but by winning a literary prize for her first book, written before her commitment in 1945.

400 pp.; 1991

5. *At the Will of the Body*   Arthur W. Frank

This is a meditative reflection on illness by a man who suffered a heart attack at thirty-nine and cancer at forty. Great for discussions.

144 pp.; 1991

6. *The Yellow Wallpaper*   Charlotte Perkins Gilman *and Other Writings*

Autobiographical title story of depression following childbirth and the classic mistreatment by a Philadelphia neurologist. The fictional narrator goes mad; Gilman saved herself and went on to write ten more books.

63 pp.; 1892

7. *Sounding the Territory*   Laurel Goldman

A portrait of a psychiatric ward written by a woman with heart and empathy.

307 pp.; 1982

8. *The Passion of Alice*   Stephanie Grant

A first novel set in an eating-disorder clinic filled with overeaters, purgers, and undereaters, where no one can shower alone: running water covers the sound of vomiting. This might be funny if this particular plague were not sweeping the country.

260 pp.; 1995

9. *I Never Promised You a Rose Garden*   Hannah Green
Classic study of a sixteen-year-old girl who retreats from reality into psychosis, and her struggle, aided by a knowledgeable psychiatrist, to reenter the world after three years in a mental hospital.

256 pp.; 1964

10. *Death Be Not Proud*   John J. Gunther
A true story of a father's recollections of his son's hard battle against the brain tumor that finally killed him at age seventeen.

261 pp.; 1953

11. *We Have Always Lived*   Shirley Jackson
     in the Castle
Jackson traces in this unusual novel how the female psyche can sometimes be rendered sociopathic.

214 pp.; 1962

12. *Girl, Interrupted*   Susanna Kaysen
The triumphantly funny story of an almost-two-year stay at Mc-Clean Hospital, a psychiatric institution in Belmont, Massachusetts, beginning in 1967, by the daughter of a famous scientist.

168 pp.; 1993

13. *Sailing*   Susan Kenney
A beautiful, even hopeful, semiautobiographical novel about the impact of incurable cancer on a marriage and the courage needed for the family's survival.

320 pp.; 1988

14. *She's Come Undone*   Wally Lamb
Troubled girlhood in a troubled family from the 1950s to the 1980s; the heroine, Dolores Price, survives mental illness and obesity. You have to love her.

465 pp.; 1992

15. *Notes from the Border*   Jane Taylor McDonnell

Searingly honest account of raising a high-functioning autistic child, Paul, who wrote the afterword, but who remains in a kind of emotional no-man's-land, intensely self-conscious of his difference.

384 pp.; 1993

16. *Ordinary Time*   Nancy Mairs

As in *Plaintext, Remembering the Bone House,* and *Carnal Acts,* the essays here share the difficulties of a marriage and a life compounded by Mairs's multiple sclerosis and bouts of depression.

238 pp.; 1993

17. *The Art Lover*   Carole Maso

Caroline, the protagonist, is on a search for clues about how to live. When Maso breaks the fictive form with a harrowing account of her friend Gary Falk's death from AIDS, the novel becomes a testament to redemption.

243 pp.; 1990

18. *Family Pictures*   Sue Miller

Story of a large Chicago family dominated by their son Randall's autism, and of the attendant stresses on a marriage.

389 pp.; 1990

19. *The Loony-Bin Trip*   Kate Millett

Diagnosed as "constitutionally psychotic," Millett was dosed for thirteen years with all manner of mind-deadening drugs. She leads us through the depravation and humiliation of institutionalized "patients" who are stripped of all human and legal necessities. She wrote *Sexual Politics*, now a classic.

316 pp.; 1990

20. *A Beautiful Mind*   Sylvia Nasar
John Nash was a brilliant mathematician at Princeton whose long battle with schizophrenia did not prevent him from winning a Nobel Prize in 1994 based on a twenty-seven-page dissertation in applied game theory, submitted forty-four years earlier. This is a thrilling if scary book.

459 pp.; 1998

21. *The English Patient*   Michael Ondaatje
Four dissimilar people who suffer from the physical and emotional damages of World War II meet in a deserted Italian villa. Complex, haunting interior monologues. This novel won Britain's Booker Prize.

307 pp.; 1992

22. *Face*   Cecile Pineda
Nominated for the American Book Award for First Work, this novel is about disfigurement, desertion, and the individual notion of self. Based on a true story.

194 pp.; 1985

23. *The Bell Jar*   Sylvia Plath
In this American poet's semiautobiographical account, Esther Greenwood, a talented writer, suffers from society's usual dismissal of the female artist.

296 pp.; 1971

24. *Patrimony: A True Story*   Philip Roth
A fine writer brings his storytelling powers to his father's struggle with a fatal brain tumor. At times the book is even funny.

238 pp.; 1991

25. *The Man Who Mistook*   **Oliver Sacks**
His Wife for a Hat

By the author of *An Anthropologist on Mars* and *Awakenings,* which presented the life stories of twenty patients afflicted by an extraordinary disease. Here Sacks explores a greater variety of neurological disorders and their effects upon the minds and lives of patients.

223 pp.; 1985

26. *Life Size*   **Jenefer Shute**

Searing first novel that describes the inner life of a sixty-seven-pound, anorexic, hospitalized young woman who rages against treatment. Don't miss this one.

230 pp.; 1992

27. *Illness as Metaphor*   **Susan Sontag**

Sontag's point is that illness is *not* a metaphor, and that the best way to confront illness is to resist metaphoric thinking. She cites images and metaphors of illness from medical and psychiatric thinking and from the greatest works of literature.

88 pp.; 1978

28. *Darkness Visible:*   **William Styron**
A Memoir of Madness

Several years ago, this author of *Lie Down in Darkness* and *Sophie's Choice* was overtaken by despair. His real healers, he said, were "seclusion and time." You might want to look at *William Styron: A Life,* by James L. W. West.

84 pp.; 1990

29. *Miss Lonelyhearts*   **Nathanael West**

Unusual novel about a newspaperman, so named because he has been assigned to write the agony column and to answer the letters from Desperate, Sick-of-It-All, and Disillusioned. *The Day of the Locust* is by West as well.

185 pp.; 1933

Fairy Tales for Grown-ups

1. ***Don Quixote, Which Was a Dream***   **Kathy Acker**
A feminist retelling of Cervantes's famous tale.

> 207 pp.; 1986

2. ***The Music of Chance***   **Paul Auster**
Parable about two men, a fireman and a gambler, who end up in a deadly game against two guys named Flower and Stone. They risk everything "on the single turn of a card."

> 217 pp.; 1990

3. ***Chimera***   **John Barth**
A modern Scheherazade and *Thousand and One Nights* story, Barth's *Chimera*, like the mythical fire-eating monster, is composed of three interrelated elements: fore, Dunyazadiad; hind, Bellerophoniad; and middle, Perseid.

> 308 pp.; 1972

4. ***Snow White***   **Donald Barthelme**
A surrealistic version of the classic fairy tale combined with a critique of consumer society that also consumes fiction.

> 180 pp.; 1967

5. *Mr. Palomar*   Italo Calvino

Mr. Palomar, a descendant of the Baron who lived in the trees, is a quester after knowledge. A witty, fantastic tale.

126 pp.; 1983

6. *Nights at the Circus*   Angela Carter

Considered by many critics to be her masterpiece, these are the adventures of the half girl, half bird named Fevvers. Carter's early death was a great loss to literature.

294 pp.; 1985

7. *The Alchemist*   Paulo Coelho

Santiago, an Andalusian boy, travels in search of treasure, but most important is his encounter with the alchemist. Over a million and a half copies of this modern fable, written by this Brazilian, have been sold.

177 pp.; 1993

8. *Pinocchio in Venice*   Robert Coover

A postmodern tour de force that is a wicked companion volume to the original Pinocchio story. Older scholar and aesthete returns to Italy to complete his magnum opus, a final great tribute to the Blue-Haired Fairy.

330 pp.; 1991

9. *The Name of the Rose*   Umberto Eco

Signs, symbols, and metaphysical speculation; if you like medieval thrillers and complicated puzzles, this can't be beat.

724 pp.; 1983

10. *October Light*   John Gardner

Picture of a family revolution, this allegorical novel is shot through with legend, memory, and myth. An old brother and sister live together, but not happily, in his house in Vermont. Even Ethan Allen becomes a character here, as do the people in a trashy paperback in the sister's room. One of Gardner's last novels; he died young in a motorcyle accident. His novel *Grendel* fits here too.

434 pp.; 1976

11. *The Old Man and the Sea*   Ernest Hemingway

Won the Pulitzer Prize and led directly to his being awarded the Nobel in 1954. In this parable-like tale, an old Cuban fisherman who catches a giant marlin is unable to keep the sharks from mutilating it before he gets to shore. Watch the symbolic number 40 in this one.

140 pp.; 1952

12. *Smilla's Sense of Snow*   Peter Hoeg

Smilla, an elegant, independent thirty-seven-year-old woman who is an expert on snow and ice, investigates the death of an Eskimo boy from Greenland named Isaiah. This morality tale is heightened by the discussion of culture, race, heritage, and destiny, all encoded in the character of Smilla's Eskimo mother and her father, a rational, unemotional Danish anesthesiologist. Skip the movie.

453 pp.; 1993

13. *The Bone People*   Keri Hulme

Winner of the Booker Prize and the Pegasus Prize for literature, this unusual novel features Kerewin Holmes, a part Pakeha (New Zealander of European descent), part Maori (New Zealander of Polynesian descent) in self-exile, living in a tower she has built with money won in a lottery. Hulme, herself a Maori, lives in Okarito, Westland, in New Zealand.

450 pp.; 1985

14. *Mrs. Caliban and Other Stories*   Rachel Ingalls
In most fairy tales, there are disappearing children, murder, per-version, and the rest; Ingalls treats all the horrors in a matter-of-fact, clear manner in these modern fables.

125 pp.; 1983

15. *Einstein's Dreams*   Alan Lightman
Lightman is a science writer (*A Modern Day Yankee in a Connecti-cut Court*), but in this unusual fiction debut he creates Einstein's possible nighttime fantasies as a twenty-six-year-old patent clerk in Switzerland, during May and June of 1905, when Einstein was working on his theory of relativity.

224 pp.; 1993

16. *The Giver*   Lois Lowry
A haunting novel in which a boy inhabits a seemingly ideal world but where there are dark secrets underlying this fragile per-fection. Any reading group could (and should) talk about this slim volume for hours.

180 pp.; 1993

17. *A River Runs Through It*   Norman Maclean
Two brothers growing up in Missoula, Montana, in the 1930s learn the art of fly-fishing from their father; when one brother's life becomes fragmented and troubled, the other brother tries to save him.

161 pp.; 1989

18. *The Magic Mountain*   Thomas Mann
In this long, celebrated novel devoid of plot, Hans Castorp, a young north German engineer, visits his cousin in a TB sanitorium high in the Swiss mountains. Fascinated by decay, he stays for seven years. Mann uses this framework to discuss all the symbolic and

philosophical problems of the twentieth century in what is definitely one of the greatest works of modern world literature.

900 pp.; 1924

19. *Moby-Dick*   Herman Melville

Remember how your high school English teacher told you the whiteness of the whale represented good and Ahab symbolized evil? Or was it the other way around? Take another look.

728 pp.; 1851

20. *Animal Farm*   George Orwell

World-famous allegory in which the animals, and the rest of us, learn that not all pigs are trustworthy, nor are all animals created equal.

155 pp.; 1945

21. *The Satanic Verses*   Salman Rushdie

This fable about Islam earned Rushdie a death sentence from Iranian fundamentalists. He followed their threat with *Haroun and the Sea of Stories*, but *Midnight's Children* is his best book.

546 pp.; 1989

22. *The Catcher in the Rye*   J. D. Salinger

Holden Caulfield has entered the vocabulary as a modern-day Huck Finn and, with his sister, Phoebe, represents (among many other interpretations) the innocence of Eden and the corruption of it by society. The paperback version published in 1964 has gone through more than forty printings. Follow up with *Franny and Zooey*, the bible of the 1960s.

277 pp.; 1951

23. *Mr. Summer's Story*   Patrick Süskind

The narrator is a nameless boy who hates his piano teacher. Mr. Summer is an eccentric recluse who strides around the countryside saying only, "Why can't you just leave me in peace!" and who pulls the boy down to earth, literally and emotionally. In Süskind's *Perfume* a baby is born under a fishmonger's table and then abandoned. Although this kid has no aroma of his own, he possesses an absolute sense of smell and his obsession, to isolate the most perfect scent of all, leads to disaster.

116 pp.; 1993

24. *Tintin in the New World*   Frederic Tuten

A French comic strip hero, Tintin, beloved by both adults and children in the glossy, oversized, imported comic book version, is introduced by an American writer into a novel and to the temptations of the real world.

239 pp.; 1993

25. *Things Invisible to See*   Nancy Willard

One of the few novels that can be described, in the best sense, as a cult novel among writers. Seemingly it is about a baseball game between dead sports heroes and the mothers of children who can be saved only if those mothers win the game, but it is actually a brilliant fictionalized discussion of good and evil. In *Sister Water,* Willard creates a cat named The Everpresent Fullness, the Buddha Uproar Cafe, and an indoor stream where fish swim into view and then vanish under the floor.

263 pp.; 1985

26. *Sexing the Cherry*   Jeanette Winterson

Rabelaisian romp in the reign of Charles II when Jordan and his mother, the Dog-Woman, live on the banks of the stinking Thames. He learns that every journey conceals another within it.

167 pp.; 1990

27 *Orlando*   Virginia Woolf

A historical fantasy, this novel charts the life of its central character from a masculine identity within the Elizabethan court to a feminine identity. An early exploration of the tension between androgyny and the conventions of sexual difference.

222 pp.; 1928

More Fairy Tale Time

This is an entirely new list of novels that allude, subtly or otherwise, to the traditions of the fairy tale, to Bible stories, and to myth. It accompanies "Fairy Tales for Grown-ups."

1. *Mr. Vertigo*   **Paul Auster**

A cocky orphan boy is adopted in 1924 at the age of nine by Master Yehudi, a mysterious Hungarian Jew who teaches young Walt Rawley the impossible—how to levitate off the ground, and to move himself through the air.

293 pp.; 1994

2. *Rule of the Bone*   **Russell Banks**

The Huck Finn myth shows up in the person of Chappie, a mall rat from upstate New York. He lights out for the territory with a runaway farm worker.

390 pp.; 1995

3. *Cora Fry's Pillow Book*   **Rosellen Brown**

The story of a small-town, working-class New Englander begins in *Cora Fry*, an earlier novel in verse, which is reprinted here. I love Rosellen Brown's voice.

179 pp.; 1994

4. *Talking to the Dead*   Helen Dunmore

Good sister, bad sister, one blonde, one brunette, two babies, lots of sex, and two murders? Dunmore is the first winner of the Orange Prize for fiction—the women-only version of the Booker Prize.

300 pp.; 1996

5. *The Sacrifice of Isaac*   Neil Gordon

First novel, actually a murder thriller, based loosely on the biblical story of Abraham and Isaac. Here, Luke Benami goes to Israel when his father, General Yosef Benami, dies of a heart attack. The novel is also about brotherly love, sacrifice, and the apparent need in some men to make war.

304 pp.; 1995

6. *The Saskiad*   Brian Hall

Hall's massive intelligence shines through everything he writes. This novel is about a twelve-year-old who longs to escape from the rundown commune where she lives with her organic farmer mother and imagines herself as the noble contemporary of Odysseus and other heroes. Real life with her own long-lost father turns out to be a bigger challenge.

380 pp.; 1997

7. *The Phantom Tollbooth*   Norton Juster

This offbeat fantasy about a little boy named Milo and his strange adventures with King Azaz the Unabridged, the unhappy ruler of Dictionopolis; Faintly Macabre, the not-so-wicked Which; and the watchdog, Tock, may be a bit precious for the 1990s reader. But since we are still searching for Juster's Rhyme and Reason, it is worth a look, if only for the Jules Feiffer illustrations.

256 pp.; 1961

8. *The Giant's House*   **Elizabeth McCracken**

I'm a McCracken fan because she is one of the young writers with a distinctive voice. In this first novel, a finalist for the National Book Award, a librarian falls in (romantic) love with a young boy who can't stop growing. Poignant and thoughtful.

259 pp.; 1996

9. *Who Will Run the Frog Hospital?*   **Lorrie Moore**

The heroine is approaching forty in this sad fairy tale, and, like all of us, she thinks about all those missed opportunities.

147 pp.; 1994

10. *A Feather on the Breath of God*   **Sigrid Nunez**

The immigrant story and the power of family never fail to mesmerize. Here, a female narrator with a Chinese-Panamanian father and a German mother grows up in a New York housing project in the 1950s and 1960s.

192 pp.; 1996

11. *The Magician's Assistant*   **Ann Patchett**

The opening line, "Parsifal is dead," does not entirely prepare you for a gay magician who owns a rug store in L.A., has AIDS, and dies of a ruptured aneurysm while holding hands with his bride. Lots of secrets in this novel, including a mother and two sisters from Alliance, Nebraska, that no one knew about.

357 pp.; 1997

12. *Morality Play*   **Barry Unsworth**

Interesting way to get some insight into what fourteenth-century England was like. Clearly, our moral dilemmas remain the same. In this story, a twenty-three-year-old priest breaks his vows of chastity and ends up as a member of a troupe of traveling actors who reenact a child's murder in order to solve it. In 1992, Unsworth won the Booker Prize for *Sacred Hunger*.

206 pp.; 1995

13. *Objects in Mirror Are Closer Than They Appear*   Katharine Weber

Weber was deservedly one of *Granta*'s fifty regional choices for the best young (under forty) writers in the United States in 1996. This first novel, about female friendship, finding and losing yourself, and much more is great for book clubs. Her latest, *The Music Lesson*, concerns an IRA theft of one of the Queen's art treasures.

262 pp.; 1995

14. *The Glass Mountain*   Leonard Wolf

A quest fantasy with modern psychological underpinnings, this novel has an ice queen, another obsessed with birds, many riddles—all permeated by some deeply disturbing Oedipal tensions.

243 pp.; 1993

15. *After Gregory*   Austin Wright

Gregory plunges into the river. Leaves his family. Kills his neighbor? Maybe. Extremely readable and gripping.

292 pp.; 1994

What an Adventure!

Many more readers seem to be gravitating toward adventure books and these give you some idea of what is readily available. The subject itself works for book clubs, even if they meet in the heart of the city and are far from the wilder regions of the world. "Save the Planet" is a related list.

1. *The Voyage of the Narwhal*   Andrea Barrett

In 1855 the *Narwhal* is about to set sail for the Arctic in search of Sir John Franklin's lost expedition. In some ways this is a classic nineteenth-century adventure story of men trapped by ice, the disappearance of a maniac captain named Zeke, and his reappearance after the crew returns to Philadelphia. But it is also a breathtaking story of family dynamics and moral dilemmas.

386 pp.; 1998

2. Daisy Bates in the Desert   Julia Blackburn

Biography of an eccentric woman, set in the aboriginal desert of Australia. Subtitled *A Woman's Life Among the Aborigines.*

232 pp.; 1994

3. *The Universe Below: Discovering*   William J. Broad
   the Secrets of the Deep Sea

Broad, a Pulitzer Prize–winning science reporter for the *New York Times*, explains how marine scientists are exploring the earth's last frontier. He also details how some "citizens" are trying to find (and make money from) the tons of lost artwork and artifacts in the sea.

415 pp.; 1997

4. *A Walk in the Woods: Rediscovering*   Bill Bryson
   America on the Appalachian Trail

The Trail is 2,160 miles long, from Springer Mountain in Georgia to Mount Katahdin in Maine. Bryson, mildly overweight and middle-aged, and his hiking partner, Stephen Katz, who took "some contaminated phenylethylamines about ten years ago" and is seriously out of shape, walked 870 miles of it—or 39.5 percent of its total. Bravo!

274 pp.; 1998

5. *USA*   John Dos Passos

One of the great human adventures is the emigration of many people into America. Trilogy consisting of *The 42nd Parallel* (1930), *1919* (1932), and *The Big Money* (1936).

The 42nd Parallel, 365 pp.; *1919,* 412 pp.; *The Big Money,* 494 pp.

6. *Gorillas in the Mist*   Dian Fossey

One of the longest field studies of primates, covering fifteen years in the lives of four gorilla families in Central Africa, ended with Fossey's murder.

326 pp.; 1983

7. *The Royal Road to Romance*   **Richard Halliburton**

This adventurer spent six hundred days biking across Germany and swimming the Hellespont in northwest Turkey. He trekked across the Himalayas, climbed Mount Fujiyama in Japan and the Acropolis in Greece, and slept out under the stars at the Taj Mahal in India. And you're complaining about your morning commute?

399 pp.; 1925

8. *Amelia Earhart's Daughters*   **Leslie Haynsworth and David Toomey**

Subtitled *The Wild and Glorious Story of American Women Aviators from World War II to the Dawn of the Space Age,* this is the exciting story of the forgotten women aviators of World War II, thirty-eight of whom died during the war and were denied military funerals, who trained to become military ferry pilots, flew without military benefits, lived in almost squalid conditions, and still outperformed men on exams and flight tests. They were also the first pilots to fly the dreaded B-26. Thirteen of them passed all the tests to qualify as astronauts. I'm proud but not surprised

322 pp.; 1998

9. *The Perfect Storm:*   **Sebastian Junger**
A True Story of Men Against the Sea

Recounts the disaster of the seventy-two-foot swordfishing boat *Andrea Gail,* which disappeared with its crew of six in October 1991, a thousand miles from Gloucester, Massachusetts, its home base. Only a propane tank and a radio beacon washed up on the beach. Junger wants to know why certain men risk their lives for swordfish, how storms are formed, and what it means to withstand hundred-foot waves.

227 pp.; 1997

10. *Into Thin Air*   Jon Krakauer

Krakauer, a veteran climber and a writer for *Outside* magazine, was a member of one of the ill-fated teams attempting a final assault on the peak of Mount Everest in 1996. Intensely personal and painful.

378 pp.; 1997

11. *Into the Wild*   Jon Krakauer

Chris McCandless, an affluent honors graduate of Emory University, starved to death in the summer of 1992. His decomposed body was found by moose hunters in an abandoned Fairbanks city bus. He left behind five rolls of film and a haunting diary of his final days, scribbled in the last two pages of a field guide to edible plants. His attempt to survive in the natural world failed, but we have much to learn from him about fear and courage.

207 pp.; 1996

12. *The Call of the Wild*   Jack London

The adventures of an unusual dog, part Saint Bernard, part shepherd, that eventually becomes the leader of a wolf pack in the Klondike gold fields.

102 pp.; 1990 (reprint)

13. *Arctic Dreams*   Barry Lopez

Subtitled *Imagination and Desire in a Northern Landscape*, this is a celebration of the arctic landscape, of the metaphorical power it has exerted on the human imagination, of the animals who live there, and of some who have made the journey: Cook and Peary, sixth-century Irish monks, and Elizabethan sailors. A new book, *About This Life: Journeys on the Threshold of Memory,* is compelling.

448 pp.; 1986

14. *Canyon Solitude: A Woman's*   Patricia C. McCairen
    Solo River Journey Through the Grand Canyon

Chronicle of a twenty-five-day solo raft trip through the canyon's gorge. Men who go on such adventures, she notes, are considered "brave and daring"; women who do so are considered odd. Let's hope that's changing.

246 pp.; 1998

15. *Sisterhood of Spies*   Elizabeth P. McIntosh

McIntosh was working as a war correspondent when the Japanese bombed Pearl Harbor. By 1943 she was employed by the Office of Strategic Services, creating what we now call "disinformation." Her compatriots were women like Maria Gulovich, who fled the German army across mountains in subfreezing weather, and Virginia Hall, known to the Nazis as "the Limping Lady" because of her artificial leg. The best known of the group was one Julia McWilliams, or as we know her, Julia Child. Makes you proud to be a woman.

282 pp.; 1998

16. *The Commodore*   Patrick O'Brian

In O'Brian's seventeenth novel, large, good-natured Captain Jack Aubrey of the British navy and his ship's doctor, Stephen Maturin, both complex men, leave England during the naval wars against Napoleon. You can read this without starting at novel number one. Some others are *Master and Commander*, *Post Captain*, *The Yellow Admiral*.

282 pp.; 1995

17. *No Mercy: A Journey into the*   Redmond O'Hanlon
    Heart of the Congo

An expedition in search of a living dinosaur? I'll go on this one! O'Hanlan has a rare and nutty way of seeing the world.

461 pp.; 1997

18. *The Travellers' Guide to Mars*   **Michael Pauls and Dana Facaros**

As the *New York Times* said, this is "a breezy and painlessly informative survey of what you could expect to find on the red planet if you had thirteen months to travel there and back and $640,000 for the estimated cost of a round-trip ticket—and if such an enterprise were technically achievable." I love this stuff.

108 pp.; 1998

19. *I May Be Some Time: Ice and the English Imagination*   **Francis Spufford**

Spufford got interested in Scott's journey to the South Pole by reading *The Worst Journey in the World* by Apsley Cherry-Garrard, who was with Scott on his 1910–12 expedition. What he is really trying to figure out is why the English, back to the Victorians and the Edwardians, felt compelled to make these journeys.

372 pp.; 1997

20. *Terra Incognita: Travels in Antarctica*   **Sara Wheeler**

Wheeler is a British travel writer who set out in 1995 to retrace the footsteps of Robert Falcon Scott (who died in Antarctica in 1912) and his colleague Ernest Shackleton. As the *New York Times* noted, "instead of limning the physical world of the pole—its geologic formations, its animal life, its atmospheric conditions—she zeroes in on the people who have charted and continue to chart the [South Pole's] stark and unforgiving terrain."

351 pp.; 1998

War Is Hell...Continued

1. *The Ghost Road*   **Pat Barker**

The human cost of World War I is illuminated here through the
life of Lieutenant Billy Prior, cured of shell shock by famed psychiatrist Dr. William Rivers at Craiglockhart War Hospital. Booker
Prize winner and third in a trilogy. Preceded by *Regeneration* and
The Eye in the Door. Close to a masterpiece.

278 pp.; 1995

2. *Dangling Man*   **Saul Bellow**

A short, intense portrait of a young man waiting to be called up
for military service and caught in the limbo between war and peace.

126 pp.; 1944

3. *Tree of Heaven*   **R. C. Binstock**

This novel, set in Nanking during the savage Japanese invasion
of China in the 1930s, is a love story about a junior officer, trained
as a botanist, and his captive, a starving, filthy, Chinese woman—
with whom he falls deeply in love.

212 pp.; 1995

4. *Muddy Boots and Red Socks*   Malcolm W. Browne

Along with David Halberstam, with whom he shared a Pulitzer for coverage of Vietnam, and Neil Sheehan, Browne is the most reliable reporter on this war. He has seen it all—from Indochina to the Persian Gulf.

366 pp.; 1993

5. *A Good Scent*   Robert Olen Butler
from a Strange Mountain

Butler's fifteen stories are told from the point of view of a Vietnamese immigrant to the American Gulf Coast whose sense of loss stems more from cultural displacement than from the war. A Pulitzer Prize winner.

249 pp.; 1993

6. *The Red Badge of Courage*   Stephen Crane

Henry Fleming volunteers to serve with the Union forces, but he is thrown into a panic when he is faced with real fighting. This story is more about the courage of common men than it is about generals, victories, and defeats. A classic not to be missed.

170 pp.; 1895

7. *The Discovery of the*   Bernal Diaz del Castillo
Conquest of Mexico

Diaz was a young soldier in the Spanish army that conquered Mexico under Cortes's leadership. It's a bloody tale of how Cortes successfully posed as Quetzalcoatl, the ruler whose return the Aztecs expected, and then managed to kill every living thing in sight.

478 pp.; 1996

8. *To the White Sea*   James Dickey

A B-29 tailgunner named Muldron is shot down over Tokyo in the last days of World War II. The lone survivor, he strikes out for Hokkaido, the northernmost Japanese island.

275 pp.; 1993

9. *Winners and Losers*   Gloria Emerson

An American classic. Emerson traveled across the United States to speak to those who fought in Vietnam or opposed that war.

448 pp.; 1976

10. *The Wars*   Timothy Findley

Margot Livesey says that this novel about a young Canadian soldier's experiences in France during World War II "is remarkable for making new the horror of war. The protagonist's protest is irresistible and completely surprising."

226 pp.; 1990

11. *Cold Mountain*   Charles Frazier

It does my heart good that a first-time novelist has deservedly won every award in sight for this beautiful Civil War love story of Ada and Inman. Bravo.

356 pp.; 1997

12. *Patches of Fire: A Story of*   Albert French
War and Redemption

This African-American novelist, a marine in Vietnam, writes a memoir about his unit and the senseless life that was the infantryman's lot. He recounts what happened after his return and how his pain almost did him in.

241 pp.; 1997

13. *The Best and the Brightest*   David Halberstam

Clear-sighted, evenhanded reporting on U.S. politics and government from 1961 to 1969, and the answers to Mailer's question, Why [Were] We in Vietnam? Also *One Very Hot Day.*

688 pp.; 1972

14. *Stones from the River*   Ursula Hegi

Oprah loved this one more than I did, but it is unquestionably useful in understanding how ordinary citizens in Germany were complicit in the near extermination of the Jews and in the creation of the Holocaust. Hegi's story of Trudi Montag, a dwarf, explains the perilous existence of the "other"—particularly in a society where Nazis ruled.

525 pp.; 1994

15. *Paco's Story*   Larry Heinemann

Winner of the National Book Award, this novel reminds readers that the blue-collar men of this country bore the brunt of Vietnam and that many of these men remain haunted.

210 pp.; 1986

16. *A Farewell to Arms*   Ernest Hemingway

Set on the Italian front during World War II, Frederic Henry, a wounded American ambulance driver, falls in love with his English nurse, Catherine Barkley. If you can get past what you know of Hemingway's sexism and his treatment of women, this is one of his best novels.

332 pp.; 1929

17. *Dispatches*   Michael Herr

Nonfiction account of the Vietnam years which makes the point that it is hard to arrive at a final truth about this experience.

260 pp.; 1977

18. *The Soldiers' Tale: Bearing*   **Samuel Hynes**
    Witness to Modern War

Hynes, a Woodrow Wilson Professor of Literature Emeritus at
Princeton, was also a Marine combat pilot in both World War II
and the Korean War. He has been working on this book—both a
meditation on war and a survey of the vast literature produced by
men in war (but no women)—for fifty years.

318 pp.; 1997

19. *A Very Long Engagement*   **Sébastien Japrisot**

A French novel about World War II, part romance, part history,
part mystery, concerning five French soldiers in January 1917 who
try to escape further military service by shooting themselves in the
hand. Very worthwhile.

327 pp.; 1993

20. *From Here to Eternity*   **James Jones**

Oh, that scene on the beach! One of the great World War II novels, and even the movie is good.

861 pp.; 1951

21. *The Truce*   **Primo Levi**

In this sequel to his 1947 Holocaust memoir, *Surviving in
Auschwitz*, Levi is liberated from the death camp by Russian soldiers and travels a long, circuitous route by rail and on foot through
a series of dirty Soviet-run displaced person camps to his home in
Turin, Italy.

380 pp.; 1979

22. *Slow Walk in a Sad Rain*   **John McAfee**

A powerful, darkly comic novel based on the author's experiences
as a Green Beret in Vietnam.

256 pp.; 1993

23. *The Naked and the Dead*   Norman Mailer
A great novel about a handful of exhausted men in the recon-naissance platoon who landed on the beach at Anopopei during World War II. Another set of questions about war was posed in *Why Are We in Vietnam?*

605 pp.; 1951

24. *Going After Cacciato*   Tim O'Brien
Generally considered the best novel about Vietnam, in this one O'Brien's hero walks out of the jungles and begins the 8,600-mile walk to "gay Paree."

338 pp.; 1978

25. *Buffalo Soldiers*   Robert O'Connor
In this one the U.S. Army is wallowing in peacetime, with plenty of time for drinking booze, chasing women, and watching TV. Specialist Ray Elwood, clerk to the battalion commander in Mannheim, Germany, deals heroin to the troops and is almost con-sumed by the system. A violent, comic, and captivating read.

324 pp.; 1993

26. *The Names of the Dead*   Stewart O'Nan
This is both a portrait of the Vietnam War in 1960 and the men who fought in A Shan Valley, and of survivor Larry Markham, who has a dead-end job in Ithaca, New York, and a wife who has left him and taken their young son with her. Also *A World Away*. Watch this young writer.

399 pp.; 1996

27. *Machine Dreams*   Jayne Anne Phillips
The war in Vietnam splinters the society around the Hampsons of Bellington, West Virginia, and leaves them, and the country,

permanently scarred and changed. Also her short-story collection, *Fast Lanes*.

331 pp.; 1984

28. *Gravity's Rainbow*   Thomas Pynchon

This National Book Award winner is about Tyrone Slothrop, an American lieutenant stationed in London during World War II. His particular gift is that his erections anticipate German rocket launchings. Demanding but extraordinary.

887 pp.; 1973

29. *All Quiet on the*   Erich Maria Remarque
Western Front

The power of this realistic novel of World War I lies in its passionate hatred of war, experienced in person by the author. After his sudden rise to world fame, he moved to Switzerland after the rightwing German press subjected him to a campaign of hatred and abuse.

256 pp.; 1929

30. *Arundel*   Kenneth Roberts

Arundel, Maine (now called Kennebunkport), is Roberts's ancestral home and that of this novel's main character, Steven Nason. He was the right-hand man to Benedict Arnold as the Revolutionary War general drove his troops northward toward the walls of Quebec.

487 pp.; 1956

31. *A Bright Shining Lie*   Neil Sheehan

Why America lost the Vietnam War is delineated in this 1989 Pulitzer Prize winner for nonfiction. When Lieutenant Colonel John Paul Vann realized that the South Vietnamese regime was corrupt and incompetent, he secretly briefed reporters (one of whom was Sheehan) on what was really happening.

861 pp.; 1988

32. *Dog Soldiers*   Robert Stone
A National Book Award winner. Stone creates a compelling account of the Vietnam drug trade.

263 pp.; 1974

33. *Slaughterhouse-Five*   Kurt Vonnegut
The hero goes to Dresden as it is about to be destroyed by the Allies, to Ilium (Ithaca, home of Cornell), and to the planet Tralfamadore. Vonnegut wrote, among others, *Cat's Cradle* and *God Bless You, Mr. Rosewater*.

215 pp.; 1969

34. *Iron Coffins*   Herbert Werner
Written by a former German officer, this book recalls why 779 U-boats sank and how the Allies defeated Hitler's plan to intercept American ships ferrying war matériel across the North Atlantic.

329 pp.; 1969

35. *In Pharaoh's Army*   Tobias Wolff
Second installment of an autobiographical record, begun with *This Boy's Life*, Wolff writes here about the Mekong Delta at the time of the Tet offensive, and of hundreds of corpses "rolled up in tatami mats and left by the roadside for pickup." Tobias Wolff is one of America's best writers.

221 pp.; 1994

14

Evil Lurks

1. *Bastard Out of Carolina*   **Dorothy Allison**
Ruth Anne Boatwright, a teenage daughter of a luckless, Southern, "white trash" mother, suffers sexual abuse from her vicious stepfather in South Carolina. Allison's latest novel is *Cavedweller.*

309 pp.; 1992

2. *Affliction*   **Russell Banks**
Wade Whitehouse, a part-time policeman, is the poster child for male violence. In the struggle between decency and brutality, Whitehouse represents a man beset by the dark side of the macho mentality. *Cloudsplitter* is sad and marvelous.

355 pp.; 1989

3. *Violence*   **Richard Bausch**
Public and private forms of brutality, including an armed robbery, dominate this masterly novel by a very fine contemporary writer. Also *Rebel Powers*.

293 pp.; 1992

4. *Meeting Evil*   **Thomas Berger**
Evil shows up this time in the person of Richie, a cheerful psychopath standing in John Felton's doorway.

256 pp.; 1992

5. *Theory of War*   Joan Brady

This novel, based on the true story of Brady's grandfather—a white man who was a slave in America—should be much better known.

257 pp.; 1993

6. *A Clockwork Orange*   Anthony Burgess

Alex, a vicious fifteen-year-old hoodlum, is the central character in this thirty-six-year-old book, a nightmare vision of the future. This is a frightening fable about good and evil, and, if you read the newspapers, you will see that a lot of it sounds eerily familiar.

192 pp.; 1962

7. *In Cold Blood*   Truman Capote

One of the first so-called nonfiction novels. A terrifying portrayal of the brutal mass murder by two psychopaths of an entire family, the Clutters, Capote captures an event that now seems horrifyingly familiar, and not just in Kansas.

343 pp.; 1965

8. *Falconer*   John Cheever

After the death of his brother, a college professor named Ezekiel Farragut ends up an unlikely convict in cellblock A, in a prison called Falconer. Cheever's best work.

226 pp.; 1977

9. *Waiting for the Barbarians*   J. M. Coetzee

Prizewinning novel by a South African, this is an allegory of the war between the oppressor and the oppressed. Here it is the Magistrate who lives in complicity with the Empire, a regime he comes to deplore. In *The Master of Petersburg,* the hero is none other than Dostoyevsky.

156 pp.; 1981

10. *Heart of Darkness* — Joseph Conrad

The story of Marlow, Conrad's famous maritime wanderer in Africa, and how he first hears the name Kurtz ("He dead"), the evil figure at the heart of darkness.

117 pp.; 1902

11. *Deliverance* — James Dickey

Four men set out from a small Southern town for a three-day camping and canoe trip. What they find is murder, sexual violence, and the violence of nature. The movie is on most people's 100 Best list.

239 pp.; 1970

12. *Play It as It Lays* — Joan Didion

Loveless sex, drugs, violence, and booze in a grim portrayal of a California world where people use each other without sympathy or conscience.

214 pp.; 1989

13. *The Diary of a Young Girl, The Definitive Edition* — Anne Frank

"I want to go on living even after my death," wrote young Anne Frank in 1944, the year she and her family were discovered in their hiding place in an Amsterdam attic. Of the eight people "living" there, only her father, Otto Frank, survived. The others, along with more than six million Jews and other minorities, were murdered by the Nazis.

340 pp.; 1995

14. *Lord of the Flies* — William Golding

Golding won the Nobel Prize for Literature in 1983 although this book was first published almost thirty years earlier. Proper

British schoolboys are marooned on a deserted island and the struggle between good and evil begins. Evil wins.

243 pp.; 1954

15. *Snow Falling on Cedars*   David Guterson

Winner of the PEN/Faulkner Award for a first novel, this became a bestseller and is on everyone's list of favorite books. This story of murder, love, and justice pivots around a Japanese American on trial in 1954.

345 pp.; 1994

16. *Dogeaters*   Jessica Hagedorn

Nominated for a National Book Award, Hagedorn's novel describes a Philippines where Hollywood dreams and tropical nightmares violently collide. American pop culture and local Filipinos mix again in *The Gangster of Love*.

251 pp.; 1990

17. *King Leopold's Ghost: A Story*   Adam Hochschild
of Greed, Terror, and Heroism in Colonial Africa

Hochschild does a masterful job of delineating the greed and atrocities committed in central Africa by many men under the protection of Leopold II, King of the Belgians. It turns out that there were numerous people with their own hearts of darkness, who were as vicious and evil as Joseph Conrad's Kurtz.

366 pp.; 1998

18. *Seventh Heaven*   Alice Hoffman

When Nora Silk arrives in a typical suburban community in the 1950s, everyone asks questions—of her and of themselves. In other words, they think she's a witch. Sound familiar? Also *Turtle Moon*, about a single mother and her complicated son.

256 pp.; 1990

19. *Oyster*   Janette Turner Hospital

Outer Maroo, a small mining town in the Australian outback, is visited by strangers looking for missing children. At the heart of this mystery is the white-robed cult Messiah, Oyster, who preaches about the end of time. Shortlisted for Australia's National Book Award. Hospital's short-story collections, *Dislocations* and *Isobars*, are strongly recommended, as is *The Last Magician*.

400 pp.; 1996

20. *The Remains of the Day*   Kazuo Ishiguro

Stevens, a model British butler in the last days of the Empire, is the cloth through whom Ishiguro weaves important questions about personality, class, culture, anti-Semitism, and the buried life.

245 pp.; 1989

21. *The Poisonwood Bible*   Barbara Kingsolver

Another white clergyman goes on a religious mission to the Congo, this time in 1959. But the real heroes are Nathan Price's wife, Orleanna, who recollects the story years later; her daughters, writing to her from Africa; and the Congolese, who reject American salvation and accept the 1998 harshness of their lives with grace

543 pp.; 1998

22. *The Fifth Child*   Doris Lessing

Contentment reigns in the Lovatt household in 1960s England until their gruesome, insatiable, hungry, demanding, and violent fifth child arrives. A must by the author of the *Children of Violence* series and *The Golden Notebook*. In my view, her novella *To Room Nineteen* is the best thing Lessing ever wrote.

133 pp.; 1988

23. *The Butcher Boy*   Patrick McCabe

Entering the deranged mind of an Irish schoolboy is not pleasant. Not for the fainthearted.

215 pp.; 1993

24. *Remembering Babylon*   David Malouf

In nineteenth-century Queensland, Australia, the dark passions of racism, brutality, and hate surface when Gemmy Fairley, "a British object," emerges from sixteen years of living with the aborigines in the wilderness.

202 pp.; 1993

25. *Billy Budd, Foretopman*   Herman Melville

Remember Captain Vere? Innocent Billy is doomed in this seafaring drama because his goodness just might subvert evil. Amazing how a story written in the 1800s can be so modern.

95 pp.; 1924

26. *Homeboy*   Seth Morgan

Savagely comic and brilliant first novel about the teeming San Francisco netherworld of junkies, pimps, drag queens, and hookers.

400 pp.; 1990

27. *A Dangerous Woman*   Mary McGarry Morris

A Vermont loony, Martha Horgan, is not the village saint, but her unspecified derangement takes the form of compulsive honesty.

358 pp.; 1991

28. *Lolita*   Vladimir Nabokov

The famous and controversial bestselling novel about Humbert Humbert, a "White Widowed Male," and a seductive twelve-year-old girl. It was shocking then and it's shocking now.

319 pp.; 1955

29. *The Rise of Life on Earth*   **Joyce Carol Oates**
This short novel sketches Kathleen's violent childhood, including a broken home, child beating, and murder. Her later exploitation by a young doctor energizes latent fury.

135 pp.; 1991

30. *Yonnondio*   **Tillie Olsen**
Unfinished story of the Holbrook family as they migrate from coal-mining town to farm to industrial slum, set in the Depression era of the 1930s; this is a lesson in how an inequitable society destroys the spirit.

133 pp.; 1974

31. *The Origin of Satan*   **Elaine Pagels**
Author of *The Gnostic Gospels*, here Pagels traces the evolution of Satan from its origins in the Hebrew Bible to the fierce Prince of Darkness he becomes in the New Testament.

214 pp.; 1995

32. *Looking for Mr. Goodbar*   **Judith Rossner**
Tery Dunn, a young schoolteacher, finds more than she wants, including murder, in the Big Apple on New Year's Eve. Remember that this was written many, many years before the infamous Levin murder case in Central Park.

284 pp.; 1975

33. *The Jungle*   **Upton Sinclair**
Published in 1906, this muckraking exposé of Chicago's meat-packing industry led directly to the passage of the Pure Food and Drug Act. Only for vegetarians, Oprah, or those who never plan to eat another hotdog.

346 pp.; 1906

34. *God's Snake*   Irini Spanidou

Fearless, passionate first novel about a brave little Greek girl, her authoritarian father, a fragile and wounded mother, and with all the simplicity and power of a Greek myth. Don't miss it. The sequel is *Fear.*

252 pp.; 1986

35. *Loitering with Intent*   Muriel Spark

When the young writer Fleur Talbot becomes the secretary to the Autobiographical Association (whose members are writing their memoirs), she runs into a con artist named Quentin Oliver and the defrocked Father Delaney, among others. In *The Prime of Miss Jean Brodie*, Spark's most famous novel, the unforgettable teacher fails to see the evil that Mussolini represents.

217 pp.; 1981

36. *The Women of Whitechapel*   Paul West
and Jack the Ripper

A madman is on the loose in 1888 London and preying on the prostitutes of the Whitechapel district. A shocking, dark thriller about Jack's victims.

420 pp.; 1991

15

Keep It Short

As with detective novels, science fiction, and children's literature, the list of wonderful short-story collections is endless. But here are some of my favorites.

1. *Mrs. Vargas and*   **Kathleen Alcala**
   the Dead Naturalist

The essence of magical realism emerges in these short stories about desert towns, lost sisters, canary singers, and ghost scientists.

170 pp.; 1992

2. *The Collected Stories*   **Isaac Babel**

Translated from the Russian by Walter Morrison. One of the greatest writers of the Communist period, Babel was killed by Stalin in 1937 or 1938. He rode with the Cossacks, edited Sholom Aleichem, and wrote about Jewish gangsters in his hometown of Odessa.

381 pp.; 1955

3. *Ship Fever: Stories*   **Andrea Barrett**

These eight tales grow out of the scientific experience, which both limits and reveals possibilities. Barrett is a writer with a full heart and a dazzling intelligence.

254 pp.; 1996

4. *Park City: New and Selected Stories*   **Ann Beattie**
Three dozen fine stories, culled from twenty-five years of writing about men and women on the domestic front.

464 pp.; 1998

5. *Labyrinths*   **Jorge Luis Borges**
A metaphysical Argentinian writer whose short stories are intellectually (as opposed to emotionally) driven; a good introduction to why he was so influential before his death in 1986.

243 pp.; 1962

6. *The Half You Don't Know*   **Peter Cameron**
Flawless stories of contemporary relationships by a writer who makes each word count. My favorite is "Excerpts from Swan Lake." Also *Andorra*, a dreamlike metaphorical novel about remembering and forgetting that is a good choice for a book club discussion.

276 pp.; 1997

7. *Plan B for the Middle Class*   **Ron Carlson**
One of the most honest contemporary writers in print, Carlson addresses the men and women in the middle years of life. Also *The Hotel Eden*—filled with wonderful stories.

208 pp.; 1992

8. *Cathedral*   **Raymond Carver**
Stories by a sometime minimalist, dead from the effects of alcoholism. Here, drained and empty characters, usually undereducated and working class, are trapped in loss, futility, and emptiness. Also *What We Talk About When We Talk About Love*.

227 pp.; 1983

9. *Bodies of Water*   **Michelle Cliff**

Abandonment is the issue running through these excellent short stories by a Jamaican-born author who now lives in the States.

155 pp.; 1990

10. *Moses Supposes*   **Ellen Currie**

Currie is a writer to watch. Here, most of the characters are believable Irish Americans.

219 pp.; 1994

11. *Krik? Krak!*   **Edwidge Danticat**

Mostly stories of Haiti from a twentyish writer whose first novel, *Breath, Eyes, Memory*, was well received.

224 pp.; 1995

12. *Winter's Tales*   **Isak Dinesen**

Margot Livesey says that "these beautiful, lucid stories remind us of the pleasures of the imagination—of knowing that something is just a story and enjoying it for that reason. That gross question of plausibility never raises its toadlike head."

313 pp.; 1993

13. *The Stories of Stephen Dixon*   **Stephen Dixon**

Selected from thirty years of Dixon's work, these are about truth, relations between the sexes, and what happens to the individual in a hostile world.

642 pp.; 1994

14. *All Around Atlantis*   **Deborah Eisenberg**

Eisenberg is a writer whom other writers read. Many of these stories concern children, pampered and/or neglected, who see more clearly than the adults.

244 pp.; 1997

15. *Constancia and Other Stories for Virgins*   Carlos Fuentes

Five magical novella-length stories by the Mexican writer concerning the eruption of the bizarre and uncanny in the lives of his characters.

340 pp.; 1990

16. *Same Place, Same Things*   Tim Gautreaux

It's not always *la bonne vie* in rural Louisiana, but this new voice tells it all, and beautifully. Even if you've never seen a bayou, you won't regret reading these stories. His debut novel is *The Next Step in the Dance.*

208 pp.; 1996

17. *Whistling and Other Stories*   Myra Goldberg

Tzuris, not hearts and flowers, is what you get in these exceptional love stories of New Yorkers battling their way through modern heterosexual encounters, the dating scene, and redefined relationships.

182 pp.; 1993

18. *Do the Windows Open?*   Julie Hecht

All of these stories, which appeared in *The New Yorker*, are about a superneurotic photographer who, like Hecht, lives in East Hampton in the winter and on Nantucket in the summer. The stories are funny and intelligent although the existential despair hangs heavy over Hecht's head.

212 pp.; 1997

19. *Cowboys Are My Weakness*   Pam Houston

Mostly in the first person, these are told by women who get mixed up with complicated men, sometimes on a raft in white water. Houston has perfect pitch; she's one to watch.

171 pp.; 1992

20. *The Elizabeth Stories*   Isabel Huggan
Often sad stories about growing up in Canada with a less than wonderful family.

184 pp.; 1987

21. *Lost in the City*   Edward P. Jones
For this collection of fourteen stories of African-American life in Washington, D.C., Jones won the PEN/Hemingway Award and was nominated for the National Book Award.

256 pp.; 1992

22. *The Pugilist at Rest*   Thom Jones
Many of Jones's eleven stories are about the war in Vietnam and its aftermath in injured lives. Jones was himself discharged from the Marines for what was thought to be schizophrenia, and later found to be epilepsy.

230 pp.; 1993

23. *Learning by Heart*   Margot Livesey
Stories about the connections people make, or, in most cases, fail to make. The title story about a girl and her stepmother is particularly important.

248 pp.; 1986

24. *All the Days and Nights*   William Maxwell
This collection contains work from the 1930s to the 1990s, including two dozen short fables. Maxwell was a fiction editor at *The New Yorker* for forty years and his prose is beloved by most working writers.

415 pp.; 1995

25. *The Complete Shorter Fiction*   Herman Melville

"Bartleby the Scrivener" is my favorite short story, bar none, and I could probably tell you ten ways that it seriously affected my life. But, as the man said, "I would prefer not to."

478 pp.; 1997

26. *Birds of America*   Lorrie Moore

Nobody can make misery sound as funny as Moore. Her characters are beset with problems—medical, reproductive, political, marital, romantic. And it all rings true.

291 pp.; 1998

27. *The Middleman and Other Stories*   Bharati Mukherjee

A National Book Critics Circle Award winner, this collection concentrates on human failings in those displaced from the East, and in the homegrown product as well.

206 pp.; 1988

28. *Open Secrets*   Alice Munro

A Great Canadian writer creates compressed stories about eccentric spinsters, librarians, and various other small-town types rebelling against the repressive, imprisoning circumstances of their lives. Also *The Beggar Maid, Lives of Girls and Women, Something I've Been Meaning to Tell You, The Progress of Love, Friend of My Youth*. The latest and best collection is *The Love of a Good Woman*.

293 pp.; 1994

29. *Music of the Swamp*   Lewis Nordan

A favorite of American Southerners. Here Sugar Mecklin turns ten, eleven, and twelve around the time his father tells him that the Mississippi Delta "is filled up with death."

191 pp.; 1991

30. *The 70 Best Tales*   Edgar Allan Poe

This is the master's voice! And if you are having trouble getting a child to read, start with "The Pit and the Pendulum." I can still remember the first time I heard it.

617 pp.; 1990

31. *Charity*   Mark Richard

Richard wrote the stories in *The Ice at the Bottom of the World,* and the novel *Fishboy*. He has lots of well-drawn oddball characters.

147 pp.; 1998

32. *Various Antidotes*   Joanna Scott

Wonderful stories, including "Chloroform Jags," "You Must Relax!" and more.

240 pp.; 1993

33. *Various Miracles*   Carol Shields

Marvelous short stories, including "Mrs. Turner Cutting the Grass," by one of the finest writers living in Canada. In *The Republic of Love,* two unlikely people in Winnipeg, a folklorist studying mermaids and a radio deejay on the graveyard shift, stumble into the territory of the title. *Swann*, a novel, is recommended too.

183 pp.; 1985

34. *Where She Brushed Her Hair*   Max Steele

Masterful short stories, including "What to Do Till the Postman Comes."

215 pp.; 1968

35. *The Collected Stories*   **William Trevor**

Includes tales from seven previous books, as well as four stories that have never appeared in America. Trevor, born in County Cork in 1928, often writes about rural Ireland.

1,261 pp.; 1996

36. *Thirteen Stories and Thirteen Epitaphs*   **William T. Vollmann**

As the *New York Times* said, this new collection of stories "can be read as a feverish contemporary travelogue . . . of Mr. Vollmann's brain." More than anything else, loss of place is the issue here.

318 pp.; 1991

37. *A Curtain of Green and Other Stories*   **Eudora Welty**

The mystery of human relationships always emerges in stories by Jackson, Mississippi's, gift to the literary world.

285 pp.; 1941

38. *The Richer, the Poorer: Stories, Sketches, and Reminiscences*   **Dorothy West**

West was a protégée of Zora Neale Hurston and the youngest member of the Harlem Renaissance. Thirteen of these nonfiction sketches are about a largely black upper-class enclave on the island of Martha's Vineyard. West also wrote two extraordinary novels, *The Living Is Easy* (1948) and *The Wedding* (1995).

272 pp.; 1996

39. *Mama Makes Up Her Mind*   Bailey White

Subtitled *And Other Dangers of Southern Living*, here are fifty true stories about rural South Georgia where the author lives and until recently taught first grade. Many of them have been heard on National Public Radio's "All Things Considered."

240 pp.; 1993

Fathers, Sons, and Brothers

1. *A Death in the Family* James Agee

A posthumously published novel based on the death of his father, when Agee was six, that won a Pulitzer Prize.

318 pp.; 1957

2. *Moon Palace* Paul Auster

Mesmerizing narrative of Marco Stanley Fogg, orphan and child of the 1960s, the novel spans three generations and moves from Manhattan (and the Chinese restaurant near Columbia University for which the novel was named) to the West, while Fogg searches for his father and the keys to his origin. Great for book clubs.

307 pp.; 1989

3. *Gabriel's Lament* Paul Bailey

Abandoned son of an irascible, annoying father idolizes the mother who left him. But you have to read to the *very* end to understand the secret here. I love this book and the ruminations it offers on misplaced loyalty.

331 pp.; 1987

4. *Go Tell It on the Mountain*   James Baldwin

Baldwin took ten years to write this first novel in order to make sense out of the relationship with the father he hated. Baldwin says he "had to understand the forces, the experience, the life that shaped him before I could grow up myself, before I could become a writer."

191 pp.; 1953

5. *The Brothers*   Frederick Barthelme

Bud is a restless teacher at a small-town college in Biloxi, Mississippi; his brother, Del, is a former public relations man who moves to his brother's town, falls in love with his brother's wife, and gets involved with a woman half his age who collects grotesque stories about death and mutilation.

262 pp.; 1993

6. *World's End*   T. Coraghessan Boyle

While Walter van Brunt searches for his lost father, the reader gets a good review of the early history of the American eastern seaboard.

456 pp.; 1987

7. *Father and Son*   Larry Brown

"Women can get weary" but (some) men, it seems, have no trouble getting violent. The 1968 Mississippi setting is perfect.

347 pp.; 1996

8. *Blue River*   Ethan Canin

Evokes the mythic theme of good brother, bad brother; written in spare, exacting prose. Beautiful.

220 pp.; 1991

9. *Body and Soul*   **Frank Conroy**

First novel by the now famous head of the Iowa Writers' Workshop, who is also an accomplished pianist—like the child-prodigy character searching for a father figure in this novel. Conroy's memoir is *Stop-Time.*

450 pp.; 1993

10. *David Copperfield*   **Charles Dickens**

Partly autobiographical, all of David's troubles begin when his widowed mother, Clara, marries the villainous Edward Murdstone. His spiritual father, Mr. Micawber, foils the unctuous scoundrel Uriah Heep.

845 pp.; 1849–50

11. *Loon Lake*   **E. L. Doctorow**

This Depression-era tale takes place at a tycoon's hidden mountain estate. In an ironic twist of the Horatio Alger story, the poor hero, Joe Korzeniowski of Paterson, New Jersey, becomes Joseph Patterson Bennett, the rich man's adopted son and heir to Loon Lake. But he is corrupted, not empowered, by the money.

258 pp.; 1980

12. *The Brothers Karamazov*   **Fyodor Dostoyevsky**

The tragedy is dominated by Father Zossima in this masterful story of religious faith and sordid crime. The struggle between the elder Karamozov and his oldest son, Dmitri, is over the father's mistress, Grushenka. Only the youngest Karamazov, Alyosha, triumphs over the family tradition of rottenness.

483 pp.; 1949

13. *Absalom, Absalom!*   **William Faulkner**

A favorite of reading clubs, here Faulkner explores the intricate family histories of the Sutpens, Compsons, Coldfields, Bons, and the Joneses. The four chapters recounting Quentin Compson's conversation with his father, Jason III, continue the story of a poor white man, Thomas Sutpen, whose dynasty building results in tragic ruin.

313 pp.; 1936

14. *Roots*   Alex Haley

Most of America watched the televised version of Haley's partly fictional account of his ancestors in Africa, and many of them began to think about the relationship of sons to fathers, missing or present.

688 pp.; 1976

15. *The Nick Adams Stories*   Ernest Hemingway

Autobiographical stories of a Midwestern boy who is being taught to hunt and fish by his doctor-father. Read them not in the order of publication, but in chronological order: "Indian Camp," "The Doctor and the Doctor's Wife," "The Killers," "Ten Indians," "The End of Something," "The Three-Day Blow," "The Battler," "Now I Lay Me," "A Way You'll Never Be," "Big Two-Hearted River," "Cross-Country Snow," and "Fathers and Sons."

268 pp.; 1972

16. *The Lies Boys Tell*   Lamar Herrin

A dying Ed Reece calls his estranged son home to help him retrace the paths of his life. This journey of reconciliation encompasses husbands and wives and the opposed camps of two generations during the Vietnam War.

267 pp.; 1990

17. *Mr. Ives' Christmas*   Oscar Hijuelos

A foundling, Ives is adopted by a saintly printer, becomes an illustrator, and marries Annie MacGuire. But the senseless murder of his son by a neighborhood punk tests his religious faith and his capacity for forgiveness. I will never forget this deeply moving novel.

248 pp.; 1995

18. *Fathers, Sons, and Brothers*   **Bret Lott**

Lott does a good job of exploring the emotions involved in being a son, a father to a child disturbed by a hurricane, and a brother to an addict. He understands how the patterns of one generation infect and affect the next.

196 pp.; 1997

19. *The Music Room*   **Dennis McFarland**

Exceptional first novel about Martin Lambert's search for answers to his brother Perry's death. The alcoholic mother is like few characters ever created in contemporary fiction. Don't miss this one. I also loved (as did both of my book clubs) *A Face at the Window,* a sophisticated ghost story really about the living.

275 pp.; 1990

20. *Death of a Salesman*   **Arthur Miller**

Although many book clubs do not read plays, Miller's Pulitzer Prize—winning drama is the story of the pathetic Willy Loman, struggling to achieve some dignity in a society that prefers betrayal, and his equally ineffective sons, Biff and Happy.

104 pp.; 1949

21. *The Sailor Who Fell from*   **Yukio Mishima**
Grace with the Sea

A devotee of the Japanese samurai tradition, and of a Japan free from Western influence, Mishima took his own life in a ritual suicide. In this impressionistic novel, a young boy secretly watches the sailor, soon to be his stepfather, make love to his mother. Suffice it to say the wedding does not take place.

181 pp.; 1965

22. *Northern Lights*   Tim O'Brien

This novel focuses on two brothers, one of whom has served in Vietnam (like O'Brien) and returned to join the other in the northern Minnesota town where they grew up. The strongest section, really about understanding relationships, emerges when the brothers are lost during a skiing trip and struggle to survive in the wilderness.

356 pp.; 1975

23. *A Personal Matter*   Kenzaburo Oe

Autobiographical novel about a father named Bird, coping with the news that his newborn son's "brain is protruding from a fault in the skull" and that "there appear to be two heads." Moving evocation of guilt, self-deception, and contradiction.

165 pp.; 1968

24. *Zen and the Art of*   Robert Pirsig
Motorcycle Maintenance

If you lived through the 1960s you've already read this autobiographical and philosophical exploration, grafted onto a motorcycle trip of a father and son going west from Minnesota.

412 pp.; 1974

25. *Fly-Fishing Through*   Howell Raines
the Midlife Crisis

Ostensibly a book about Raines's avocation, but more profoundly about his seven-year feud with his father and brother and his relationship with his dead friend Dick Blalock.

352 pp.; 1993

26. *East of Eden*   John Steinbeck

Classic brother story in which the ne'er-do-well survives the shock of discovering his mother's profession, while the pure and upright brother disintegrates when confronted with the truth. *Of Mice and Men* is an unforgettable story of two brothers.

602 pp.; 1952

27. *Unto the Sons*   Gay Talese

The well-known journalist and novelist traces his heritage from southern Italy to Ocean City, New Jersey, principally by focusing on his father's life.

636 pp.; 1992

28. *Messages from My Father*   Calvin Trillin

It's great to have a book where you find yourself smiling the entire time you are reading. Trillin's love for his father, Abe, a great but somewhat complicated guy, is delightful and uplifting.

117 pp.; 1996

29. *Fathers and Sons*   Ivan Turgenev

Largely a novel about ideas, including an 1860s movement in Russia called nihilism, this is also a classic tale of conflict between a father's ideas and the iconclasm and skepticism of the son.

243 pp.; 1930

30. *Rabbit Is Rich*   John Updike

Won the Pulitzer Prize and the National Book Award in 1982 and was preceded by *Rabbit, Run* and *Rabbit Redux*. Followed, inevitably, by *Rabbit at Rest*. In this one Rabbit (Harry Angstrom), like America in the 1970s, has peaked, and the person who is the locus of his intimations on mortality is his son, the troubled Nelson, who returns home after three years at Kent State University.

467 pp.; 1982

31. *The Promise of Light*   Paul Watkins

A novel about personal legacy and responsibility, Watkins's fourth novel concerns Ben Sheridan, a first-generation Irish American who learns that the man who raised him was not his father.

271 pp.; 1993

32. *Justice*   Larry Watson

Critics generally loved *Montana 1948*, about a small-town family in Bentrock. Here Watson explores their earlier lives—even back to 1899.

226 pp.; 1995

33. *The Solid Mandala*   Patrick White

The twins—mad, gentle Arthur and conventional, fearful Waldo—are the strongly contrasted brothers in this Jungian novel by the Australian winner of the Nobel Prize for Literature who died in 1990. "What I could not accept at the time was the invitation to fly to Stockholm and receive the award in person. This refusal must remain incomprehensible to all those who don't understand my nature or my books."

309 pp.; 1966

34. *Silent Passengers*   Larry Woiwode

The *New York Times* says that "Woiwode's characters are mostly parents and children sorting through complicated relationships. . . . In "Owen's Father" a son recovers memories by staring at a photograph.

131 pp.; 1993

17

Mothers and Daughters

1. *Paula*   **Isabel Allende**

Every parent's worst fear is recounted here: As Allende's daughter is dying, the famous Chilean novelist tells the stories of her family's life. Allende is NOT a conventional person and she has the guts to live her life her way. Brava.

336 pp.; 1994

2. *Bitter Grounds*   **Sandra Benítez**

Winner of the American Book Award. Three generations of Salvadoran women share a secret. A poetic novel rich in history, it resonates with the love of mothers for daughters.

445 pp.; 1997

3. *During the Reign of*   **Joan Chase**
   the Queen of Persia

Almost a cult novel among writers, this story of three generations of women and their farm in northern Ohio is narrated through the collective point of view of four teenage girls.

215 pp.; 1983

4. *The Mirror*   Lynn Freed

This South African novelist became known in the United States for *Home Ground*. Here, seventeen-year-old poor Agnes La Grange leaves England just after World War II, gets involved with her South African Jewish employer, and gives birth to Leah. That relationship is the core of the novel and it packs a wallop.

219 pp.; 1997

5. *Hideous Kinky*   Esther Freud

Semiautobiographical first novel by an actress who is the great-granddaughter of Sigmund Freud and the daughter of the artist Lucien Freud. Told from a five-year-old's point of view as she and her sister are schlepped through Morocco in the 1960s by their nonconformist mother. In *Summer at Gaglow* she presents four generations of a ruined family looking for some place to call home.

186 pp.; 1992

6. *A Mother and Two Daughters*   Gail Godwin

In the stormy late 1970s, three women—Cate, Lydia, and their mother, Nell—come together in a small North Carolina town after the death of Leonard Strickland, father and husband.

564 pp.; 1982

7. *Men and Angels*   Mary Gordon

A religious fanatic named Laura enters the life of Anne Foster, an art historian, while Anne is herself drawn into the life of Caroline Watson, an artist who has been dead for forty-five years.

239 pp.; 1985

8. *A Journey with Elsa Cloud*   Leila Hadley

A voyage eastward to New Delhi and Dharamsala (the residence of the exiled Dalai Lama) by a gifted travel writer/mother from hell in search of her twenty-five-year-old pain-in-the-butt daughter (to whom she hasn't spoken in two years). It takes all these pages to work this one out!

600 pp.; 1997

9. *In a Country of Mother*s   A. M. Homes

Really a psychological thriller, this novel concerns a twenty-four-year-old daughter whose adoptive mother still calls her every night at 11:00 P.M. Her therapist, whose infant daughter was given up for adoption twenty-four years ago, is also a big part of her problem.

275 pp.; 1993

10. *Pride of Family*   Carole Ione

Subtitled *Four Generations of American Women of Color*, this is the nonfictional story of a clan of artistocratic black mothers and daughters.

224 pp.; 1991

11. *Comfort Woman*   Nora Okja Keller

Beccah, of Korean and American heritage, has to cope with her strange mother, Akiko, who is indeed strange because she was sold away from her Korean family during World War II—as part of her sister's dowry—and forced by the Japanese into the job of "comfort woman," a prostitute for Japanese soldiers. She was saved by an American missionary who became her now-deceased husband.

213 pp.; 1997

12. *Annie John*   Jamaica Kincaid

Disquieting story of a childhood in Antigua with a hateful mother and a daughter lost in loneliness. The story continues, in a sense, in *Lucy*.

160 pp.; 1985

13. *The Mother Knot*   Jane Lazarre
Powerful autobiographical account of the shock and pain of childbirth, the transformation of identity, and the ensuing ambivalent feelings, including those of love.

188 pp.; 1976

14. *The Good Mother*   Sue Miller
A contemporary version of the age-old struggle between maternal and sexual love emerges when Leo Cutter, an artist, enters the world of Anna Dunlap and her daughter, Molly.

310 pp.; 1986

15. *The Night Sky*   Mary Morris
This novel is a disturbing tale about the loneliness and fear Ivy Slovak experiences when she is alone in New York with her infant son and the memories of the mother who deserted her when she was seven.

287 pp.; 1993

16. *Beloved*   Toni Morrison
One of America's best writers tells the post–Civil War story of an escaped slave, Sethe, who lives in a small house in Ohio with, among others, a disturbing, compelling intruder—perhaps the ghost of her daughter, Beloved. Also *Sula* and *The Bluest Eye*.

275 pp.; 1987

17. *'night, Mother*   Marsha Norman
Winner of the 1983 Pulitzer, this play centers on Jessie, who has decided to commit suicide, and her mother, Thelma, who realizes that she is powerless to prevent it.

89 pp.; 1983

18. *Housekeeping*   **Marilynne Robinson**

Robinson's reputation continues to rest on this one novel, the story of an adolescent girl's journey to self-consciousness, and of the ways Ruth is alienated from her sister, Lucille, after their mother's suicide. Aunt Sylvie is an unforgettable nonconformist.

219 pp.; 1980

19. *Her First American*   **Lore Segal**

Writers and editors recommend this book, set in the 1950s, to each other. It's about immigrants, black-white relationships, a mother-daughter dance, love, alcoholism, and the rebirth and the waste of human spirit. Don't miss it.

287 pp.; 1985

20. *Anywhere but Here*   **Mona Simpson**

Not everyone (thankfully) has a mother who leaves her on the side of the road and then comes back with an offer of ice cream cones. But this twisted mother drives from Wisconsin to California to make her daughter into a child star "while [she is] still a child." Unforgettable portrait of a mother nobody wants.

406 pp.; 1986

21. *In My Mother's House*   **Elizabeth Winthrop**

Three-generation story of buried secrets, the ghosts of memory, and the ways in which they impact on the Websters, particularly the women, strong New Englanders from the 1800s to the present.

523 pp.; 1988

Questioning the Miraculous

1. *The House of the Spirits*   **Isabel Allende**

Allende contrasts Esteban Trueba's patriarchal attitude with the imaginative spiritual life of his wife, Clara, and spotlights the violence done to women. The model for Clara was Allende's own mother.

368 pp.; 1985

2. *Baby of the Family*   **Tina McElroy Ansa**

From the moment of her birth in a rural black hospital in Georgia, Lena McPherson, born with a caul over her face, is recognized by all the nurses as a special child, with the power to see ghosts and predict the future.

265 pp.; 1989

3. *The Forms of Water*   **Andrea Barrett**

In this one a retired monk escapes from a rest home. Barrett, a fine writer, also wrote *The Middle Kingdom*.

292 pp.; 1993

4. *Giles Goat-Boy*   **John Barth**

Barth's writing reminds the reader of the boisterous tone of Cervantes, and here the modern university is transformed into a universe by an academic who has gone nuts. Is the book's author a computer? Barth also wrote *Lost in the Funhouse* and *Sabbatical*.

710 pp.; 1966

5. *Jack Maggs*   **Peter Carey**

Magwitch, the fierce Australian convict that Charles Dickens created for *Great Expectations,* is tranformed here into a sympathetic hero. Carey wrote *Illywhacker*, an extraordinary, surreal tale supposedly written by a 139-year-old man, and *Bliss,* which is, so to speak, hell.

600 pp.; 1998

6. *Wise Children*   **Angela Carter**

Her eleventh and final novel, this mock memoir is narrated by an endlessly imaginative postmodernist old woman, and tells the story of unusual illegitimate twin daughters.

234 pp.; 1992

7. *Taratuta/Still Life with Pipe*   **José Donoso**

Two novellas about a young man's obsession with a now-forgotten painter and the ways in which fiction and history intertwine.

160 pp.; 1993

8. *Rebecca*   **Daphne du Maurier**

All about Manderley, the place where "the dead come back and watch the living." Gothic suspense at its best.

446 pp.; 1938

9. *Carmen Dog*   Carol Emshwiller

Hilarious, radical version of housewives devolving into snarling mutts while their pets become more human and start helping out at home. The heroine, Pooch, runs away to New York (where else?) to become an opera singer.

161 pp.; 1990

10. *The Beet Queen*   Louise Erdrich

Spans forty years, beginning when a brother and sister, abandoned by their peculiar mother, arrive by boxcar in Argus, a small off-reservation town in North Dakota, to live with their aunt Fritzie and her husband, Pete. This is a novel about miracles, the magic of natural events, and the mystery in the human condition.

338 pp.; 1986

11. *A Passage to India*   E. M. Forster

Forster's greatest novel is set in India and examines the relations between the English and the Indians in the early 1920s. The scenes near the caves and the death of Mrs. Moore both lead to great discussions about this topic heading.

322 pp.; 1924

12. *JR*   William Gaddis

The story of Das Rheingold, the dwarfish Alberich—a novel with Wagnerian overtones, but really about money making, business, depersonalization, and the individual loss of recognition.

725 pp.; 1975

13. *One Hundred*   Gabriel García Márquez
Years of Solitude

Written by one of Latin America's greatest writers, this is the story of the rise, fall, birth, and death of the mystical town of Macondo, as seen through the history of the Buendia family. *The Gen-*

eral in His Labyrinth transmutes historical truth about Simón Bolívar, the liberator who tried to free South America from Spanish domination, into magical narrative.

285 pp.; 1990

14. *Black Narcissus*   **Rumer Godden**

A small band of nuns settles in the Himalayas, and they are disturbed either by the old fakir in the garden or the mountain itself.

294 pp.; 1939

15. *Mariette in Ecstasy*   **Ron Hansen**

Bestselling story of a young postulant's claim to divine possession and religious ecstasy in a small convent in upstate New York over a quarter of a century ago. Lots of questions for the reader to answer. Great for book clubs.

192 pp.; 1991

16. *Winter's Tale*   **Mark Helprin**

In the year 2000, New York becomes the golden city people have always desired, complete with a milkhouse that can fly, a manic billionaire who commutes to East Hampton by blimp, and a love affair between a second-story man and Beverly Penn, the daughter of the mansion.

673 pp.; 1983

17. *Dune*   **Frank Herbert**

Herbert is interested in the tensions between humanity and the environment. The sequence of *Dune* books form a serious space opera, complete with Galactic Empires, storm troopers, etc.

412 pp.; 1965

18. *Steppenwolf*   **Hermann Hesse**

In Hesse's best-known novel, the protagonist, Harry Haller, is introduced into the Magic Theatre—a fantastic realm devoted to liberating the senses—by Hermine, a free-spirited androgyne. Those interested in Eastern philosophy will like *Siddhartha*.

309 pp.; 1929

19. *Carmichael's Dog*   **R. M. Koster**

World-famous author of successful science-fiction tetrology is possessed by the demons of lust, envy, sloth, avarice, wrath, and, especially, pride.

320 pp.; 1992

20. *The Hour of the Star*   **Clarice Lispector**

This last postmodern novel by the Brazilian short-story writer and novelist is about the socioeconomic problems of a naive, proletarian girl. Lispector is known for first-person, stream-of-consciousness, epiphanic moments.

96 pp.; 1986

21. *Feather Crowns*   **Bobbie Ann Mason**

Fire-and-brimstone revival meetings, quintuplets, and death, all in Kentucky, where Mason lives. An American parable with universal resonances.

454 pp.; 1993

22. *Song of Solomon*   **Toni Morrison**

A tour de force and one of my all-time favorites about mystical flights, shamans, mother love, and the power of myth. The scene where Milkman Dead visits his mother's grave is unforgettable.

341 pp.; 1978

23. *The Wind-Up Bird Chronicle*   Haruki Murakami

Time says that Murakami is the "postwar successor [to] the Big Three of modern Japanese literature: Mishima, Kawabata and Tanizaki." His *Norwegian Wood* sold more than two million copies. Here he digs deeply into Japan's past.

640 pp.; 1997

24. *The Flight from the Enchanter*   Iris Murdoch

Not surprising (since Murdoch was an Oxford don) that one critic described this novel as "a very brainy fairy tale," and another said it was a "modern *Nightmare Abbey*." Thoroughly enjoyable and much better than Murdoch's later novels.

316 pp.; 1956

25. *Maqroll*   Alvaro Mutis

Three novellas featuring Maqroll the Gaviero (the Lookout), an adventurer whose dubious schemes include smuggling, managing a brothel, and an unwitting involvement with South American guerrillas.

288 pp.; 1992

26. *The Famished Road*   Ben Okri

Winner of the Booker Prize, Okri presents a crowded, impoverished African village where visitors arrive from the spirit world.

500 pp.; 1992

27. *Godmother Night*   Rachel Pollack

Love story of two women and their daughter, Kate, all of them wooed year after year by Mother Night and her five red-haired, leather-clad bikers.

355 pp.; 1996

28. *Tropical Night Falling*   Manuel Puig

Poignant last novel before the author's untimely death in 1990. Two elderly Argentinian sisters living in Rome gossip about the people in their apartment complex.

192 pp.; 1991

29. *The Witching Hour*   Anne Rice

Rowan Mayfair, a San Francisco neurosurgeon who brings a drowned man back to life, is descended from witches. The setting is Rice's actual house in the Garden District of New Orleans. In *Lasher,* the queen of the coven flees the demon, whom she hates but finds irresistible.

965 pp.; 1990

30. *Was*   Geoff Ryman

Fantastic, if not exactly magical, politics in this novel, and Ryman won the 1985 World Fantasy Award for holding up a looking glass to it.

371 pp.; 1992

31. *Frankenstein*   Mary Shelley

Let's get it straight: Frankenstein is the *scientist*! He's the one who creates the "hideous progeny," last seen as he traveled across the frozen shore to loose havoc on the world.

192 pp.; 1818

32. *Memento Mori*   Muriel Spark

A collection of London grotesques between the ages of seventy and one hundred, all of them old friends or acquaintances, get the same phone message from an unidentified caller. The voice says, "Remember You Must Die." This is Spark at her best.

224 pp.; 1959

33. *Dracula*   **Bram Stoker**

As "the whole man" crawled down the castle wall, what could the reader think? "What manner of man—or creature—is this?"

382 pp.; 1897

34. *Beauty*   **Sheri Tepper**

When her wicked aunt's curse is fulfilled on Beauty's sixteenth birthday, she finds herself alone amid millions and millions of humans.

412 pp.; 1991

35. *The White Hotel*   **D. M. Thomas**

Shortlisted for the Booker, this combines Freudian psychoanalytic ideas, the evil of modern history, and plenty of sex.

274 pp.; 1981

36. *The Invisible Man*   **H. G. Wells**

A mad scientist concocts a potion that makes him invisible; then he begins to terrorize the inhabitants of a small town. So, how'd he do it? And why?

235 pp.; 1897

Go West

1. *Strange Angels*   **Jonis Agee**
   Set in the Nebraska sandhills, this is a world of cowboys, honky-tonk bars, small towns, and huge stretches of rolling prairie.

                                              405 pp.; 1993

2. *All but the Waltz*   **Mary Clearman Blew**
   These are essays about an ordinary but also remarkable Montana family, about whom we come to care deeply.

                                              223 pp.; 1991

3. *Desierto*   **Charles Bowden**
   Subtitled *Memories of the Future*, Bowden evokes here the Southwestern desert and the men and women who inhabit it: tycoons, drug kingpins, the aboriginal Seris and Yaquis, and the author himself.

                                              225 pp.; 1991

4. *Palm Latitudes*   **Kate Braverman**
   Three women dominate this novel set in the barrio of Los Angeles: a whore, Francisca Ramos; a young housewife and mother, Glo-

ria Hernandez; and an aged mestizo, Marta Ortega. Braverman also wrote *Lithium for Medea*.

384 pp.; 1988

5. *The Ox-Bow Incident*   Walter V. T. Clark

This novel about a Nevada lynching was followed by *The Track of the Cat* about brothers hunting for a mountain lion.

309 pp.; 1940

6. *Deadwood*   Pete Dexter

Set on the Dakota frontier in the days of Wild Bill Hickok.

365 pp.; 1986

7. *Dancing at the Rascal Fair*   Ivan Doig

Set in the great Montana highlands. By the author of *This House of Sky* and *English Creek*, the other volumes in this trilogy.

405 pp.; 1987

8. *The River Why*   David James Duncan

The story of Gus Orviston, fly-fishing genius, and his adventures with a woman, a river, many trout, several dogs, a philosopher, a salmon, and a colorful cast of backwoods characters.

294 pp.; 1983

9. *Drinking Dry Clouds*   Gretel Ehrlich

Linked stories of whites and Japanese Americans interned at Wyoming's Heart Mountain during World War II. Since Ehrlich lives on a ranch in northern Wyoming, it's not surprising that she wrote *The Solace of Open Spaces*.

160 pp.; 1991

10. *Wildlife*   **Richard Ford**
Set in Great Falls, Montana, it chronicles the ways a family's sense of itself is changed by surrounding and rampant forest fires.
177 pp.; 1990

11. *The Meadow*   **James Galvin**
An unusual, touching, one-hundred-year history of a meadow in the arid mountains of the Colorado-Wyoming border.
230 pp.; 1992

12. *The Jump-Off Creek*   **Molly Gloss**
A portrait of a pioneer woman, Lydia Sanderson, and her struggles as she homesteads alone in the Blue Mountains of Oregon in the 1890s.
186 pp.; 1989

13. *The Big Sky*   **A. B. Guthrie**
Guthrie moved a quarter century into the past to portray the West, from Kentucky to Oregon.
386 pp.; 1947

14. *Desperadoes*   **Ron Hansen**
Geoffrey Wolff called this novel "one of the great prose entertainments of recent years" and it's generally considered to be one of the great contemporary novels of the West.
273 pp.; 1979

15. *Seven Rivers West*   **Edward Hoagland**
Hoagland lives in New York City but he re-creates the Native American West of the 1880s in the fictional town of Horse Swim.
319 pp.; 1986

16. *Already Dead: A California Gothic*   Denis Johnson

If you're looking for a nice relaxing tale about the wonders of la la land and the Pacific Rim, this is not it. As the *New York Times* said, in Denis Johnson's contemporary Gothic, "everyone is on something, killing someone or about to be killed." I would add words like *demonic, obsessive, freaked-out, burned-out, left out,* etc. But in its way it is terrific!

435 pp.; 1997

17. *Riding the White Horse Home*   Teresa Jordan

Ranch life and social customs in Wyoming, written in beautiful prose.

219 pp.; 1993

18. *Sometimes a Great Notion*   Ken Kesey

This novel about a family and a lumbering feud in Oregon is a more impressive and important book than his hugely popular *One Flew Over the Cuckoo's Nest.*

628 pp.; 1964

19. *Hole in the Sky*   William Kittredge

Searing indictment of his own self-destructive life and of the ways his family's agribusiness empire laid waste to an Edenic swatch of Oregon countryside.

238 pp.; 1992

20. *All New People*   Anne Lamott

A beautifully honest book about life as a single mother in California; her son, Sam; and the support of her church and AA groups. *Bird by Bird,* she says, contains *Some Instructions on Writing and Life.* I say that it is priceless.

166 pp.; 1989

21. *The Legacy of Conquest*   **Patricia Limerick**
Subtitled *The Unbroken Past of the American West.* Limerick is a popular and respected favorite of westerners.

396 pp.; 1987

22. *If You Lived Here, You'd Be*   **Sandra Tsing Loh**
   Home by Now
"I want $: I want nice things." The *Los Angeles Times* calls it "a deceptively droll portrait of Los Angeles as a giant mousetrap, baited with all the ridiculous junk that money can buy."

224 pp.; 1997

23. *Young Men and Fire*   **Norman Maclean**
A National Book Critics Circle Award–winning account of the 1949 Mann Gulch fire in Montana that killed thirteen young Forest Service smoke jumpers trapped between the flames and a mountain ridge. More profoundly, this is a book about mortality, and the way accidents often control fate.

301 pp.; 1992

24. *Rain or Shine*   **Cyra McFadden**
McFadden writes about her wildly dysfunctional family, particularly her father, a radio announcer on the macho rodeo circuit.

177 pp.; 1986

25. *The Bushwacked Piano*   **Thomas McGuane**
Here the popular McGuane satirizes cowboys and con men from Michigan to Montana. Also *Ninety-Two in the Shade.*

220 pp.; 1971

26. *Streets of Laredo*   **Larry McMurtry**

A Texas bounty hunter goes south of the border as he pursues a train robber and killer. *Lonesome Dove* is McMurtry's best-known book.

843 pp.; 1993

27. *The Milagro Beanfield War*   **John Nichols**

After Joe Mondragon taps into the main irrigation channel on a patch of now-arid land, his beanfield becomes the rallying point for the small farmers and sheepmen. Downstate in the capital the Anglo water barons and powerbrokers have their own multimillion-dollar land development ideas.

445 pp.; 1974

28. *The Nightbird Cantata*   **Donald Rawley**

In spare, lyrical prose Rawley leads us through three months during an Arizona summer when L.P., a ten-year-old child of a wealthy but self-indulgent mother, is sent off in the care of Betty, his grandmother's maid, to live in black South Phoenix.

245 pp.; 1998

29. *Beyond Deserving*   **Sandra Scofield**

In this second novel, Scofield creates three couples woven together by extended-family ties in a small Oregon town. It won an American Book Award and a New American Fiction Award, as did *Gringa*, her debut book. *Walking Dunes*, her third novel, tells David Puckett's story of life on the wrong side of the tracks in a 1950s Texas town.

310 pp.; 1992

30. *Making History*   Carolyn See

See traces the tragedies of a fragile family living in Los Angeles on the edge of the Pacific Rim. This writer understands the nuances of California life better than anyone.

276 pp.; 1991

31. *A Cold Day for Murder*   Dana Stabenow

For ten years I've been saving pennies in a giant pickle bottle on top of the fridge for my trip to Alaska. I now have enough money to get to Newark Airport. In the meantime, the mystery series featuring Kate Shugah, an Aleutian Indian and a former investigator for the DA's office in Anchorage, will have to suffice.

199 pp.; 1992

32. *Where the Bluebird*   Wallace Stegner
Sings to the Lemonade Springs

The late writer both celebrated the West and criticized the illusions that have been built around it. Also *Angle of Repose* and *The Sound of Mountain Water*.

240 pp.; 1992

33. *The Eagle Bird*   Charles Wilkinson

As Wallace Stegner said, "Wilkinson understands western attitudes, western inferiorities, western limitations, western pride and arrogance. He is hopeful that the West will arrive at workable compromises before it is destroyed by the big corporations of the extractive industries, or by its more native stockraisers and lumbermen and miners." Amen.

203 pp.; 1992

New York Stories

1. *New York Trilogy*   **Paul Auster**

In *City of Glass,* Quinn, a mystery writer, receives a phone call in the middle of the night from someone who is looking for "Paul Auster. Of the Auster Detective Agency." Thus begins *City of Glass,* Volume 1 in this Kafka-like adventure. Volume 2 is *Ghosts,* followed by *The Locked Room.* In my view, Auster is one of the best writers in the United States.

203 pp.; 1985

2. *Mr. Sammler's Planet*   **Saul Bellow**

Artur Sammler, born in Cracow but with the manners of an Oxford don, looks back on civilized England and the animals who ran the death camps in World War II. Recommended too are *The Victim* and *Herzog.*

316 pp.; 1970

3. *Manhattan, When I Was Young* **Mary Cantwell**

More a youthful memoir about a lousy marriage, her frigidity, a sick child, and the fashion magazine world in 1953 than a book strictly about New York, but nevertheless it is sad and memorable. Preceded by *American Girl* and followed by *Speaking with Strangers.*

214 pp.; 1995

4. *Breakfast at Tiffany's: A*   Truman Capote
Short Novel and Three Stories

Holly Golightly takes New York, but in most of our minds she will forever look like Audrey Hepburn.

179 pp.; 1958

5. *Happy All the Time*   Laurie Colwin

Funny, poignant tale of romance and complications. Colwin died suddenly at forty; her posthumously published novel is *A Big Storm Knocked It Over.*

213 pp.; 1978

6. *Sleeping Arrangements*   Laura Cunningham

Unusual memoir (that reads like good fiction) of an orphaned Bronx girl, Rosie, raised by two bachelor uncles and their nutty mother, "Esther in Hebrew, Edna in English, and Etka in Russian." Don't miss it.

195 pp.; 1989

7. *Sister Carrie*   Theodore Dreiser

One of America's finest naturalistic novels, here the city is a metaphor for the survival of the fittest: the Midwesterner Carrie Meeber survives, and the ill-fated Hurstwood ends up in Potter's Field.

557 pp.; 1900

8. *Approaching Eye Level*   Vivian Gornick

Living alone in New York City is both joyful and lonely. This follows Gornick's 1987 memoir, *Fierce Attachments,* about her complicated relationship with her widowed mother and her neighbors in the Bronx.

164 pp.; 1996

9. *The Blindfold*   **Siri Hustvedt**

Iris (S-i-r-i) Vegan, an impoverished graduate student in New York City, encounters four characters who try to shape and alter her identity. A brilliant debut.

221 pp.; 1992

10. *Slaves of New York*   **Tama Janowitz**

Collection of tales about various women in New York—a jewelry designer, an East Village performance artist, and a well-born prostitute, among others, who waft, half-cheerful, half-lost, through the big city.

278 pp.; 1986

11. *Gentlemen Prefer Blondes*   **Anita Loos**

This is not on any politically correct list, but if you read between the lines, this just might be a feminist text!

217 pp.; 1925

12. *This Side of Brightness*   **Colum McCann**

Yes, I know McCann is Irish, but he writes here about Treefrog, a homeless man of Irish, black, and Chippewa ancestry whose life is defined by the subway and train tunnels that burrow beneath Manhattan.

288 pp.; 1998

13. *Bright Lights, Big City*   **Jay McInerney**

Considered by many to be the diary of life in the Big Apple during the 1980s, it falls someplace between a beach book and a literary novel. McInerney is a wunderkind of the so-called brat pack of contemporary fiction.

182 pp.; 1984

14. *Brown Girl, Brownstones*   **Paule Marshall**

Semiautobiographical novel by a writer who was born in Brooklyn of parents who emigrated from Barbados during World War II.

310 pp.; 1959

15. *Up in the Old Hotel*   **Joseph Mitchell**

Consists of four of Mitchell's five books—*McSorley's Wonderful Saloon, Old Mr. Flood, The Bottom of the Harbor*, and *Joe Gould's Secret*—along with some pieces never reprinted since their use in *The New Yorker* between 1938 and 1964.

718 pp.; 1993

16. *In Nueva York*   **Nicolasa Mohr**

Short, interlocking stories that depict life in one of New York City's Puerto Rican communities.

194 pp.; 1977

17. *New York Days*   **Willie Morris**

Morris, the former editor in chief of *Harper's,* recalls the heady literary world in the Big Apple in the 1960s, in the decade of Vietnam and the assassinations.

396 pp.; 1993

18. *Benediction at the Savoia*   **Christine O'Hagan**

Irish-Catholic life in 1960s Jackson Heights, Queens; fifteen minutes from Manhattan but insular and unchanging. For all the impact of glitzy New York City on these people, they might as well have been in Toledo.

325 pp.; 1992

19. *New York Cookbook*   Molly O'Neill

New York is not New York without dim sum, falafel, Jamaican meat pies, Hungarian szekely, paratha, and focaccia. And a bagel with a *schmear* wouldn't hurt either. The stories of New York's neighborhood cooks by the *New York Times* food columnist are great! And your book club needs something to eat anyhow.

509 pp.; 1992

20. *Bigfoot Dreams*   Francine Prose

Hilarious story of Vera Perl, star reporter for a sleazoid tabloid, and what happens when one of her invented stories turns out to be true. Prose's more sophisticated and deeper writing emerges in *Guided Tours of Hell: Novellas.*

289 pp.; 1986

21. *Call It Sleep*   Henry Roth

Undisputed American masterpiece about an immigrant Jewish boy, David Schearl, in the slums of New York City. Followed thirty-four years later by the four volumes *Mercy of a Rude Stream: A Star Shines over Mt. Morris Park* (childhood), *A Diving Rock on the Hudson* (school days), *From Bondage* (adolescence), and *Requiem for Harlem* (his years at City College). Violence in the streets, the terror of poverty, his own sexual conflicts and those of his parents—no one has dealt with this kind of material more effectively.

447 pp.; 1934

22. *The Adirondacks:*   Paul Schneider
A History of America's First Wilderness

The best part of this book is not the explication of three hundred years in the history of what is now the Adirondack Park but the idea, as the *New York Times* reviewer pointed out, "that wilderness is not only a human invention but a New York invention!"

416 pp.; 1997

23. *Leaving Brooklyn*   Lynne Sharon Schwartz

A novel about double vision; one kind is physical—a wandering eye resulting from a birth injury—and the other is an emotional insight into the world beyond postwar Brooklyn in the 1950s.

160 pp.; 1989

24. *Bronx Primitive*   Kate Simon

After Kaila and her family leave the Warsaw ghetto for America at the end of World War II, her neighborhood around 178th Street and Lafontaine Avenue in the Bronx becomes home; this Old Country childhood in the New World is not all sweet *or* nurturing.

179 pp.; 1982

25. *A Tree Grows in Brooklyn*   Betty Smith

Unforgettable American masterpiece about a young girl's coming-of-age at the turn of the century.

432 pp.; 1947

26. *Straitjacket and Tie*   Eugene Stein

A phantasmagoric Manhattan where Phillip Rosenbaum has a psychotic breakdown and communicates with extraterrestrials through radio channels no one else can hear. A funny, poignant book.

256 pp.; 1993

27. *No Lease on Life*   Lynne Tillman

As the *New York Times* noted, "Tillman's underachieving, underpaid heroine is a proofreader named Elizabeth Hall, a formerly middle-class WASP in a neighborhood [the East Village] mingling third-world hurly-burly with post-apocalyptic tribalism." But she is no dainty character, this Elizabeth, and you'll remember her long after you finish the book.

179 pp.; 1998

28. *Old New York*   Edith Wharton

Four masterly short novels of New York during the nineteenth century, with lots of insight into the tribal rites of that time.

306 pp.; 1964

29. *Bonfire of the Vanities*   Tom Wolfe

You've heard the one about how anything that can go wrong, will? This is a cartoon version of New York, complete with class warfare and seething ethnic resentments, all filtered through the decidedly reactionary view of Wolfe.

659 pp.; 1987

Southern Comfort

1. *Souls Raised from the Dead*   Doris Betts

This wise, poignant novel, set in the Piedmont region of North Carolina, is about the death of a child and the ensuing grief. Also *Heading West*. Betts is a favorite of other Southern writers.

339 pp.; 1994

2. *Terminal Velocity*   Blanche McCrary Boyd

A staid book editor leaves Boston, goes to California, and joins a group of radical lesbians in a commune called Red Moon Rising. Boyd, by the way, is the Southerner who wrote *The Redneck Way of Knowledge*.

255 pp.; 1997

3. *All Over but the Shouting*   Rick Bragg

A Pulitzer Prize–winning reporter for the *New York Times* rises from grim poverty in Alabama. And his much-beloved Mama, Margaret Bragg, is at the center of the story.

329 pp.; 1997

4. *Other Voices, Other Rooms*   **Truman Capote**
First novel told through a thirteen-year-old's eyes in Deep South Mississippi and laden with grotesque, mystical overtones, and homosexual urges.

231 pp.; 1948

5. *Prince of Tides*   **Pat Conroy**
Spanning forty years, this is the story of Tom Wingo, his gifted and troubled twin sister, Savannah, and the dark and violent past of the extraordinary South Carolina family into which they were unfortunately born.

567 pp.; 1986

6. *Forms of Shelter*   **Angela Davis-Gardner**
The heart of this beautifully written novel is the betrayal of a girl child—by an absent father, a childish and complicit mother, an evil and devious stepfather, and a confused brother. Don't miss this one.

276 pp.; 1991

7. *Walking Toward Egypt*   **Clyde Edgarton**
Title is from a hymn (words and music by Edgarton), the favorite of Mattie Rigsbee, an independent Southern dame of seventy-eight. Somehow she gets involved with a teenage juvenile delinquent named Wesley.

215 pp.; 1991

8. *Fried Green Tomatoes*   **Fannie Flagg**
    at the Whistle Stop Cafe
More than you think goes on in rural Alabama, including a sexual relationship they left out of the movie.

403 pp.; 1987

9. *Ellen Foster*   Kay Gibbons

Stark and affecting story of a young country girl in North Carolina whose mother commits suicide and whose father, a tobacco farmer, drinks himself to death. Her newest is *On the Occasion of My Last Afternoon.*

146 pp.; 1987

10. *The Anna Papers*   Ellen Gilchrist

Anna Hand, dying of cancer, returns to Charlotte, North Carolina, to sort out her unresolved conflicts with her sister, old lovers, her brother, and his out-of-wedlock daughter.

277 pp.; 1988

11. *Oldest Living Confederate*   Allan Gurganus
Widow Tells All

Lucy Marsden, ninety-nine, half-blind, mother of nine children, and the best friend of a former slave, is also the widow of the Civil War's last surviving soldier.

718 pp.; 1984

12. *Boomerang*   Barry Hannah

Tender weaving of fiction and autobiography as the narrator meets Yelverston, a sixty-two-year-old man whose stature and sad nobility astound him.

150 pp.; 1989

13. *Southern Cross: The*   Christine Leigh Heyrman
Beginnings of the Bible Belt

Trust me on this one. You can't understand the American South without paying attention to "that old-time religion," the evangelical faith of the region. Heyrman writes about the 1740s to the 1830s when the Baptists and the early preachers were affirming the rights of both women and blacks to bear witness publicly and sometimes together.

352 pp.; 1997

14. *Dreams of Sleep*   Josephine Humphreys

The power of place and the effects of memory reverberate in a house in Charleston, South Carolina, in the debut novel of one of the best writers in the South. *Rich in Love* comes later.

232 pp.; 1984

15. *To Kill a Mockingbird*   Harper Lee

The 1961 Pulitzer Prize–winning novel about a small-town lawyer in Alabama who stands up for what is right when a black man is accused of rape. Told from the perspective of his daughter, Scout.

296 pp.; 1960

16. *Carolina Moon*   Jill McCorkle

Finally—a book about a woman past sixty who is sexy, free-spirited, and full of energy. Quee Purdy, a fixture in Fulton, North Carolina, is a delight. *Final Vinyl Days* is McCorkle's latest collection of short stories.

260 pp.; 1996

17. *Shiloh and Other Stories*   Bobbie Ann Mason

Stories about working-class people in Kentucky who experience the tension between history and progress as the rural areas where they live become urbanized.

247 pp.; 1982

18. *Gone With the Wind*   Margaret Mitchell

My deceased mother (raised in Jacksonville, Florida, and Savannah, Georgia) and my deceased father (raised in Atlanta) have both turned over in their graves since hearing that I left this book out of the first edition. Sometimes you just can't see the magnolias for the honeysuckle. Or something like that.

1,024 pp.; 1936

19. *A Good Man Is Hard to Find*   Flannery O'Connor
O'Connor died young of lupus but left us stories filled with grotesque characters who epitomize the false piety and moral blindness of her Southern characters. She wrote two novels, *Wise Blood* and *The Violent Bear It Away.*

251 pp.; 1955

20. *Love in the Ruins*   Walker Percy
A great apocalyptic satire and very funny. Percy is the author of *The Moviegoer* and *The Last Gentleman.*

403 pp.; 1971

21. *Kate Vaiden*   Reynolds Price
In this one Price fashions a twentieth-century Moll Flanders. He creates wonderful female characters, but in his books they all suffer—big time.

306 pp.; 1986

22. *The Devil's Dream*   Lee Smith
Smith is a favorite of reading clubs, and her *Fair and Tender Ladies* is lovely. She writes a kind of Southern Gothic, including lots of loony aunts and cousins.

311 pp.; 1992

23. *Hall of Mirrors*   Robert Stone
The ultimate book with a New Orleans setting, Stone's first novel is the story of three drifters who are swept into town at the

end of Mardi Gras and plunged into the seamy world of Louisiana politics.

411 pp.; 1966

24. *A Summons to Memphis*   Peter Taylor

His last novel, about a family's secrets, is *In the Tennessee Country*. Dislocation and remorse were his issues.

209 pp.; 1986

25. *A Confederacy of Dunces*   John Kennedy Toole

Epic comedic novel about Ignatius J. Reilly, a thirty-year-old self-proclaimed genius in New Orleans who is out to reform the entire twentieth century. This is Toole's only novel; he committed suicide at age thirty-two in 1969.

415 pp.; 1980

26. *The Optimist's Daughter*   Eudora Welty

Laurel Hand returns from Chicago to Mississippi after her father's death and tries to come to terms with the small town that he loved and what it means in her own life. *Losing Battles* and *Delta Wedding* are also recommended.

180 pp.; 1969

27. *You Can't Go Home Again*   Thomas Wolfe

The title has entered the language, but here a successful novelist searches everywhere for his own identity—perhaps so he can go home?

743 pp.; 1934

My Kind of Place

Of course any successful novel or meaningful memoir should evoke a sense of place. But the choices on this list have a special connection.

1. *The Dollmaker*   **Harriette Arnow**
One of the first books to represent Kentuckians as the valiant people they are, this novel focuses on the confrontation between the individual conscience and socioeconomic forces.

549 pp.; 1954

2. *Remembering*   **Wendell Berry**
In this fourth of Berry's novels about the citizens of Port William, Kentucky, he reminds us that more is usually less, and that "membership" in a family, a country, or a place is more powerful than are the questionable benefits of acquisition, possession, and accumulation. I love this book.

124 pp.; 1988

3. *The Road to Wellville*   T. Coraghessan Boyle

A historical farce set in 1907 Battle Creek, Michigan, where cornflake inventor Dr. John Harvey Kellogg's world-famous sanitarium attracts a mix of health nuts and hustlers.

476 pp.; 1993

4. *Life in the Iron Mills*   Rebecca Harding Davis

Davis was one of the most prominent ninetenth-century U.S. writers of realist regional fiction; her son was Richard Harding Davis, the newspaperman. This piece was first published in an April 1861 issue of *The Atlantic Monthly* and brought back into public consciousness by Tillie Olsen in the 1980s. Very much worth reading.

174 pp.; 1972

5. *A Frozen Woman*   Annie Ernaux

A French novelist, the daughter of a grocer mother and a father who scrapes the vegetables and keeps house, Ernaux could have been expected to profit by these nontraditional examples of personhood. Instead she turns into a woman with her own "silent, sparkling kitchen," which is killing her "with flour and strawberries." I like this book very much.

160 pp.; 1981

6. *Storming Heaven*   Denise Giardina

You can learn plenty here about West Virginia coalfields and coal miners.

293 pp.; 1988

7. *The Dead of the House*   Hannah Green

Finally reissued shortly before Green died, this fictionalized account of her childhood in an Ohio village beautifully illustrates life on the shores of Lake Michigan.

180 pp.; 1972

8. *Italian Days*   **Barbara Grizzuti Harrison**

More than a travel journal, this is a pilgrim's tale and a wonderful explanation of how an encounter with another culture can change a life. One of my daughter's favorites.

477 pp.; 1989

9. *The Road Home*   **Jim Harrison**

This novel resonates with the characters' Nebraska roots, their white and Oglala Sioux heritages, and Harrison's preoccupation with the connectedness between generations and the earth and its human inhabitants. To some degree he continues the story begun in his 1988 novel, *Dalva*.

446 pp.; 1998

10. *Grand Opening*   **Jon Hassler**

Covering more than a year in the life of the Foster family, this poignant and upsetting vision of small-town life in 1944 Plum, Minnesota, chronicles the small-minded fights between Lutherans and Catholics, and the disorientation of a good family in a bad place. Hassler also wrote *The Love Hunter*, *Simon's Night*, and *Staggerford*.

309 pp.; 1987

11. *PrairyErth*   **William Least Heat-Moon**

An intensive look at a 744-square-mile piece of Chase County, Kansas. As he says, "the land, like a good library, lets a fellow extend himself, stretch time . . . slip the animal bondage of the perpetual present . . . a journey into the land is a way into some things and a way out of others." Amen. Also *Blue Highways*.

648 pp.; 1990

12. *All the Pretty Horses*   Cormac McCarthy
Winner of both the National Book Award and the National Book Critics Circle Award, it's the story of a sixteen-year-old East Texan who leaves home in 1950, heads for Mexico, ends up in prison, and returns to Texas wiser but forever scarred.

301 pp.; 1992

13. *Dreams of My Russian Summer*   Andreï Makine
This French novel about a youth trying to cope with Soviet life won every award in sight, including the Prix Goncourt and the Prix Medicis in France and accolades from the *New York Times, Los Angeles Times,* and *Boston Book Review.*

320 pp.; 1998

14. *In the Palm of Darkness*   Mayra Montero
An American herpetologist is searching for a specimen of the blood frog in the mountains of Haiti, a once-lush land reduced to a dry, inhospitable place. This is the first of Montero's novels to be translated into English.

181 pp.; 1997

15. *Cultivating Sacred Space: Gardening for the Soul*   Elizabeth Murray
I'm one of those people who got stuck in an apartment but should be living on two wooded acres. So this book, which is and isn't about gardening, is perfect for me. It's definitely about cultivating the spirit, reflecting on nature, finding the holy, and tending to the soul.

160 pp.; 1997

16. *Dakota: A Spiritual Geography*   Kathleen Norris
Many readers recommended Norris. Here she talks about the contemplative life in the western regions of North and South Dakota.

222 pp.; 1993

17. *A Place Called Home*   **Mickey Pearlman**

As I found out in editing this collection of twenty memoirs, everyone leaves home and everyone finds a place to call home. Exodus, it turns out, is genesis.

257 pp.; 1996

18. *The Drowning Room*   **Michael Pye**

In the Dutch colony of New Amsterdam in the frozen winter of 1642, a distraught woman tries to warm her husband's corpse back to life.

252 pp.; 1995

19. *Deep in the Green:*   **Anne Raver**
     An Exploration of Country Pleasures

Lots of lovely and loving essays, especially the one on ladybugs, by a *New York Times* garden columnist.

280 pp.; 1995

20. *Outside Passage*   **Julia Scully**

Subtitled *A Memoir of an Alaskan Childhood*, the state is a main character here. Julia and her sister end up in San Francisco and Seattle orphanages after their father's leg is amputated and he commits suicide. Her resilient mother returns to Nome to buy a rough-and-tumble roadhouse. As usual, you could not make this stuff up!

219 pp.; 1998

21. *The Woman Who Married a Bear*   **John Straley**

A mystery that takes place in the Alaskan port city of Sitka, it combines modern Alaskan life with the experiences and folklore of Alaska's indigenous peoples.

225 pp.; 1992

Save the Planet

1. *Desert Solitaire*   **Edward Abbey**

The famed environmentalist knew well how to step back from the world in this nonfiction work in order to really see it.

269 pp.; 1968

2. *A Natural History of the Senses*   **Diane Ackerman**

When you understand how you *see* the world, you will fight to preserve it.

331 pp.; 1990

3. *Platte River*   **Rick Bass**

A petroleum geologist who lives on a remote ranch in northern Montana, Bass has written three novellas illuminating mankind's relationship to the natural world. Also great is *The Ninemile Wolves*, about the reintroduction of those animals into the wild. Three more wonderful novellas appear in *The Sky, The Stars, The Wilderness*.

224 pp.; 1994

4. *Plain and Simple: A Woman's Journey to the Amish*   Sue Bender

Not strictly about the *physical* environment, but a good read about an urban woman finding peace in the spiritual environment of the Amish in Iowa and Ohio.

152 pp.; 1989

5. *Natural Affairs*   Peter Bernhardt

One of the most interesting books I've read in a long time, the subtitle, *A Botanist Looks at the Attachments Between Plants and People*, says it all. Bernhardt wrote *Wily Violets and Underground Orchids*.

225 pp.; 1993

6. *Women in the Field: America's Pioneering Women Naturalists*   Marcia Myers Bonta

Several readers wrote to me about this one and I'm glad they did. I love the outdoors, the study of which was dominated by men from the late eighteenth through the early twentieth century. So I am grateful for Bonda's biographies of twenty-five women in the field: naturalists, botanists, entomologists, ornithologists, and agrostologists.

272 pp.; 1991

7. *The Crystal Desert*   David G. Campbell

A personal account of a remarkable place at the bottom of the world, the "banana belt" of the Antarctic Peninsula, and of its plants, rocks, and glaciers.

308 pp.; 1992

8. *Silent Spring*   Rachel Carson

Probably the most influential book of the last fifty years, Carson, who wrote the bestselling *The Sea Around Us*, documented here how the pesticide industry was destroying the natural world. Because of Carson, DDT was banned and the environmental movement was launched. She is my hero.

464 pp.; 1962

9. *The Songlines*   Bruce Chatwin

This is a story of ideas. Set in an almost uninhabitable region of central Australia, where invisible pathways across the continent are known to us as songlines, two companions explore, among other questions, why man is the most restless and dissatisfied of animals. *In Patagonia* is, to say the least, about wandering and exile. Great for discussion.

293 pp.; 1987

10. *Pilgrim at Tinker Creek*   Annie Dillard

Winner of the Pulitzer Prize, this work reflects Dillard's urgent longing for a hidden God, for whom she searches in commonplace, natural events in her own neighborhood.

271 pp.; 1974

11. *The Everglades: River*   Marjorie S. Douglas
of Grass

Douglas's book is probably the reason we still have what is left of the Florida Everglades. She died recently at 108, but for many years warned us about what would happen (and to some extent it did) if the developers and commericial builders got their trucks on these unique wetlands.

448 pp.; 1947

12. *Sea Change: A Message*   Sylvia A. Earle
of the Oceans

Earle, a marine biologist and former chief scientist of the National Oceanic and Atmospheric Administration, has logged so many hours as a deep-sea diver that she once called herself the "Sturgeon General." She begs us to save the oceans "from ruin."

361 pp.; 1994

13. *The Trees in My Forest* **Bernd Heinrich**

An award-winning naturalist who writes like a poet, Heinrich tries to illustrate the vital link among humans, trees, birds, insects, and the creatures of the forest. Is there some way to make this required reading for everyone—while we still have a few trees left?

256 pp.; 1998

14. *A Country Year* **Sue Hubbell**

Hubbell, a self-taught naturalist, took refuge for twelve years in the Missouri Ozarks and turned to commercial beekeeping to make a living. Rare and sweet.

221 pp.; 1986

15. *Sand County Almanac* **Aldo Leopold**

This book by a noted naturalist poses the question of "whether a still higher 'standard of living' is worth its cost in things natural, wild, and free. For us of the minority, the opportunity to see geese is more important than television, and the chance to find a pasque-flower is a right as inalienable as free speech." Leopold died fighting a grass fire on a neighbor's farm in 1948.

226 pp.; 1949

16. *Hope, Human and Wild:* **Bill McKibben**
True Stories of Living Lightly on the Earth

McKibben is looking for examples of communities where people can live well and yet do less damage to nature. Are there ways to live that "produce decent human lives with less money, less energy, less wood. Less stuff." Can we make this required reading?

227 pp.; 1995

17. *Coming into the Country*   John McPhee

Alaska, the last wilderness, is threatened, and McPhee travels down an arctic river by kayak beyond the civilized frontiers to tell us what we are about to lose. Also *The Pine Barrens.*

438 pp.; 1977

18. *Bird of Life, Bird of Death*   Jonathan Evan Maslow

This naturalist and a photographer went to Guatemala in July 1983 to observe the quetzal, thought by many to be the most beautiful bird in the hemisphere.

240 pp.; 1986

19. *Gathering the Desert*   Gary Paul Nabhan

Wonderful study of the desert flora and ethnobiology of the Sonora Desert, with a fine portrait of some of the Indians of North America.

209 pp.; 1985

20. *The Island Within*   Richard K. Nelson

Nelson, an anthropologist, settled with his family in a small town on the Pacific Northwest coast in order to explore a nearby island. Instead he ended up exploring the meaning of place itself and learning in the process about the wisdom of Native Americans.

280 pp.; 1991

21. *Ecological Literacy*   David Orr

This readable argument about sustainable living was recommended by a reader, Claudia Ebeling.

210 pp.; 1992

22. *Grizzly Years*   Doug Peacock

After Vietnam, Campbell crawled into the vastness of the Rocky Mountain wilderness and met another veteran, the American grizzly. He has spent twenty years arguing powerfully for the preservation of all things wild. We should listen to him.

288 pp.; 1990

23. *Living by Water*   Brenda Peterson

Subtitled *Essays on Life, Land, and Spirit* and published in Alaska, Peterson writes about aquatic biology, natural history, and ecology.

144 pp.; 1991

24. *Skywater*   Melinda Worth Popham

Many of the main characters here are coyotes, named after the trash that litters the desert. Poetic and important discussion too of the tailings from abandoned copper mines that have poisoned the groundwater. I love this book.

243 pp.; 1990

25. *Cadillac Desert*   Marc Reisner

This book documents the growth of the Bureau of Reclamation, responsible for Hoover, Shasta, and Grand Coulee dams, and its bitter rivalry with the U.S. Army Corps of Enginers. Neither pork-barrel politics nor utopian schemes have yet solved the West's most relentless problem: water.

517 pp.; 1986

26. *Song for the Blue Ocean: Encounters*   Carl Safina
Along the World's Coasts and Beneath the Seas

I grew up with a brother who often took me deep-sea fishing off the coast of Florida, so I am plenty depressed about the dwindling populations of wild edible creatures that this research ecologist discovers on his journeys. Read this book! He will make you care even if you never see the sea.

384 pp.; 1998

27. *The Meadowlands: Wilderness*   Robert Sullivan
Adventures at the Edge of a City

I live ten minutes from the abused but beautiful New Jersey Meadowlands, a place filled with swamps and birds and wildlife. Let us hope that one of the less money-hungry politicians will prevent its being paved over for another shopping center.

224 pp.; 1998

28. *Walden*   Henry David Thoreau

The most famous naturalist of them all ruminates about the change of seasons in a New England woods, nineteenth-century society, the good life, and—best of all—solitude.

207 pp.; 1854

29. *Refuge*   Terry Tempest Williams

An extraordinary book, hard to categorize. It is part memoir about the many women in her family who have died from cancers caused by irresponsible U.S. atomic testing in Utah, and part description, in this case of the flooded Bear River Migratory Bird Refuge near Great Salt Lake, and the emotional and physical impact of that phenomenon on the writer. *Don't miss it.*

304 pp.; 1991

30. *Red-Tails in Love: A Wildlife*   Marie Winn
Drama in Central Park

Are you saying that New York City was not the first place you'd look for red-tailed hawks? But this book chronicles the *six* years during which Pale Male, a young male hawk, attempts to feed and raise his family with Mom #3. And Winn, a writer for the *Wall Street Journal*, beautifully describes the wildlife—raccoons, turtles, woodpeckers, and myriad other birds who live in the park.

304 pp.; 1998

31. *Run, River, Run*   Ann Zwinger

Zwinger is also the author of *Downcanyon: A Naturalist Explores the Colorado River Through Grand Canyon*. She convinces the reader of the power of firsthand experience and of honest description.

317 pp.; 1975

Native American Ideas

Most of the work here is by Native Americans.

1. *The Lone Ranger and Tonto Fistfight in Heaven*   Sherman Alexie

Twenty-two widely praised short stories by a member of the Spokane Nation, often about the alcoholism, malnutrition, and suicidal self-loathing that plague *some* Native Americans. In *Indian Killer* someone is scalping white men in Seattle.

223 pp.; 1993

2. *The Sacred Hoop*   Paula Gunn Allen

Allen, a Laguna Pueblo poet, novelist, and scholar, argues that colonization transformed and obscured what were once woman-centered cultures. She explores a range of female deities, American Indian women's history, the place of lesbians in Indian culture, and the importance of mothers and grandmothers to Indian identity.

285 pp.; 1986

3. *Notches*   **Peter Bowen**

These Montana mysteries, featuring Gabriel Du Pré, show that Bowen has a sure knowledge of both Western and Native American traditions. Here some of the characters are Métis and Blackfeet.

224 pp.; 1997

4. *Night Flying Woman*   **Ignatia Broker**

This is an Ojibway narrative of life in the nineteenth century and the story of the author's great-great-grandmother, Ni-bo-Wi-se-gwe, or Night Flying Woman.

135 pp.; 1983

5. *Daughters of Copperwoman*   **Anne Cameron**

Ann Worswick recommends this book about the lives and myths of Indian women on Vancouver Island.

150 pp.; 1981

6. *From the River's Edge*   **Elizabeth Cook-Lynn**

John Tatekeya, a cattleman, discovers what it means to be a Dakotah in the white man's court when the Missouri River Power Project floods reservation lands and forty-two of his prized horned Herefords are stolen.

147 pp.; 1991

7. *Custer Died for Your Sins*   **Vine Deloria, Jr.**

Published when the American Indian Movement (AIM) was just a year old, this book was the clarion call of a new militancy among Native Americans. It has been updated with a new preface.

279 pp.; 1969

8. *A Yellow Raft in Blue Water*   **Michael Dorris**

This is a thrice-told tale of three women: Rayona, a fifteen-year-old who is part black; her American Indian mother, Christine; and the fierce and mysterious Ida, a mother and grandmother whose secrets and dreams braid the three lives together.

372 pp.; 1987

9. *Tracks*   Louise Erdrich

Tracks is the prequel to *Love Medicine* and *The Beet Queen*, and with *Bingo Palace* completes a Native American tetralogy. *Tracks* is told in three different voices—that of Nanapush, a wise leader of the Chippewa; Fleur, torn between her Chippewa and Christian beliefs; and Pauline, the witchlike avenger.

226 pp.; 1988

10. *Firesticks*   Diane Glancy

These are surrealistic, experimental stories (or firesticks) by a Cherokee poet. Recurring themes are transformation through flight and the stitching together of cultures.

142 pp.; 1993

11. *The Jailing of Cecilia*   Janet Campbell Hale
Capture

Engrossing story by a member of the Coeur d'Alene tribe of northern Idaho that takes off when Cecilia Eagle Capture, a married mother of two and a law student at Berkeley, is arrested for drunk driving on her thirtieth birthday. Also *Bloodlines: Odyssey of a Native Daughter*, a collection of autobiographical essays about growing up in a troubled Native American family.

201 pp.; 1985

12. *In Mad Love and War*   **Joy Harjo**
Winner of the Poetry Society of America's William Carlos Williams Award for 1990, these are poems written by a member of the Creek tribe who teaches at a western university. An exceptional collection.

65 pp.; 1990

13. *Rising Voices*   **Arlene B. Hirschfelder**
                                  and Beverly B. Singer
Writings of young people, including sixty-two poems and essays, that mirror the richness and sorrow of the Native American experience. *Happily May I Walk* (by Hirschfelder) is also highly recommended.

115 pp.; 1992

14. *Mean Spirit*   **Linda Hogan**
Extraordinary fictionalized account of what happened when oil was discovered on land in Oklahoma, in the 1920s and 1930s, and Osage Indians began to die. Rampant fraud, intimidation, and murder—perpetrated by white people—are revealed.

374 pp.; 1990

15. *Green Grass, Running Water*   **Thomas King**
First-rate comic novel about Lionel Red Dog, a Canadian Blackfoot stereo and TV salesman, his Uncle Eli Stands Alone, and his sister Latisha (who runs the Dead Dog Cafe). Read *Medicine River* too.

360 pp.; 1993

16. *The Deaths of Sybil Bolton*   **Dennis McAuliffe, Jr.**
McAuliffe's Osage grandmother died in 1925 at age twenty-one from either suicide or homicide. He tries here to solve the mystery.

In those years the Osage of Oklahoma were oil rich and regularly murdered by jealous whites.

337 pp.; 1994

17. *Wind from an Enemy Sky*   D'Arcy McNickle

The dean of American Indian writers, McNickle, a Flathead, writes of the tragedy caused by the building of a dam and by the stubbornness of misunderstanding in two opposing worlds.

256 pp.; 1978

18. *In the Spirit of Crazy Horse*   Peter Matthiessen

To quote Dee Brown, this is "the first solidly documented account of the U.S. government's renewed assault upon American Indians that began in the 1970s."

628 pp.; 1983

19. *House Made of Dawn*   N. Scott Momaday

Pulitzer Prize–winning novel of a proud stranger in his native land.

192 pp.; 1968

20. *Woven Stone*   Simon Ortiz

An omnibus consisting of three previous books—*Going for the Rain, A Good Journey*, and *Fight Back: For the Sake of the People, For the Sake of the Land*—by an Acoma Pueblo who is one of America's best poets.

350 pp.; 1992

21. *Wolfsong*   Louis Owens

Tom Joseph, a young Indian who is away at college, returns for his uncle's funeral and finds himself caught up in the old man's fight to save the wilderness from destruction.

249 pp.; 1991

22. *The Grass Dancer*   **Susan Power**

Set on a Sioux reservation in North Dakota, this novel uses folk motifs to emphasize how the actions of our ancestors affect our contemporary lives. Power, an enrolled member of the Standing Rock Sioux, received an A.B. from Harvard, a J.D. from Harvard Law School, and an M.F.A. from the Iowa Writers' Workshop.

393 pp.; 1994

23. *Grand Avenue*   **Greg Sarris**

Sarris, who is part Native American, part Filipino, and part Jewish, is a professor of English at UCLA and the elected chief of the Miwok tribe. This novel in stories tells the tales of the Pomo Indians, Mexicans, Portuguese, and African Americans who live near this street in the northern California town of Santa Rosa. Also *Watermelon Nights*.

229 pp.; 1994

24. *Ceremony*   **Leslie Marmon Silko**

Tayo, a young American Indian who was a Japanese prisoner of war during World War II, returns to the Laguna Pueblo reservation to search for resolution. That quest leads to the ancient stories of his people. Silko's *Almanac of the Dead* is a controversial, end-of-the-world-is-coming novel.

262 pp.; 1977

25. *Deluge*   **Albertine Strong**

Wenebojo, the Trickster, surfaces in this novel about a Chippewa family called the Oshogays. At least that's what the narrator believes.

277 pp.; 1997

26. *A Lakota Woman's Story* Madonna Swan

Mark St. Pierre, a professor at Colorado Mountain College, records here multiple versions of the Lakota legends told to him by Swan, as well as stories of the ten years she spent in sanitoriums fighting her tuberculosis. There is some confusion about how much is Swan and what St. Pierre contributed.

209 pp.; 1990

27. *Two Old Women* Velma Wallis

Subtitled *An Alaska Legend of Betrayal, Courage and Survival,* this story is based on an Athabaskan Indian legend passed along from mothers to daughters for many generations on the upper Yukon River in Alaska. One of thirteen children, Wallis was born in Fort Yukon, a place reachable only by airplane, dog sled, snow machine, or riverboat.

160 pp.; 1993

28. *Talking Indian* Anna Lee Walters

Walters, a Pawnee/Otoe living on the Navajo reservation in Arizona, collects her autobiography, short stories, historical tribal documentation, and more.

222 pp.; 1992

29. *Winter in the Blood* James Welch

The thirty-two-year-old narrator, a sensitive and intelligent Blackfeet Indian, symbolizes the dispossession of his people and the nation's indifference to their fate. In *The Indian Lawyer,* Sylvester Yellow Calf, a graduate of Stanford Law, is a long way from the Blackfeet reservation in Browning, Montana. Also *Fool's Crow.*

176 pp.; 1974

30. *Pieces of White Shell:*   Terry Tempest Williams
     A Journey to Navajoland
This first book won the 1984 Southwest Book Award and is a memoir of time spent teaching on a Navajo reservation. Williams also wrote *Coyote's Canyon* and *The Secret Language of Snow*.

162 pp.; 1984

31. *Black Eagle Child*   Ray A. Young Bear
Intricate stories about religion, myth, dreams, poverty, and injustice by a Mesquakie writer who re-creates his life in Iowa in the 1950s through the 1970s.

261 pp.; 1992

25

A Jewish View

1. *Wartime Lies*   **Louis Begley**

First novel by a Manhattan lawyer who escaped the Nazis as a boy in Poland. Here the Jewish boy Maciek also survives, spends the war years in his aunt's care, and learns that deception saves *and* destroys. In *About Schmidt* the "hero" is an anti-Semitic lawyer.

198 pp.; 1991

2. *Seize the Day*   **Saul Bellow**

One day in the life of Tommy Wilhelm, whose "spirit, the peculiar burden of his existence, lay upon him like an accretion, a load, a hump . . . of nameless things which it was the business of his life to carry about."

118 pp.; 1956

3. *The Book of J*   **Harold Bloom**
                                        and David Rosenberg

Scholars agree that the first strand in Genesis, Exodus, and Numbers was written by someone they call J, who lived in the tenth century. Using Rosenberg's new translation, Bloom asserts that this unknown writer was of Shakespeare's stature, and was most probably a woman. Oh, I'm shocked, just shocked!

340 pp.; 1990

4. *The Gifts of the Jews:*   **Thomas Cahill**
How a Tribe of Desert Nomads
Changed the Way Everyone Thinks and Feels

Cahill says that "the Jews gave us the Outside and the Inside— our outlook and our inner life . . . Most of our best words, in fact— new, adventure, surprise; unique, individual, person, vocation; time, history, future; freedom, progress, spirit; faith, hope, jus- tice—are the gifts of the Jews." And it's refreshing, to say the least, that someone with a distinctly Irish name has stated clearly that Ju- daism and Christianity are not, as many people would like to be- lieve, really more or less the same religion—only with different holidays and ceremonies. Mazel tov, Mr. Cahill.

291 pp.; 1998

5. *Inherit the Mob*   **Zev Chafets**

So, Uncle Max dies, and what does his respectable journalist nephew inherit? Nu, it's the last of the great American Jewish gangs.

312 pp.; 1991

6. *Tough Jews*   **Rich Cohen**

Many of the Jewish gangsters in Brownsville (Brooklyn) fre- quented a diner owned by Cohen's great-grandparents. He heard all the "mysahs" (stories), and he knows from stick-ups, and the days when the Jewish gangster was not exactly chopped liver. This book is hilarious and a different look at a minority whose heroes are not usually named Big Greenie Greenberg, Charlie (The Bug) Work- man, and Tick-Tock Tannenbaum.

271 pp.; 1998

7. *King of the Jews*   **Leslie Epstein**
Brilliant work of black humor, set in a small community in Poland, this is the story of I. C. Trumpelmann, the director of an orphanage no one wants to leave.

352 pp.; 1993

8. *The Provincials*   **Eli N. Evans**
Subtitled *A Personal History of Jews in the South*, Evans records their history, from the early 1800s when they fled the northern ghettos, to the present. The "Jews," he says, "were not aliens . . . but blood and bones part of the South itself." Also *The Lonely Days Were Sundays*.

331 pp.; 1973

9. *Man's Search for Meaning*   **Viktor Frankl**
Frankl was Nazi concentration camp inmate number 119,104, but he spent his life proclaiming that you do not recover from victimization by seeing yourself as a victim. "Decisions, not conditions," are what mental health is about. "What is demanded of man is not, as some existential philosophers teach, to endure the meaninglessness of life, but rather to bear [one's] incapacity to grasp its unconditional meaningfulness in rational terms. Logos is deeper than logic." Amen.

221 pp.; 1946

10. *Jews Without Money*   **Michael Gold**
This is the classic American urban proletariat novel. It documents that distinctive American experience, immigrant poverty.

234 pp.; 1930

11. *Snow in August*   **Pete Hamill**
Lovely novel by a famous New York editor about the friendship of an Irish Catholic boy and a Czechoslovakian

refugee, a rabbi in Brooklyn during the 1940s, who both love baseball.

503 pp.; 1997

12. *Safe in America*   **Marcie Hershman**

Three generations of a Cleveland family struggle with the question of how to keep those we love safe in an unsafe world. Hershman's intelligence also shines forth in her first book, *Tales of the Master Race*, which is a must.

285 pp.; 1995

13. *In a Hotel Garden*   **Gabriel Josipovici**

Written almost entirely in dialogue, this short novel about Ben's encounter with a strange and wonderful Jewish woman in the Dolomite Alps raises the question of how we come to terms with the destruction of the European Jews in this century.

148 pp.; 1995

14. *The Jew in the Lotus*   **Rodger Kamenetz**

A chronicle of a historical dialogue among several rabbis and the Dalai Lama. *Stalking Elijah*, his newest, tries to answer this question: "How does one live in the modern world and hold on to one's Jewish faith?"

384 pp.; 1997

15. *The Painted Bird*   **Jerzy Kosinski**

One of the most disturbing books ever written, this is terror and savagery as perpetrated against a dark-haired boy, either a Jew or a gypsy, fleeing the Holocaust. Kosinski, who committed suicide, was the author of *Passion Play* and *Steps*, among others.

251 pp.; 1965

16. *The Reawakening*   Primo Levi
The Italian author and Holocaust survivor gave us more than these two statements to think about for the rest of our lives: "God cannot exist if Auschwitz exists" and "War is always."

217 pp.; 1963

17. *Number the Stars*   Lois Lowry
A Young Adult book by a non-Jew, this tells the correct story of the Danish triumph in saving its Jewish citizens, and dispels the myth of the Star of David supposedly worn by King Christian. The truth, however, is even more laudable and exemplary.

137 pp.; 1989

18. *The Assistant*   Bernard Malamud
A mundane environment, a small grocery store run by a poor Jew in a New York City borough, is the setting for a tale of oppression and the regenerative power of suffering. Provokes great discussions.

297 pp.; 1957

19. *The Shawl*   Cynthia Ozick
Includes a short story and a novella, "Rosa." In "The Shawl," Rosa Lublin witnesses the murder of her infant daughter at the hands of a concentration camp guard. Thirty years later in "Rosa" she is "a madwoman and a scavenger," living in Florida. Powerful, required reading for everyone. A newer book, *The Puttermesser Papers,* traces the incredible life and afterlife of a New York woman.

70 pp.; 1983

20. *Later the Same Day*   Grace Paley
The third volume of stories about real people who struggle for meaning in their lives, written by the longtime antiwar, civil

rights, and women's rights activist. *The Little Disturbances of Man* and *Enormous Changes at the Last Minute* are equally good.

211 pp.; 1985

21. *Deborah, Golda, and Me*   Letty Cottin Pogrebin

Being Female and Jewish in America, the subtitle, pretty much sums it up; Pogrebin struggles here to reconcile her life as a Jew and a feminist. Great for discussion.

400 pp.; 1991

22. *The Chosen*   Chaim Potok

Accessible picture of Orthodox Jews in Brooklyn by the popular author of *My Name Is Asher Lev.*

271 pp.; 1968

23. *Solomon Gursky Was Here*   Mordecai Richler

A Canadian Jew, Richler writes here about a young scholar ruined by his obsession with a clan of Canadian Jewish bootleggers. Richler wrote *The Apprenticeship of Duddy Kravitz*, on which the movie was based.

432 pp.; 1990

24. *Lovingkindness*   Anne Roiphe

New York feminist faces her own conflicting feelings when her daughter decides to marry an Orthodox man in Israel and to become Orthodox herself. Great for discussion, even if you're not Jewish.

279 pp.; 1987

25. *The Counterlife*   Philip Roth

Nathan Zuckerman of *The Ghost Writer*, *Zuckerman Unbound*, and *The Anatomy Lesson* arrives in Israel. Roth plays on all the usual stereotypes in order to defuse them.

324 pp.; 1986

26. *The Magic We Do Here*   Larry Rudner

A golden-haired Jew disguises himself during the Holocaust and survives to tell the stories of millions of Jews who have "disappeared in the mist." His posthumously published novel, *Memory's Tailor,* was prepared for publication by a teaching colleague, novelist John Kessel.

212 pp.; 1988

27. *Scum*   Isaac Bashevis Singer

Controversial novel about the now rich and respectable Max, who revisits the scenes of his past on Krochmalna Street in Warsaw where he spent his past as a poverty-stricken youth.

218 pp.; 1991

28. *Maus: A Survivor's Tale I* and *II*   Art Spiegelman

Two stories about Auschwitz survivors, Vladek and Anja Spiegelman, told in comic book form. Winner of the Pulitzer Prize Special Award. They should be read as one.

159 pp.; 1986

29. *The Forgotten*   Elie Wiesel

Malkiel Rosenbaum's father persuades him to visit the events of his father's wartime experiences in Romania fighting the Nazis. *Memoirs: All Rivers Run to the Sea* takes us from the Nobel Peace Prize laureate's childhood through his experiences and survival in Nazi death camps to his role as witness for the dead and the survivors.

304 pp.; 1992

30. *Bread Givers*   Anzia Yezierska

Yezierska, who was born in a mud hut on the Russian-Polish border, wrote this autobiographical novel to condemn patriarchal Jewish attitudes toward women. Also *Hungry Hearts* and *Salome of the Tenements* for a look at the Jewish immigrant experience through a woman's eyes.

297 pp.; 1925

26

Mi Vida Latina

1. *How the Garcia Girls*   Julia Alvarez
Lost Their Accents

The displaced daughters of Dr. Garcia belong to the uppermost echelon of Spanish Caribbean society, descendants of the conquistadores, but in this novel they are exiles in the Bronx.

290 pp.; 1991

2. *Albuquerque*   Rudolfo Anaya

During a bitter mayoral race in Albuquerque a young man of Indian and Anglo ancestry learns about his true parentage. *Bless Me, Ultima,* published in 1972, has sold more than 275,000 copies.

293 pp.; 1992

3. *Borderlands/La Frontera:*   Gloria Anzaldua
The New Mestiza

A lesbian feminist, Anzaldua's subject is the devalued identity of Chicano immigrants, and the cultural and sexual identity problems which she says are perpetrated by U.S. racism. She is also the coeditor of *This Bridge Called My Back: Writings by Radical Women of Color.*

203 pp.; 1987

4. *A Place Where the Sea Remembers*   Sandra Benítez
Winner of the Barnes & Noble Discover Great New Writers Award, these interconnected stories explore the triumphs and tragedies of everyday life in a Mexican village. Her prose sings!

163 pp.; 1993

5. *Paradise*   Elena Castedo
Richly deserved nomination for a National Book Award. Solita, the ten-year-old daughter of refugees from Franco's Spain, is whisked off to El Topaz, the lush hacienda of a wealthy eccentric, by her mother. The child would have been safer in the ghetto.

328 pp.; 1990

6. *So Far from God*   Ana Castillo
Castillo explores the politics of the erotic woman. In her *Women Are Not Roses*, lower-class women are in a double bind; they often have to choose between an erotic relationship and class struggle.

252 pp.; 1993

7. *Woman Hollering Creek*   Sandra Cisneros
This collection of stories offers tales of women on both sides of the U.S.–Mexico border. It follows *The House on Mango Street*, winner of the 1985 American Book Award from the Before Columbus Foundation.

192 pp.; 1991

8. *Drown*   Junot Diaz
Diaz created more noise in the New York publishing world than I've heard in a long time. In five of the ten connected stories his narrator is Ramon de las Casas ("Yunior") who comes from the Dominican Republic to New Jersey. You can feel the influence of the late Raymond Carver here.

208 pp.; 1996

9. *Consider This, Señora*   **Harriet Doerr**

Fans of *Stones for Ibarra* have been waiting a long time for this one. Set again in Mexico, this novel examines the lives of a group of American expatriates who face some big adjustments.

241 pp.; 1993

10. *Intaglio: A Novel in*   **Roberta Fernandez**
     Six Stories

Winner of the Multicultural Publishers Exchange Best Book of Fiction, this novel examines the deep-rooted culture of women born at the turn of the century on the U.S.–Mexico border.

160 pp.; 1990

11. *The Old Gringo*   **Carlos Fuentes**

Ambrose Bierce, the American writer, soldier, and journalist, spends his last mysterious days in Mexico among Sancho Villa's men. His encounter with Tomas Arroyo, one of Villa's generals, is symbolic of the conflict between these two cultures.

199 pp.; 1985

12. *Dreaming in Cuban*   **Cristina Garcia**

Graceful, insightful first novel about three generations of Cuban women living in Havana, Cuba; Brooklyn, New York; and near the sea in Cuba. Her newest is *The Agüero Sisters*.

256 pp.; 1992

13. *The Magic of Blood*   **Dagoberto Gilb**

Twenty-six stories of Mexican Americans in the Southwest trying to eke out a living. It won the PEN/Ernest Hemingway Foundation Award.

287 pp.; 1993

14. *The Mambo Kings Play Songs of Love*   Oscar Hijuelos

Pultizer Prize–winning portrait of a man, his family, and his community—all in 1950s New York. Even Desi Arnaz shows up.

416 pp.; 1989

15. *Zapata Rose in 1992 & Other Tales*   Gary D. Keller

Expanded version of *Tales of El Huitlacoche*. Title story describes the reawakening in 1992 of Emiliano Zapata and the ways his presence inspires *indios*, *campesinos*, and *mestizos* in the Western Hemisphere.

326 pp.; 1993

16. *Aunt Julia and the Scriptwriter*   Mario Vargas Llosa

A comic, ribald, sophisticated tale of life and love in Lima in the 1950s. In other words, Mario falls in love with his thirty-two-year-old aunt.

374 pp.; 1982

17. *Nilda*   Nicolasa Mohr

Mohr, a Puerto Rican who lives in Brooklyn, won the *New York Times* Outstanding Book of the Year for *Nilda*. *El Bronx Remembered* was a finalist for the National Book Award.

292 pp.; 1973

18. *Sun Stone*   Octavio Paz

One of the great modern long poems by Mexico's leading poet. Get the edition with the translation by Muriel Rukeyser.

59 pp.; 1957

19. *Days of Obligation: An*   **Richard Rodriguez**
    Argument with My Mexican Father

Mexico and the United States are portrayed as moral rivals upon the landscape of California, where Rodriguez lives; the United States in this book has a culture of tragedy; Mexico revels in youthful optimism.

230 pp.; 1992

20. *When I Was Puerto Rican*   **Esmeralda Santiago**

A real-life coming-of-age story about what it means to be Puerto Rican both on the island and as an immigrant in New York City. Her first novel is *América's Dream*.

274 pp.; 1994

21. *Tropical Synagogues: Short Stories*   **Ilan Stavans**
    by Jewish–Latin American Writers

Jews make up less than 4 percent of a population that numbers some 260 million. But these twenty-three stories by twenty-one writers from Argentina, Brazil, Guatemala, Mexico, Peru, and Venezuela tell much about immigration, assimilation, anti-Semitism, and the struggle to remain Jewish in a heavily Catholic region.

239 pp.; 1993

22. *The Shadow of the Shadow*   **Paco Ignacio Taibo II**

A spellbinding novel that takes place in Mexico City in 1922 where a group of intellectuals get caught up in a political conspiracy.

288 pp.; 1991

23. *Down These Mean Streets*   **Piri Thomas**

An autobiographical novel, this is one of the best-known works about growing up Puerto Rican in New York City. Thomas grew up in El Barrio.

333 pp.; 1967

24. *Under the Feet of Jesus*   Helena María Viramontes

After living in Irvine, California, for twelve years, Viramontes was inspired to write about the migrant workers she observed in that area. As she says, "When people sit down to eat their salads or bite their apples, I want them to think about the *piscadores* [harvesters] that brought that food to their tables."

180 pp.; 1995

African-American Images

Includes fiction and nonfiction by and about African Americans.

1. *Going to Meet the Man*   **James Baldwin**
This collection of short stories includes "Sonny's Blues." *The Fire Next Time* grew from a long magazine essay on the Black Muslims and the civil rights struggle.

249 pp.; 1965

2. *Slaves in the Family*   **Edward Ball**
It's almost impossible to express the depth of my admiration for Ball, a white man born in Savannah, educated at Brown, and a columnist for *The Village Voice* who traveled all over the United States to meet some of the 75,000 to 100,000 living Americans who are descendants of the slaves owned from 1698 to 1865 by the Ball family (on twenty plantations and through six generations) until the Union troops arrived and forced emancipation. His encounters with black families—some of whom are his blood kin—and the photographs of the black and white people caught up in America's worst nightmare are alone worth the price of the book.

489 pp.; 1998

3. *Gorilla, My Love*   Toni Cade Bambara

First collection of short stories by the late writer, followed by *The Sea Birds Are Still Alive*, and *The Salt Eaters*, which includes the widely anthologized "My Man Bovanne."

177 pp.; 1972

4. *Your Blues Ain't Like Mine*   Bebe Moore Campbell

This novel recalls the racially motivated murder of Emmett Till, a black teenager killed for whistling at a white woman in Mississippi in 1955. Followed by *Singing in the Comeback Choir*.

352 pp.; 1992

5. *Good Times*   Lucille Clifton

This collection and *Good News About the Earth*, both by the Maryland poet, optimistically portray the value of the family and the ghetto as home.

85 pp.; 1969

6. *Notes of a Hanging Judge*   Stanley Crouch

A collection of essays by the well-known social critic who makes a lot of sense on the subject of racism. Also *The All-American Skin Game: Or, The Decoy of Race, The Long and Short of It, 1990–1994*.

296 pp.; 1990

7. *Invisible Man*   Ralph Ellison

Ellison won the National Book Award for this novel and created a new mode of fiction by combining social realism with elements of surrealism. This is arguably the most distinguished American work of its time.

429 pp.; 1953

8. *A Lesson Before Dying*   Ernest J. Gaines

The author of *The Autobiography of Miss Jane Pittman* tells the story of two black men in a small Cajun Louisiana community in the 1940s: Jefferson—convicted of murder and condemned to death—and Wiggins, a university-trained teacher who becomes his teacher and friend.

256 pp.; 1993

9. *Thirteen Ways of*   Henry Louis Gates, Jr.
   Looking at a Black Man

A collection of essays profiling diverse figures like James Baldwin and General Colin Powell.

226 pp.; 1997

10. *Praying for Sheetrock*   Melissa Fay Greene

Intimate reporting about a black community in rural Georgia that moved from passivity to civil rights militancy to calm.

352 pp.; 1991

11. *Ain't I a Woman?*   bell hooks

As one bookseller said, this volume "challenges every accepted notion about the lives of black women." Hallelujah. Also *Bone Black: Memories of Girlhood*.

205 pp.; 1981

12. *In My Place*   Charlayne Hunter-Gault

At one time a national correspondent for the *MacNeil-Lehrer NewsHour*, Hunter-Gault reflects on her childhood and young adulthood and on her historic role as one of two black students who desegregated the University of Georgia in 1961.

192 pp.; 1993

13. *Their Eyes Were*   **Zora Neale Hurston**
Watching God

Classic of black literature, this is the story of a strong-spirited woman's quest for love and self-fulfillment. Read Hurston's autobiography, *Dust Tracks on a Road,* as well.

286 pp.; 1937

14. *Middle Passage*   **Charles Johnson**

Winner of the National Book Award, in this novel an emancipated and very educated slave stows away on a ship bound for Africa. His new novel is *Dreamer.*

160 pp.; 1990

15. *The Healing*   **Gayl Jones**

Jones's debut novel, *Corregidora,* was published in 1975 when she was twenty-five. Here, Harlan Jane Eagleton, who at different times is a Louisville beautician, manager for a female rock star, and a faith healer, discovers—after a knife is plunged into her chest—that she has the gift of healing.

336 pp.; 1998

16. *I've Known Rivers:*   **Sara Lawrence-Lightfoot**
Lives of Loss and Liberation

The author profiles six successful African Americans in their middle years through a method she calls "human archaeology," and responds to E. Franklin Frazier's *The Black Bourgeoisie,* where, she says, he accuses middle- and upper-middle-class black people of being "bourgeois assimilationists" and "cartoon characters" who care only for money, status, and power. She also wrote *Balm in Gilead.*

654 pp.; 1994

17. *The Color of Water*   **James McBride**

Subtitled *A Black Man's Tribute to His White Mother,* this memoir/oral history by McBride, whose father was the son of a black minister and whose mother was the daughter of a failed itinerant Orthodox rabbi from rural Virginia, deserves the many accolades it received. All mothers would wish for such a hymn from a son.

223 pp.; 1996

18. *Leaving Pipe Shop:*   **Deborah E. McDowell**
   Memories of Kin

Ostensibly about the author's return, after more than twenty years, to the Alabama town where she grew up in the 1950s and 1960s, to investigate her father's death. Also an evenhanded look at the civil rights era as it intimately affected the so-called average people.

287 pp.; 1996

19. *Waiting to Exhale*   **Terry McMillan**

Bestselling novel about four African-American women who are waiting to exhale when (and if) they finally meet their misters right! In spite of *Exhale*'s huge success, many readers prefer *Disappearing Act*.

416 pp.; 1992

20. *Daddy Was a Number Runner*   **Louise Meriwether**

The first African-American novel to assess the effects of the Depression on a black family, it is a true picture of the poverty and despair in the ghetto.

208 pp.; 1970

21. *Playing in the Dark*   **Toni Morrison**

The Nobel Prize–winning author calls for literary scholarship that will help all Americans understand how black experience is interwoven in American literature.

91 pp.; 1993

22. *RL's Dream*   Walter Mosley

The author of the mysteries *White Butterfly*, *A Red Death,* and *Black Betty* writes here of Soupspoon Wise, an aging musician, who reminisces about his encounter with the ghost of an enigmatic blues genius.

267 pp.; 1995

23. *The Women of Brewster Place*   Gloria Naylor

Seven women end up on a blind alley leading into a dead-end street, but their spirits and stories are anything but impoverished. Also *Bailey's Cafe*, following *Linden Hills* and *Mama Day*. In 1998 she produced *The Men of Brewster Place*.

192 pp.; 1982

24. *The Street*   Ann Petry

An American classic and a historical document about violent and impoverished life in the city, especially for a woman trying to raise a son. Perry is the author of *Miss Muriel and Other Stories*.

436 pp.; 1946

25. *High Cotton*   Darryl Pinckney

A dense, rich, first novel about an alienated but well-educated and nonconformist black man who is obsessed with racial identities.

320 pp.; 1992

26. *All-Bright Court*   Connie Porter

In this first novel Porter describes twenty years in the lives of the black residents of a housing project in the shadow of Buffalo's steel mills. Watch this writer.

240 pp.; 1991

27. *Caucasia*   **Danzy Senna**

Margo Jefferson commented in her *New York Times* review that "race is hard to think, talk or write about with undefensive clarity and noncloying intimacy, partly because it can play so many parts in so many dramas," but that Senna writes successfully about the issue of "mulattoes, [who] aren't only a gauge of race relations, [but] a gauge of the cultural complexities you choose—or choose not—to live with."

353 pp.; 1998

28. *Betsey Brown*   **Ntozake Shange**

The story of a thirteen-year-old girl, poised between the enchantment of childhood and the possibilities of adulthood. Set in St. Louis in 1957, the story reveals the effects of both racism and integration. Shange, a playwright, is the author of *for colored girls who have considered suicide/when the rainbow is enuf.*

196 pp.; 1985

29. *Miss Ophelia*   **Mary Burnett Smith**

Isabel Anderson, called Belly, a feisty eleven-year-old, is shipped off to a secluded town in 1940s Virginia to tend to her sickly Aunt Rachel. There she has piano lessons with a shadowy figure, the well-traveled and well-read Miss Ophelia, from whom she learns more than music. Smith has a lovely voice and a fluid style.

277 pp.; 1998

30. *The Content of Our Character*   **Shelby Steele**

Subtitled *A New Vision of Race in America*, Steele argues that it is time for blacks to stop thinking of themselves as victims. This did not endear him to some members of the left, but ensured his celebrity on the right, and gave everyone in the middle plenty to think about.

175 pp.; 1990

31. *I Been in Sorrow's*   **Susan Straight**
    Kitchen and Licked Out All the Pots

Like all good writers, Straight misses nothing in her portrait of Marietta Cook, born in the Gullah-speaking Low Country of South Carolina. She ends up among the luxury condominiums and freeways in the promised land of California.

355 pp.; 1992

32. *The Color Purple*   **Alice Walker**

Epistolary novel in which the sisters Celie and Nettie epitomize the friendship black women must have with each other in the midst of the oppression they face in their relationships with black men and whites in general. Don't miss this book; even the movie was great.

253 pp.; 1982

33. *Jubilee*   **Margaret Walker**

Music is the leitmotif in this novel about Elvira Ware Brown, called Vyry, one of fifteen children and a slave in nineteenth-century America. She was the actual great-grandmother of the author. Unforgettable. Walker is best known for her first book, *For My People*.

497 pp.; 1966

34. *When Death Comes*   **Valerie Wilson Wesley**
    Stealing

The editor of *Essence* introduces P.I. Tamara Hayle in this exciting first mystery about the murders of four sons in Newark, New Jersey.

221 pp.; 1994

35. *Philadelphia Fire*   **John Edgar Wideman**

Novel inspired by the 1985 bombing (ordered by the black mayor) of a Philadelphia row house occupied by black people in a cult called Move. Also *Brothers and Keepers* and his exceptional short stories.

208 pp.; 1990

36. *Dessa Rose*   Sherley Anne Williams

In this novel Williams challenges the accuracy of the black female experience as portrayed in William Styron's *Confessions of Nat Turner*. Frances Doherty suggests that you read Willa Cather's *Sapphira and the Slave Girl* at the same time.

236 pp.; 1986

37. *Native Son*   Richard Wright

A masterpiece that reflects the poverty and hopelessness of life in the inner city, and what it means for some blacks in America.

624 pp.; 1940

An Asian Ethos

This is a diverse list, including books by Asian Americans, books by Asians that have been translated into English, and work by non-Asians about the Far and Near East.

1. *The Doctor's Wife*   Sawako Ariyoshi
This novel takes place in the late eighteenth century and is a strangely moving story of both a mother-in-law/daughter-in-law conflict and the first operation for breast cancer by the family's favorite son, Hanaoka Seishu. Translated from Japanese.

174 pp.; 1978

2. *The Secrets of Mariko: A*   Elisabeth Bumiller
Year in the Life of a Japanese Woman and Her Family
I found this account by a reporter at the *New York Times* to be truly fascinating. And I feel very sad for Mariko. Boy, is she stuck!

338 pp.; 1995

3. *Monkey Bridge*   Lan Cao
A haunting, bittersweet account of a Vietnamese girl's experiences as an emigrant to the United States. It reaches beyond the Vietnam War to exile.

272 pp.; 1997

4. *The Rape of Nanking: The*   Iris Chang
   Forgotten Holocaust of World War II
Surprising nonfiction bestseller about the atrocities committed by Japanese soldiers against Chinese civilians in 1937. It is past time for this outrage to be exposed.

290 pp.; 1998

5. *Wild Swans: Three Daughters of China*   Jung Chang
I've yet to read a story of a woman from any era whose life in China even approached happiness. In this nonfiction book Chang beautifully evokes (1) her grandmother, whose feet were bound and who was given at age fifteen to a warlord general as a concubine; (2) her mother, who became a senior official under Mao; and (3) her own life as a barefoot doctor after she was exiled at the edge of the Himalayas.

524 pp.; 1991

6. *Donald Duk*   Frank Chin
The main character is a twelve-year-old kid, confused about his ethnic heritage, with a name he most certainly doesn't like.

173 pp.; 1991

7. *The Concubine's Children*   Denise Chong
Chong, a Canadian economist and journalist, traces the path of her maternal grandfather, the wife he left in China in 1913, and his "replacement wife," his Canadian concubine and her two children,

both born in Vancouver. This complicated family story is about more than racism and poverty; it is beautiful and haunting.

266 pp.; 1995

8. *Clear Light of Day*   **Anita Desai**

Nominated for the Booker, this novel as well as *Fire on the Mountain*, which won India's National Academy of Letters Award, depict the struggle that middle-class Indian women face in harmonizing societal demands with their own needs.

192 pp.; 1980

9. *Hullabaloo in the Guava Orchard*   **Kiran Desai**

Sampath Chawla, a failed Indian postal worker who reads the private letters of his neighbors, winds up one day in the branches of a guava tree. From there he looks like a wise man.

209 pp.; 1998

10. *The Spirit Catches You*   **Anne Fadiman**
and You Fall Down

Although Fadiman is not Asian, and the book is in part about epilepsy and the medical establishment in California, it gave me rich insights into the Hmong people now living in America. This book won the 1997 National Book Critics Circle Award for nonfiction; it richly deserved it, and in my opinion was the best nonfiction book of 1997. Don't miss it.

288 pp.; 1997

11. *The Ivory Swing*   **Janette Turner Hospital**

Winner of Canada's Seal Award in 1982, this novel, set in India, presents a woman's pivotal moment of struggle and self-recognition: a poignant story of an outsider who temporarily intersects with an alien world.

252 pp.; 1982

12. *When Heaven and*   Le Ly Hyslip
    Earth Changed Places

Award-winning account of the author's youth in wartime Vietnam; followed by *Child of War, Woman of Peace,* which explains how a peasant girl, twice widowed, lives through rape, poverty, and desertion and ends up worth more than a million dollars.

374 pp.; 1989

13. *Typical American*   Gish Jen

Simultaneously charming and powerful look at the Chang family as they come to New York for education and safety, and find moneyhunger and fried chicken franchises. *Mona in the Promised Land* (Scarsdale, New York!) is even funnier.

296 pp.; 1991

14. *The Floating World*   Cynthia Kadohata

In a unique coming-of-age story, a Japanese-American adolescent goes on the road with Obasan, her grandmother, and the rest of the family, and visits her father, a chicken sexer in Arkansas.

196 pp.; 1989

15. *Tripmaster Monkey*   Maxine Hong Kingston

In her first work of fiction, Kingston creates Wittman Ah Sing, a word-drunk Chinese American one year out of Berkeley, who dreams of writing a huge work encompassing novels and folktales, finding his grandmother, and of living when the Beats ruled San Francisco.

340 pp.; 1989

16. *Obasan*   Joy Kogawa

Kogawa, a Canadian, writes here of the internment of the Japanese in Canada during World War II. *Obasan* won both the Books in

Canada First Novel Award, and the Canadian Author's Association Book of the Year Award.

250 pp.; 1982

17. *China Boy*   Gus Lee

Funny coming-of-age novel set in 1950s San Francisco. Offers a very different vision of America by a writer who attended West Point and received a law degree from the University of California.

322 pp.; 1991

18. *The Disappearing Moon Cafe*   Skye Lee

Kae Ying Woo searches for the "bones" or memories of her ancestors just as her great-grandfather, Wong Gwei Chang, walked the tracks of the Canadian Pacific Railway in British Columbia nearly a hundred years before, looking for the actual bones of his dead countrymen.

237 pp.; 1991

19. *The Accidental Asian:*   Eric Liu
   Notes of a Native Speaker

Eric Liu's position is that Asian Americans should "conceive of assimilation as more than a series of losses—and to recognize that what is lost is not necessarily sacred." The son of a successful immigrant from Taiwan, a graduate of Yale, and a former speechwriter for Clinton, he rejects what he calls the espousals of "Chineseness" associated with Amy Tan and others.

206 pp.; 1998

20. *Falling Leaves*   Adeline Yen Mah

Subtitled *The True Story of an Unwanted Chinese Daughter*, this autobiography defines the word "rejection." Heartbreaking.

278 pp.; 1998

21. *Talking to High Monks in the Snow*   Lydia Minatoya

Memoir about growing up as a Japanese American in the Albany of the 1950s, the relocation of the author's parents during World War II, and her subsequent visit to Japan in the 1980s to reconcile the problems of actuality and inheritance.

288 pp.; 1992

22. *Sour Sweet*   Timothy Mo

This novel about a Chinese man, Chen, living in one of London's seedier neighborhoods, was shortlisted for the Booker. Chen must deal with his ambitious wife as well as the Hung family, a traditional Triad society that governs life in his community. Mo is one of Britain's hottest writers.

278 pp.; 1985

23. *The Holder of the World*   Bharati Mukherjee

The lives of two American women intersect across three centuries.

285 pp.; 1993

24. *Bone*   Fae Myenne Ng

Ng takes readers into the hidden heart of San Francisco's Chinatown, to a world of a family's secrets, hidden shame, and the lost bones of a "paper father." The relationship between sisters is most interesting here.

194 pp.; 1993

25. *The Joy Luck Club*   Amy Tan

In 1949 four Chinese women begin meeting in San Francisco to play mah-jongg, invest in stocks, eat dim sum, and "say" stories. If you change the names, this is in many ways the story of all immigrants and the generation that succeeds them. Astounding debut novel that transcends ethnicity, place, and time; followed by *The Kitchen God's Wife*.

288 pp.; 1989

26. *Talking to the Dead*   Sylvia Watanabe

Beautifully linked stories of an ancient world and a modern one, and a journey through the minefields of adolescence, betrayal, madness, racism, and disillusion. Written by a Japanese American from Hawaii. Terrific.

127 pp.; 1992

27. *Homebase*   Shawn Wong

Four generations of one Chinese-American family have their roots in a laborer who arrived in northern California in the nineteenth century to find the elusive paradise Gum Sahn, or Gold Mountain. Also *American Knees*.

98 pp.; 1991

28. *In Desert Run: Poems and Stories*   Mitsuye Yamada

The setting for the title story is the camp in Idaho where Yamada's family was interned during World War II; it describes the emotional landscape of a woman who has never felt completely safe since then. Yamada was born in Japan and grew up in Seattle.

112 pp.; 1988

29. *Seventeen Syllables*   Hisaye Yamamoto

Yamamoto won the 1986 American Book Award for Lifetime Achievement. Several of the stories are concerned with her mother's experience in the relocation camps for Japanese Americans during World War II, and the problems of the Nisei and Issei in the United States.

134 pp.; 1988

Gay Writes

1. *Nightwood*   **Djuna Barnes**

A novel about a lesbian love affair by the well-known writer who was a central figure in the 1920s literary community in Paris.

211 pp.; 1946

2. *Coming Out Under Fire*   **Allan Berube**

Ten years in the writing, this is a vivid portrait of the life and times of gay men and women during World War II. They fought two wars: one for their country, another for their own survival.

287 pp.; 1990

3. *Gentlemen, I Address You Privately*   **Kay Boyle**

Originally published more than sixty years ago and revised in 1990. Munday, an English priest defrocked for playing "Poeme de l'Extase" during collection, exiles himself to Normandy. There he becomes sexually involved with Ayton, a Cockney sailor. Included here for historical value and an early look at homosexuality.

227 pp.; 1933

4. *Rubyfruit Jungle*   Rita Mae Brown
Like her heroine in this novel, Brown was an orphan born out of wedlock. A former lesbian separatist, her latest book, *High Hearts*, is about Southern women who, disguised as men, fought in the Civil War.

217 pp.; 1973

5. *The Weekend*   Peter Cameron
Charming short novel about a young gay man, his current boyfriend, and the family of his dead lover.

241 pp.; 1994

**6. *A Home at the End*   Michael Cunningham
    *of the World***
Jonathan Glover and Bobby Morrow, childhood friends from Cleveland, and Clare, a veteran of New York's erotic wars, try to create a new kind of family in New York City and upstate.

343 pp.; 1990

7. *Odd Girls and Twilight Lovers*   Lillian Faderman
A lesbian feminist and Distinguished Professor of English at California State University in Fresno, Faderman wrote *Scotch Verdict*, about two nineteenth-century Victorian lesbians who were brought to trial. This is the definitive study of lesbian life in America from the turn of the century to today.

373 pp.; 1991

8. *Murder at the Nightwood Bar*   Katherine V. Forrest
Forrest writes the Kate Delafield mysteries and in this one, the LAPD detective, a midforties lesbian, solves a case of child abuse. *Apparition Alley* is the new one.

220 pp.; 1987

9. *What the Dead Remember*   Harlan Greene

An exquisitely told Southern novel about a young boy growing up in Charleston, South Carolina, and his coming-of-age there as an adult.

180 pp.; 1991

10. *The Well of Loneliness*   Radclyffe Hall

Largely autobiographical, this is Hall's attempt to deal with lesbian identity in novel form. She was prosecuted for obscenity and the novel was suppressed.

506 pp.; 1928

11. *A Country of Old Men:*   Joseph Hansen
The Last Dave Brandstetter Mystery

Hansen created the gay detective story with a series of twelve mysteries featuring gay insurance investigator Dave Brandstetter and won the 1992 Lambda Literary Award.

248 pp.; 1991

12. *Dancer from the Dance*   Andrew Holleran

This is the classic disco era "gay novel," which more or less defined the genre.

250 pp.; 1978

13. *Let the Dead Bury the Dead*   Randall Kenan

Kenan creates Horace Cross, a member of the oldest and proudest black family in Tims Creek, North Carolina, four generations of whom are caught in tradition and transformation.

257 pp.; 1993

14. *The Normal Heart*   Larry Kramer

Longtime activist and probably the most vociferous speaker on AIDS and the failure of America to treat it in time, this includes an introduction by the novelist Andrew Holleran and a foreword by the late Joseph Papp.

123 pp.; 1985

15. *Angels in America*   Tony Kushner

Subtitled *A Gay Fantasia on National Themes*, this award-winning, well-received Broadway play follows Part One: *Millennium Approaches*.

90 pp.; 1993

16. *The Lost Language of Cranes* David Leavitt

Following *Family Dancing* and *Equal Affections*, Leavitt writes here of the troubled marriage of Rose and Owen Benjamin. His newest is *The Page Turner*.

319 pp.; 1986

17. *Zani: A New Spelling of My Name* Audre Lorde

A self-described "radical, Black, lesbian, feminist," Lorde died young. This is her autobiography, which she called a "biomythography." She is best known as a poet, as in *Undersong: Chosen Poems*.

256 pp.; 1982

18. *The Object of My Affection* Stephan McCauley

In this one George Mullen is gay, Nina Borowski is straight *and* pregnant; they're best friends and roommates; a kooky, sweet, unusual tale of New York life.

316 pp.; 1987

19. *Tales of the City*   Armistead Maupin

Portrait of the agonies and absurdities of modern urban life in San Francisco in one volume of a series of Maupin tales.

271 pp.; 1978

20. *Now It's Time to Say Goodbye*   **Dale Peck**

Although I wasn't as taken by *Martin and John* as some other critics, this story of a small Kansas town called Galatea, a hive of bigots, powerfully restates the idea of how ancient history is always new. Very violent.

458 pp.; 1998

21. *S/he*   **Minnie Bruce Pratt**

"Poetic, intelligent and personal writing on sex and gender without a trace of academic 'queer theory' genderspeak." So says the writer Martha Coventry.

189 pp.; 1995

22. *Everything You Have Is Mine*   **Sandra Scoppettone**

Growing reputation for Scoppettone's lesbian private eye, Lauren Laurano, who shares her life with longtime lover, a psychotherapist named Kit, in a somewhat grimy New York.

261 pp.; 1991

23. *Conduct Unbecoming*   **Randy Shilts**

Epic-length book based on more than 1,100 interviews, it traces the history of discrimination against gays in the military, dating back to the Revolution.

784 pp.; 1993

24. *Virtually Normal: An*   **Andrew Sullivan**
Argument About Homosexuality

An editor of *The New Republic*, Sullivan is also a member of the minority he discusses and seems fair to both the heterosexual view and that of his own community.

209 pp.; 1995

25. *The City and the Pillar*   Gore Vidal

Vidal, who assiduously rejected modernism and the modern novel, wrote one of the first books to touch on homosexual themes. *Myra Breckinridge* is considered to be a transsexual novel.

249 pp.; 1948

26. *The Front Runner*   Patricia Nell Warren

Considered a gay *Catcher in the Rye*, this is the story of Billy Conners, who realizes at sixteen that he's a little different, a little "weird." Touching.

346 pp.; 1974

27. *Oranges Are Not the Only Fruit*   Jeanette Winterson

Semiautobiographical first novel, a coming-out story of a British girl in the 1960s who is adopted into an evangelical household in the dour industrial midlands.

177 pp.; 1987

Don't-Miss
Nineteenth-Century Novels

1. *Little Women and Good Wives*   **Louisa May Alcott**
Originally published in two parts, the first half introduces Jo, Meg, Amy, and Beth and the overperfect Marmee; in the second part Beth dies and Jo marries. Repeat after me: This is not a children's book; this is not a children's book; this is . . .

643 pp.; 1868–69

2. *Emma*   **Jane Austen**
Austen's dates are 1775–1817, but since she is often considered to be the greatest English novelist, her best novel—with her most successful heroine, Emma Woodhouse—is included here.

378 pp.; 1816

3. *Looking Backward*   **Edward Bellamy**
In late nineteenth-century America, Bellamy laid bare the social inequities and offered the reforms that would lead to a utopian society. Your reading group might combine this with other utopian novels (*Erewhon* by Butler) or dystopias (anti-utopian novels) like Orwell's *1984*.

234 pp.; 1888

4. *Jane Eyre*   Charlotte Brontë

No one is truly educated without reading this one. Mr. Rochester has become an archetypal figure and then, of course, there's the madwoman in the attic.

434 pp.; 1847

5. *Wuthering Heights*   Emily Brontë

Here are the Byronic Heathcliff and the Romantic Cathy in the multilayered and ever-fresh story of two disparate British families in an isolated, harsh, and beautiful environment. The third Brontë sister, Anne, wrote *The Tenant of Wildfell Hall*.

315 pp.; 1847

6. *The Way of All Flesh*   Samuel Butler

A few years beyond 1900, but this novel belongs on this list. Butler describes parent-child relationships during the Victorian era, using several generations of the Pontifex family, who bred maladjusted, introverted children.

423 pp.; 1903

7. *The Leatherstocking Tales*   J. Fenimore Cooper

The Pioneers (1823), *The Last of the Mohicans* (1826), *The Pathfinder* (1840), *The Deerslayer* (1841), and, ending, narratively, with *The Prairie* (1827), the closing chapter in the great American saga of the frontiersman Natty Bumppo and his Indian friend Chingachgook.

402 pp.; 1823–41

8. *Bleak House*   Charles Dickens

My favorite of the Dickens novels. Considering the current view of lawyers in the United States, the lawsuit between Jarndyce and Jarndyce, based on "another well-known suit in Chancery, not yet decided, which was commenced before the close of the last century and in which more than double the amount of seventy thousand pounds has been swallowed up in costs," is contemporary reading at its best.

808 pp.; 1852–53

9. *The Adventures of*   Arthur Conan Doyle
Sherlock Holmes

The pipe, the cape, and Watson—all part of the milieu of the ultimate British detective. He is available to a whole new generation on PBS's *Mystery!*

279 pp.; 1892

10. *The Mill on the Floss*   George Eliot

Probably the most widely read novel by the author of *Middlemarch*, here Maggie Tulliver leads a dull life and cares for her largely worthless and unlikable brother. Great for discussions about responsibility and denial.

595 pp.; 1860

11. *The Damnation of Theron Ware*   Harold Frederic

They made me read this one in graduate school, but I'm glad now. (And no one will ever beat *you* on a trivia test after you read it!) An exposé of the cultural barrenness of the American small town, this is the ancestor of *Main Street* and *Elmer Gantry*.

287 pp.; 1896

12. *Mary Barton*:   Elizabeth Gaskell
A Tale of Manchester Life

British working-class life and a recession in an industrial town. Good picture of the then-nascent trade unions.

487 pp.; 1848

13. *The New Grub Street*   George Gissing

Autobiographical work about the effects of poverty on the free-dom of the writer. Gissing rebelled against Victorian society and had a wretched life, but left us this very fine novel. Many readers suggested *The Odd Woman*.

543 pp.; 1891

14. *Jude the Obscure*   Thomas Hardy

In my opinion, Hardy's best (and last) novel about the short and miserable life of a man thwarted by fate, weakness, and society. Don't miss it.

493 pp.; 1895

15. *The Scarlet Letter*   Nathaniel Hawthorne

Hester Prynne wears the "A" for adultery; her lover, the minister, is ruined by his hidden guilt, and her husband goes nuts—all in seventeenth-century America.

283 pp.; 1850

16. *Les Misérables*   Victor Hugo

When Hugo was banished for twenty years to the Channel Is-land of Guersey for opposing Louis Napoleon's coup of 1851, he wrote his best and most famous novel. All four parts are concerned with Jean Valjean, a man who triumphs over internal and external evils. Get the version abridged by James K. Robinson.

334 pp.; 1862

17. *Daisy Miller*   Henry James

The most popular of James's novels. Here his usual American in-nocents in Europe are represented by the truly blemishless and sympathetic Daisy. If you find James boring, as many readers do, choose this one.

83 pp.; 1878

18. *The Country of the Pointed Firs*   Sarah Orne Jewett
Usually considered a New England regional realist, Jewett's preference for the rural is always obvious. Women are central in her work, and she is definitely worth reading.

306 pp.; 1896

19. *The Egoist*   George Meredith
Patterne is jilted by Durham; he falls in love with Middleton. She falls in love with Whitford; Laetitia Dale, nobody's favorite, is prevailed upon to marry the "incorrigible egoist." Trust me. You'll love it.

393 pp.; 1879

20. *McTeague: A Story of San Francisco*   Frank Norris
Norris died at thirty-two, following an operation, but left this story of a sadomasochistic marriage, featuring, of all people, a dentist as hero. (He ends up, by the way—for those of us who have had root canal—chained to a corpse in the middle of Death Valley.)

324 pp.; 1881

21. *The Story of an African Farm*   Olive Shreiner
Her only nonposthumous novel, Shreiner yearns for a life beyond that offered by South African colonialism, and rejects Victorian materialism and spiritual dryness. Shreiner, an antiracist and anti-imperialist writer who died in 1920, is a central figure in modern white South African literature.

375 pp.; 1883

22. *Dr. Jekyll and Mr. Hyde*   R. L. Stevenson
Classic romantic adventure based on the dual personalities of a single man representing beauty and the beast.

62 pp.; 1886

23. *Uncle Tom's Cabin*   **Harriet Beecher Stowe**

Subtitled *Life Among the Lowly*, this novel, in spite of its impossibly good and/or evil characters, greatly raised the public consciousness about slavery. And it is a great choice for book clubs. If you get to Hartford, Connecticut, visit her house; she lived next door to Mark Twain.

116 pp.; 1852

24. *Vanity Fair*   **W. M. Thackeray**

The prototype of all climbers, Becky Sharp is a witty, clever, accomplished young woman who is determined to break into fashionable society by any means possible. You could read this one in the Hamptons (while eating a three-dollar blueberry muffin), for example!

754 pp.; 1847

25. *Phineas Finn*   **Anthony Trollope**

An Irish political boss loses his beloved and rejects the hand and fortune of a rich widow. Good way to understand nineteenth-century Irish politics. *Barchester Towers* is the novel with the odious chaplain Mr. Slope. *He Knew He Was Right* (1869) is the usual academic favorite.

367 pp.; 1869

26. *Huckleberry Finn*   **Mark Twain**

Sequel to the *Adventures of Tom Sawyer*, this is a more somber and polished novel. The Mississippi River as time and possibility, friendship between a man and a boy, and lighting out for the territory—all themes in American literature—were born here.

435 pp.; 1884

Early
Twentieth-Century Writing

1. *Winesburg, Ohio*   **Sherwood Anderson**

Still holds up as an examination of the many grotesques in small-town America, always struggling as individuals against the norms of society.

303 pp.; 1919

2. *Death of the Heart*   **Elizabeth Bowen**

The vulnerability of the orphaned Portia in this novel recalls Bowen's own insecure childhood, "motherless since [she] was thirteen," "shuttling between two countries: Ireland and England," an outsider everywhere.

418 pp.; 1938

3. *The Professor's House*   **Willa Cather**

The greatest American author to have written about the prairies, populated at the end of the nineteenth and early twentieth century by Norwegians, Swedes, Bohemians, and Germans. Here a scholarly professor in a Midwestern university is approaching old age; the subplot concerns the Cliff Dwellers in the Southwest. Also *A Lost Lady*, *My Mortal Enemy*, and *O Pioneers!* I would recommend this one for book clubs.

283 pp.; 1925

4. *Men and Wives*   Ivy Compton-Burnett
A Victorian family is dominated by the archetypal maternal power figure, Harriet Haslam.

288 pp.; 1931

5. *Lord Jim*   Joseph Conrad
One of Conrad's major themes is the fragility of the bonds that hold an individual to society. In this adventure story Jim is involved in the disgraceful affair of the Patna and its pilgrim passengers.

417 pp.; 1900

6. *The Enormous Room*   e. e. cummings
Autobiographical novel set in the filthy jail where he was imprisoned, and where the captors are worse than their prisoners.

271 pp.; 1922

7. *As I Lay Dying*   William Faulkner
Don't be afraid of the multivoiced stream-of-consciousness technique as the Burden family carries Addie's coffin to her hometown for burial. By any standards, this short novel is a not-to-be-missed masterpiece.

250 pp.; 1930

8. *This Side of Paradise*   F. Scott Fitzgerald
This first novel established Fitzgerald at age twenty-three as the golden boy of the Jazz Age. Amory Blaine, a self-absorbed Princeton undergrad, becomes part of the Lost Generation, "grown up to find all Gods dead, all wars fought, all faith in man shaken."

282 pp.; 1920

9. *Howards End*   E. M. Forster
One of the great laserlike looks at personal and social relationships among the upper classes in Britain. If you haven't written your will yet, read this first.

393 pp.; 1919

10. *In This Our Life*   Ellen Glasgow
In this Pulitzer Prize–winning book Glasgow advocates some experimentation with sexual relationships, far removed from the mores of her old colonial Virginia family.

467 pp.; 1941

11. *Brave New World*   Aldous Huxley
Prophetic look at the problems of genetic engineering. You might combine this with the reading of a more recent dystopian (anti-utopian) novel like *The Giver*, by Lois Lowry.

288 pp.; 1958

12. *A Portrait of the*   James Joyce
Artist as a Young Man
These connected stories of a boy's childhood in Catholic Dublin form a central work in modern literature. Also *Dubliners*.

299 pp.; 1916

13. *The Rainbow* and *Women in Love*   D. H. Lawrence
These are Lawrence's best novels, in spite of the fact that an entire generation of readers hid *Lady Chatterley's Lover* under their socks. (Or was it the mattress?) A fine look at young married life.

The Rainbow: 467 pp.; 1915
Women in Love: 464 pp.; 1920

14. *Babbit*   Sinclair Lewis

The title has entered the language to represent the small-town businessman who is consumed by his own materialism and social climbing.

898 pp.; 1923

15. *Of Human Bondage*   F. Somerset Maugham

A great storyteller usually derided by literary critics, this is his most important and autobiographical novel—about a handicapped boy and his life as an artist.

648 pp.; 1915

16. *Flowering Judas and*   Katherine Anne Porter
Other Stories

Many of Porter's stories (all better than *Ship of Fools*, which is awful) focus on the moment of epiphany when women realize that they have often been deluded about their lives. "The Jilting of Granny Weatherall" is a particular favorite.

285 pp.; 1935

17. *The Catherine Wheel*   Jean Stafford

The struggle in Stafford's work is always between spiritual and/or sexual death versus the demands of culture and society.

281 pp.; 1925

18. *The Grapes of Wrath*   John Steinbeck

A Pulitzer Prize winner, this novel expresses best Steinbeck's concern for the poverty and hopelessness of those driven from their homes by the Depression—like the Joads who migrate from Oklahoma to California—and his sympathy for the agricultural workers of the then-decidedly non–Golden State.

619 pp.; 1939

19. *The Judge*   Rebecca West

Born Cecily Isabel Fairfield in Ireland, West took the name of Ibsen's heroine in *Rosmershalm*. This novel explores two generations of the women's suffrage movement.

430 pp.; 1922

20. *The Custom of the Country*   Edith Wharton

The current favorite of Wharton scholars, this pits an American fortune hunter, the insatiably ambitious and beautiful Undine Spragg from Apex, Kansas, against the European aristocracy. Unusual in that Wharton uses a woman to represent materialism and greed.

370 pp.; 1913

21. *Mrs. Dalloway*   Virginia Woolf

While Clarissa Dalloway plans her dinner party, with all the accoutrements of her social class and status, Septimus Smith, emotionally damaged by World War I, draws closer to suicide. One of modernism's greatest novels and one of my all-time favorites.

296 pp.; 1925

22. *Native Son*   Richard Wright

Bigger Thomas, a black chauffeur, accidentally kills a white girl and then murders his black girlfriend. His relationship with his white lawyer will resonate for today's reader.

359 pp.; 1940

Other Lands, Other Voices

1. *Year of the Elephant*   **Leila Abouzeid (Morocco)**
This is the counterpoint to Paul Bowles's *The Sheltering Sky*. She writes from the inside of a society that strictly limits women, and makes Morocco seem a lot less trendy and inviting.

129 pp.; 1989

2. *Anthills of the Savannah*   **Chinua Achebe (Nigeria)**
By the author of *Things Fall Apart*, this view of modern Africa uses the conflict between the city and tribal villages, drought, and third-world politics as background.

216 pp.; 1988

3. *The Information*   **Martin Amis (Great Britain)**
Envy of an unsuccessful novelist for the one who makes it—in this case, his best friend. This is the London literary scene at its worst.

374 pp.; 1995

4. *Underground River*   Ines Arredondo (Mexico)
and Other Stories

Set in northwestern Mexico at the beginning of this century, these stories are largely about erotic perversity. Arredondo published only three small volumes of stories during her lifetime but she is still one of modern Mexico's most highly regarded writers.

128 pp.; 1996

5. *Flaubert's Parrot*   Julian Barnes (Great Britain)

A peculiar, quirky writer with a big following, this was followed by *The Porcupine* and *A History of the World in 10½ Chapters*. In *Talking It Over* Barnes deals with the familiar question: What's real in fiction and who's in charge?

190 pp.; 1985

6. *The Lost Honor of*   Heinrich Böll (Germany)
Katharina Blum

Böll won the Nobel Prize for Literature in 1972 and is well known for his staunch commitment to artistic freedom. This novel is a mystery story turned on its head since the killer—and you probably won't blame her—is revealed at the outset.

140 pp.; 1975

7. *Possession*   A. S. Byatt (Great Britain)

In this modern Victorian novel two academics research the lives of two poets; the story climaxes on a storm-tossed night in the churchyard where one of the poets is buried. This won England's Booker Prize.

555 pp.; 1990

8. *The Officers Camp*   Giampiero Carocci (Italy)

Considered by many to be a small masterpiece, this memoir of two years in a German concentration camp begins in 1943, after the fall of Mussolini, when Carocci and another officer were captured by the Germans.

218 pp.; 1997

9. *Mazurka for*   Camilo José Cela (Spain)
Two Dead Men

A 1989 Nobel Prize–winning story of the Spanish Civil War, the death of "Lionheart" Gamuzo, and how he is avenged by his brother Tanis. For both events the blind accordion player Gaudencio plays the same mazurka.

272 pp.; 1992

10. *Nervous Conditions* Tsitsi Dangarembga
(Zimbabwe)

Debut novel of a girl's coming-of-age and a narrative of the devastating human loss involved in the colonization of one culture by another.

204 pp.; 1989

11. *Murther and Walking Spirits* Robertson Davies
(Canada)

A murdered writer's ghost relives his family's history on a movie screen. The critic who killed him is watching too.

357 pp.; 1991

12. *The Radiant Way*   Margaret Drabble
(Great Britain)

This tenth novel, Drabble's best, is the story of three Englishwomen. We follow them for the next five years, as the seventies give way to the eighties and the world changes around them.

408 pp.; 1987

13. *The House on Moon Lake* Francesca Duranti (Italy)

This third Duranti book won the Bagutta, Martina Franca, and City of Milan prizes. This is the story of Garrone, who translates an obscure novel, and how that act rewards and menaces his own existence. It was followed by *Happy Ending* and *Personal Effects*, a favorite of mine.

181 pp.; 1986

14. *The Rape of Shavi*   Buchi Emecheta (Nigeria)

Set partly in an imaginary country by the edge of the African Sahara and partly in England, this is a portrait of people confronted for the first time with the ways of the civilized world.

178 pp.; 1983

15. *Deep River*   Shusaku Endo (Japan)

Thirty years after *Silence,* Endo combines Christian faith with Buddhist acceptance in this novel about a group of mostly soulless Japanese tourists who converge on the river Ganges in India. Endo has won all of his country's major literary prizes and his work is published in twenty-five countries.

224 pp.; 1995

16. *Secrets*   Nuruddin Farah (Somalia)

I'd definitely recommend this novel about civil war to adventurous book clubs. Since its publication, Farah is persona non grata in his native land and lives in Nigeria. It won the Neustadt International Prize for literature. There's plenty of sex in this novel.

298 pp.; 1998

17. *Ruin*   Beppe Fenoglio (Italy)

A seminal work of Italian neorealism by someone widely considered to be one of the most influential Italian writers of the twentieth century. Fenoglio lived from 1922 to 1963.

94 pp.; 1992

18. *The Bookshop*   Penelope Fitzgerald (Great Britain)

This slim novel examines the smallness and pinched "quality" of a small town in England where Florence Green opens a bookshop that is rejected by her seaside community. Many critics consider *The Blue Flower* to be a masterpiece.

123 pp.; 1997

19. *A State of Siege*   Janet Frame (New Zealand)

Malfred Signal returns to an idyllic island after her mother dies. Terror reigns on the first night when an intruder pounds on the door and the still-unconnected telephone does not work. As in all of her work, the place under siege is really the inner landscape of the human heart.

246 pp.; 1966

20. *A Wife for My Son*   Ali Ghalem (Algeria)

Difficult to believe that this Algerian version of *A Doll's House* was also written by a man, especially in this part of the world, but the oppression of this young woman in and by Muslim society rings true. Like Ibsen's Nora, when she has enough of the fetters that tie her to the traditional woman's role, she leaves. I wholeheartedly recommend it.

211 pp.; 1984

21. *Family Sayings*   Natalia Ginzburg (Italy)

Novel that relies on Ginzburg's memory and her evocation of the past, particularly of her youth in Turin, where she was raised as an atheist. (Her mother was Catholic, her father Jewish.) She married Leone Ginzburg, who died in prison in 1944 after imprisonment by the fascists.

181 pp.; 1967

22. *Requiem*   Shizuko Go (Japan)

Often called the Japanese version of *The Diary of a Young Girl* (Anne Frank), this novel tells the story of a girl whose parents, brother, and friends are killed in World War II. War, as always, remains futile.

122 pp.; 1992

23. *My Son's Story*   Nadine Gordimer (South Africa)

A Nobel Prize—winning author writes here of a "colored" anti-apartheid activist and the white woman he loves.

277 pp.; 1990

24. *The Call of the Toad*   Günter Grass (Germany)

Considered by many to be Germany's greatest living writer, the author of *The Tin Drum* writes here about middle-aged love, German and Polish schemes, and capitalism run amok.

248 pp.; 1992

25. *The Grisly Wife*   Rodney Hall (Australia)

Part of a trilogy, which includes *The Second Bridegroom* and *Captivity Captive.* This one focuses on women, especially Catherine Byrne, a nineteenth-century missionary who moves from England to Australia with "her nut-case prophet husband and his band of 8 female true believers, called by him the Household of Hidden Stars" (*New York Times*).

262 pp.; 1993

26. *The Wall* **Marlen Haushofer (Austria)**

This novelist lived only from 1920 to 1970. Her dystopian novel, a philosophical parable of human isolation, is recognized now for its important place in the tradition of feminist fiction.

244 pp.; 1962

27. *Too Loud a Solitude* **Bohumil Hrabil (Czechoslovakia)**

For thirty-five years Hant'a rescues books from the jaws of the hydraulic press before he compacts the trash. This baroque tale celebrates the indestructibility of the spoken word. Hrabal wrote *Closely Watched Trains* and *I Served the King of England*.

98 pp.; 1990

28. *Moving House: Stories* **Pawel Huelle (Poland)**

Huelle comes from the Baltic seaport of Gdansk, a city inhabited by Germans, Jews, and others before World War II. Its population was homogeneous when it became the birthplace of the Solidarity movement. That city is really his subject.

248 pp.; 1995

29. *My Life as a Dog* **Reidar Jonsson (Sweden)**

The first novel about a parentless boy in a trilogy by this Swedish writer, and followed by *My Father, His Son*. In the second novel Jonsson follows Ingemar Johansson into adulthood, the merchant marines, and his troubled marriage.

201 pp.; 1990

30. *The Metamorphosis* **Franz Kafka (Czechoslovakia)**

Even if you read this one in college, a great discussion can evolve from why Gregor Samsa awakens one morning to find that he is now a giant insect—instead of a man.

65 pp.; 1946

31. *The Unbearable*   **Milan Kundera**
    Lightness of Being   **(Czechoslovakia)**

Tomas, a surgeon; Tereza, a dependable woman; Sabina, a free-spirited artist; and her good-hearted lover Franz—all exist in a world shaped by irrevocable choices, fortuitous events, and plenty of sex. As the cynics say, be careful what you ask for. Also *The Book of Laughter and Forgetting*.

314 pp.; 1984

32. *Palace of Desire:*   **Naguib Mahfouz (Egypt)**
    The Cairo Trilogy II

A Nobel Prize–winning author writes about the emergence of Egypt from colonization.

422 pp.; 1991

33. *Beginning with My Streets*   **Czeslaw Milosz**
                                        (Poland)

Essays and recollections about time, religion, sin, friendship, etc. from the 1980 Nobel laureate in literature.

288 pp.; 1992

34. *The Trench*   **Abdalrahman Munif (Lebanon)**

The second volume of the *Cities of Salt* trilogy, this novel chronicles the life of a fictional Arab town as it is transformed by the discovery of oil.

554 pp.; 1991

35. *Hardboiled Wonderland*   **Haruki Murakami**
    and the End of the World   **(Japan)**

Murakami's hero is Ben Johnson, the cowboy turned character actor who "played in all those great John Ford movies." As *Newsweek* said, "Pop culture references are like Popeye's spinach in

Murakami's fiction. It's hard to believe this was written by a Japanese and easy to believe that he lives in the USA now."

400 pp.; 1991

36. *The Man Without Qualities* Robert Musil (Austria)

Unfinished long novel recommended by many patient readers who like Proust and Joyce. A new version in two volumes, with a fine translation, was published in 1995.

2 vols.; 1,774 pp.; 1953

37. *A Bend in the River*   V. S. Naipul (Indian, born in Trinidad)

This is a chillingly accurate portrait of Africa in decay. Also *The Enigma of Arrival*.

354 pp.; 1979

38. *To Know a Woman*   Amos Oz (Israel)

A retired Israeli secret service officer struggles to understand his mother, mother-in-law, daughter, and his dead wife. Great for book clubs. And follow up with *Don't Call It Night*.

262 pp.; 1991

39. *The White Castle*   Orhan Pamuk (Turkey)

This is the first of his four novels to be translated into English. A Venetian scholar in the final days of the Ottoman Empire is brought to slavery in Constantinople, where he teaches a man who is his physical double.

161 pp.; 1991

40. *Caetana's Sweet Song*   Nelida Piñon (Brazil)

The second of her eight novels to appear in English, this picaresque novel contains a multitude of self-deluded questers. The novel is set in 1970, during Brazil's military dictatorship.

402 pp.; 1992

41. *A Dance to the Music*   **Anthony Powell**
of Time   **(Great Britain)**

Reissued in four volumes of three books each (although originally published as twelve separate novels), these chronicle English society between the wars, beginning with the narrator's life at Eton in 1921. I've gotten over my snit about having to slug through a lot of Powell (pronounced Pole) in graduate school and in retrospect I'd hardly recommend *A Question of Upbringing* and *Casanova's Chinese Restaurant*. You will be swallowed up in Nicholas Jenkins's life. See *A Buyer's Market, The Acceptance World, At Lady Molloy's, The Kindly Ones, The Valley of Bones, The Soldier's Art, The Military Philosophers, Books Do Furnish a Room, Temporary Kings,* and *Hearing Secret Harmonies.*

239 pp., 1962; 229 pp., 1964;
274 pp., 1971; 214 pp., 1976

42. *Eugene Onegin*   **Alexander Pushkin (Russia)**

As Susan Martin says, this book is "painfully accurate for anyone who has ever been in love."

238 pp.; 1979

43. *Excellent Women*   **Barbara Pym (Great Britain)**

Many readers reminded me that I had inadvertently left out Barbara Pym, a writer whose prose is spare and whose sense of humor is unique, in the first edition of *What to Read*.

256 pp.; 1952

44. *Blindness*   **José Saramago (Portugal)**

Winner of the 1998 Nobel Prize in Literature, this Portuguese writer, not well known in North America, wrote *Baltasar and Blimunda* and *The Gospel According to Jesus Christ,* among others

294 pp.; 1998

45. *Sicilian Uncles*   Leonardo Sciascia (Italy)
Four novellas, all ironic political thrillers, by one of Italy's best
writers.

205 pp.; 1986

46. *Cracking India*   Bapsi Sidwa (Pakistan)
An eight-year-old girl is caught up in the partition of India in
1947. This novel is at once heartbreaking and funny.

289 pp.; 1991

47. *Ake: The Years of*   Wole Soyinka (Nigeria)
   Childhood
Although best known as a Nobel Prize–winning playwright,
Soyinka has written in many genres, including fiction.

230 pp.; 1981

48. *The Eye of the Storm*   Patrick White (Australia)
White won the Nobel Prize shortly after publication of this
novel. It focuses on the last weeks of an elderly woman who reminisces about her life and the tranquillity she experienced fifteen
years earlier when she was temporarily stranded on an island.

608 pp.; 1973

49. *Mr. Mani*   A. B. Yehoshua (Israel)
Chronicles six generations in the Mani family from the mid-
nineteenth century to the mid-1980s, beginning in the present and
moving, as memory moves, back to the past.

369 pp.; 1992

50. *Dear Departed*   Marguerite Yourcenar
                                        (born in Belgium)

This is the first volume of her ancestral trilogy, which omits any discussion of Yourcenar's homosexuality. However, if you think your family is some story, read this! Highly recommended.

346 pp.; 1991

It's a Mystery to Me

MYSTERIES BY WOMEN

1. *Alias Grace*   **Margaret Atwood**

Draws on an actual nineteenth-century case in which an Irish immigrant housemaid, Grace Marks, was convicted of murdering her Toronto employer and his mistress. Marks spends the next thirty years in an assortment of jails and asylums. Atwood recounts the story in fictional form and adds an interesting glimpse into the then rudimentary science of psychology.

468 pp.; 1996

2. *A Bleeding of Innocents*   **Jo Bannister**

Three outsiders, Inspector Liz Graham, Detective Chief Inspector Frank Shapiro, and Irish Detective Sergeant Cal Donovan, appear together in the British CID. Bannister writes strong characters.

218 pp.; 1993

3. *Snapshot*   **Linda Barnes**

Six-foot-one-inch-tall red-haired Boston P.I. Carlotta Carlyle receives a snapshot of a newborn baby in the mail, and in the next several weeks more photographs of the same child arrive. Barnes's fifth work is about obsession, hypocrisy, and corruption. *Steel Guitar* and *The Snake Tattoo* are good too.

325 pp.; 1993

4. *Lady Audley's Secret*   Mary Elizabeth Braddon
This Victorian mystery, much admired by William Thackeray, went through eight editions in the first year of publication and sold approximately one million copies.

286 pp.; originally 1887

5. *Death on the Nile*   Agatha Christie
When Christie died in 1976 at the age of eighty-five, she had written sixty-six mystery novels, thirteen short-story collections, a book of poems, a volume of Christmas verse and stories, and her autobiography. In this one, the inestimable Hercule Poirot is relaxing on a luxury liner when the sound of a shot disturbs the peace. Her female sleuth, Miss Jane Marple, appeared first in *Sleeping Murder* and finally in *The Murder at the Vicarage*. *The Murder of Roger Ackroyd* traces Hercule Poirot on his most baffling case.

340 pp.; 1938

6. *I'll Be Seeing You*   Mary Higgins Clark
Clark writes traditional mysteries, this one about a mugging and a Jane Doe victim who looks just like the newspaper reporter investigating the case.

317 pp.; 1993

7. *Bloodlines*   Susan Conant
This mystery is about the disreputable characters who sometimes supply pet shops. Diane Sweet, owner of Puppy Luv, is visited by Conant's hero, dog writer Holly Winter. Hours later Diane is dead and the rescue malamute, Missy, has disappeared. All of her light-

hearted mysteries, like *Gone to the Dogs*, *A New Leash on Death*, *Dead and Doggone,* are for animal lovers of all kinds.

271 pp.; 1992

8. *All That Remains*   Patricia D. Cornwell

Five young couples suffer strange deaths in Virginia. Cornwell's cool detective, Dr. Kay Scarpetta, chief medical examiner (and a forensic pathologist) for the state, investigates. This one was followed by *Cruel and Unusual*. Her first novel, *Postmortem*, won the Edgar, Creasey, Anthony, and Macavity Awards in the same year. Try *Unnatural Exposures* too. A new one is *Point of Origin*.

373 pp.; 1992

9. *Eulogy for a Brown Angel*   Lucha Corpi

Corpi, a poet, gives her sleuth occasional clairvoyant moments that provide hints of subtle menace. Good ear for Latino rhythms.

189 pp.; 1992

10. *Death in a Tenured Position*   Amanda Cross

As in all the Cross mysteries, the literary detective, Kate Fansler, redoubtable academic and amateur sleuth, solves the case. Read *A Trap for Fools* too. In her "other" life, Cross is Carolyn Heilbrun, a literary scholar.

285 pp.; 1981

11. *Not That Kind of Place*   Frances Fyfield

Author of *A Question of Guilt*, Fyfield is in the British tradition of Sayers, Christie, Ruth Rendell, and P. D. James. In this one, a naked, hastily buried body of a woman is found buried in the woods near the village of Branston. In *Without Consent*, the killer specializes in psychic havoc. Fyfield is a practicing solicitor in London, specializing in criminal law.

214 pp.; 1990

12. *Well-Schooled in Murder*   Elizabeth George

This is George's third novel featuring Detective Inspector Thomas Lynley of New Scotland Yard. In this one, a boy is missing from a private school and is found murdered; something evil is going on where the elite are educated. In *Missing Joseph,* there is a tiny British village and a murdered vicar but no hint of Agatha Christie.

356 pp.; 1990

13. *Backlash*   Paula Gosling

Who could be killing the cops in Grantham? Could it be other cops? Lieutenant Jack Stryker tries to find out. *Monkey Puzzles* won the British Crime Writers Association Gold Dagger Award.

191 pp.; 1989

14. *"G" Is for Gumshoe*   Sue Grafton

"A" Is for Alibi, *"D" Is for Deadbeat*, *"F" Is for Fugitive*—you get the idea—all starring Kinsey Millhone, a tough cookie in Santa Theresa, California, who is also resourceful and sensitive. She keeps her .32 handgun wrapped in an old sock. A recent issue, *"N" Is for Noose,* will rope you in.

261 pp.; 1990

15. *Written in Blood*   Caroline Graham

Chief Inspector Barnaby investigates the death of Gerald Hadleigh just hours after the members of Midsomer Worthy's Writers' Circle retire for the night. Her first Inspector Barnaby novel, *The Killings at Badger's Drift,* was selected by the Crime Writers Association as one of the top one hundred crime novels of all time.

387 pp.; 1995

16. *Love nor Money*   **Linda Grant**
Catherine Sayler is Grant's sleuth. Here she unravels a murder and a network of child sexual abuse. Also *Blind Trust*, about computer scams.

277 pp.; 1991

17. *The Horse You Came In On*   **Martha Grimes**
Superintendent Richard Jury of Scotland Yard and his aristocratic sidekick Melrose Plant are in Baltimore, dealing with the unrelated(?) murders of an Edgar Allan Poe scholar, a museum curator, and a derelict. *The Old Contemptibles* is fine too.

332 pp.; 1993

18. *Strangled Prose*   **Joan Hess**
The widow Claire Malloy supports herself and her teenaged daughter by running a small bookstore in a college town. When she reluctantly hosts a book-signing party, the author is strangled shortly afterward. Also *Malice in Maggody* and *A Really Cute Corpse*.

183 pp.; 1986

19. *The Talented Mr. Ripley*   **Patricia Highsmith**
Ripley is a creepy, endearing antihero; Highsmith is a poetic writer of mysteries. Some would make the case that she is the absolute best.

295 pp.; 1992

20. *A Taste for Death*   **P. D. James**
Adam Dalgliesh, James's best sleuth, is back in this one just in time to investigate the deaths of Sir Paul Berowne, rich and cultivated, and of an alcoholic tramp, both found dead in the vestry of a London church. Her other famous detective is Cordelia Grey, particularly good in *An Unsuitable Job for a Woman*. Read *Devices and*

Desires, *Children of Men*, and *Original Sin*—especially if you are interested in the publishing world.

459 pp.; 1986

21. *Lying in Wait*   J. A. Jance

Seattle is the setting for mysteries featuring homicide cop J. P. Beaumont. He's on the trail of a child killer in *Until Proven Guilty*. Here his teenage girlfriend is, thirty years later, the widow of a homicide victim.

386 pp.; 1994

22. *Grievous Sin*   Faye Kellerman

Which parent hasn't worried about this: Who would steal a newborn baby from her mother? Blackmail, a dumb nurse, and a weight lifter appear in this chilling tale. Read *Days of Atonement* and *Serpent's Tooth* too.

368 pp.; 1993

23. *Angel of Death*   Rochelle Majer Krich

As the *Los Angeles Times* said, what's "a nice Jewish woman— mother [6 children], wife, educator, daughter of Holocaust survivors—doing writing mystery novels about serial killers, rapists, abusers, psychopaths, racists and the problem of sexual harassment in the Los Angeles Police Department?" *Where's Mommy Now?* won the Anthony Award for best paperback mystery.

356 pp.; 1994

24. *Murder at the Gardner*   Jane Langton

Traditional American mystery writer who is charming and witty. Her Homer Kelly mysteries are set in Nantucket, one of America's most beautiful places, and around Boston. Also *Emily D. Is Dead*. Myths, folktales, and nursery stories play their parts in *The Face on the Wall*.

353 pp.; 1988

25. *Charm City*   Laura Lippman

A feature writer for the *Baltimore Sun*, Lippman won the Edgar for Best Paperback Original for this one. Read *Baltimore Blues* too. She knows her crab cakes.

304 pp.; 1997

26. *The Hangman's Beautiful*   Sharyn McCrumb
Daughter

McCrumb won the Edgar for *Bimbos of the Death Sun*; the sequel was *Zombies of the Gene Pool*, about murder at a sci-fi convention. This one is set in Appalachia, where horrible murders take place at the Underhill farm. *She Walks These Hills* is fine.

306 pp.; 1992

27. *Bootlegger's Daughter*   Margaret Maron

This is the first appearance of lawyer Deborah Knott of North Carolina. Maron made history by winning the Edgar, Agatha, Macavity, and the Anthony Awards for best novel, and followed this with *Killer Market*. She also writes about Sigrid Harold of New York in *Fugitive Colors* and *Corpus Christmas*.

261 pp.; 1992

28. *Wolf in the Shadows*   Marcia Muller

Sharon McCone, Muller's investigator, takes an unauthorized leave of absence from All Souls, the do-good legal collective in San Francisco where she has worked since 1977, and is involved instead with illegal immigrants in San Diego's underground community. *Trophies and Dead Things* is good too. Considered by Grafton to be the "founding mother" of contemporary female private eyes.

384 pp.; 1993

29. *Blanche on the Lam*   Barbara Neely

The detective here, Blanche White (notice the name), is a middle-aged, working-class African American.

180 pp.; 1992

30. *Guardian Angel*   Sara Paretsky

V. I. (Victoria Iphigenia) Warshawski, Paretsky's detective, daughter of a Jewish-Italian mother, runs into her smug ex-husband at a charity concert, her neighbor Hattie Frazell slips in the tub, and V.I. finds herself in the middle of the biggest political scandal to hit Chicago in years. Paretsky has a fan named Bill Clinton. *Indemnity Only*, *Deadlock*, and others.

469 pp.; 1992

31. *The Face of a Stranger*   Anne Perry

Perry's province is the Victorian era. In this novel William Monk, a London police detective who has forgotten everything because of an accident, must deal with the brutal murder of Major the Honorable Joscelin Grey, Crimean war hero and popular man about town. Rape and prostitution are the subjects in *The Silent Cry*.

328 pp.; 1990

32. *The Holy Thief*   Ellis Peters

Brother Cadfael, the extraordinary twelfth-century herbalist-detective of the medieval Abbey of St. Peter and St. Paul returns in a tale of unholy murder. *The Heaven Tree Trilogy* contains *The Heaven Tree*, *The Green Branch,* and *The Scarlet Seed* (listed under Edith Pargeter).

246 pp.; 1992

33. *A Dark-Adapted Eye*   Ruth Rendell

An Edgar Award winner, this is a psychological mystery of childhood and family. This Brit is on everybody's best mystery writer list. In *Simisola,* C. I. Wexford has to confront his own racism. Also *The Tree of Hands* and *Road Rage.*

264 pp.; 1986

34. *Gaudy Night*   Dorothy Sayers

A classic mystery without a murder, this love story has a satisfying ending. Her mysteries of the 1920s also include Lord Peter Wimsey.

469 pp.; 1936

35. *She Walks in Beauty*   Sarah Shankman

Samantha Adams, amateur detective and reporter from Atlanta, has just turned forty and is in no mood to cover the Miss America Pageant. She suspects foul play and a treacherous runway and she's right about both. Sam appears also in *First Kill All the Lawyers*, *Then Hang All the Liars,* and *Now Let's Talk of Graves.*

289 pp.; 1991

36. *North of Montana*   April Smith

Adventures of a female FBI agent in Los Angeles, Ana Grey, written in rat-a-tat style by a TV writer and producer nominated twice for Emmys for her work on *Cagney & Lacey.* Although this is a first novel, Ballantine Books reportedly paid $550,000 for the paperback rights. Need I add that the movie is forthcoming?

295 pp.; 1995

37. *The Axman's Jazz*   Julie Smith

Based on a real-life serial killer in 1919 New Orleans. This time around, Skip Langdon, Smith's detective, gets involved with a multitude of self-help groups and twelve-step programs. *New Orleans Mourning* won the Edgar and is highly recommended. In *Jazz Funeral* the producer of the New Orleans Jazz and Heritage Festival is stabbed to death in his kitchen. In *New Orleans Beat* it's life on the

TOWN—a bulletin board community of some one thousand computer nuts, including a murder victim and his killer.

341 pp.; 1991

38. *The Franchise Affair*   Josephine Tey

This novel is based on the real disappearance of a young girl and on the difference between what we assume is guilt and who we assume is innocent. *The Daughter of Time* is the all-time favorite book of many readers.

272 pp.; 1948

39. *The Lies That Bind*   Judith Van Gieson

Van Gieson's protagonist is Neil Hamel, a tough, funny Albuquerque lawyer. Here she gets mixed up with, among other things, real estate boondoggles, Santa Fe's polo set, psychic entrepreneurs, and the homeless.

256 pp.; 1993

40. *Anna's Book*   Barbara Vine (Ruth Rendell)

By an Edgar-winning author, this wonderful novel concerns the diary entries of Anna, a turn-of-the-century Danish immigrant and her granddaughter. Don't miss *A Fatal Inversion, King Solomon's Carpet, The Chimney Sweeper's Boy,* and *No Night Is Too Long*—where the murderer thinks he is being pursued by his victim's ghost!

394 pp.; 1993

41. *The Red Scream*   Mary Willis Walker

Winner of the 1994 Edgar Award for Best Mystery. Texas-based crime reporter Molly Cates gets into a lot of trouble when her first crime book, based on the exploits of a serial killer, is published.

324 pp.; 1994

42. *The Ice-House*   **Minette Walters**

Murder in the English countryside but otherwise a nontraditional and psychologically acute story of female friendships, vindictive villagers, and child abuse. Much more here than expected, including a sexy and appealing police inspector.

240 pp.; 1992

43. *The Suspect*   **L. R. Wright**

This graceful Canadian novelist writes here about a murder in a sleepy little town; this time the culprit is eighty years old and the victim is eighty-five. Interwoven is another story of abuse, guilt, honor, and compassion. Highly recommended even if you don't usually read mysteries. Her newest book is *A Touch of Panic*.

217 pp.; 1985

MYSTERIES BY MEN

1. *Zia Summer*   **Rudolfo Anaya**

Anaya is good at evoking the Spanish, Mexican, and Indian cultures that suffuse his native Southwest. Here a thirty-year-old P.I. investigates the murder of his cousin, Gloria Dominic, whose dead body, drained of blood and with a zia sign carved on her stomach, has surfaced in Albuquerque.

400 pp.; 1995

2. *Out on the Cutting Edge*   **Lawrence Block**

Matt Scudder, a defrocked New York cop, is the hard-drinking hero here, although in this one he's off booze. Block's books are as much about New York, beyond the Sixth Precinct and Midtown North, as they are about crime. *A Long Line of Dead Men*, *A Walk Among the Tombstones,* and *Everybody Dies* are all terrific.

260 pp.; 1989

3. *A Dead Man in Deptford*   **Anthony Burgess**

Burgess, who died in 1993 at age seventy-six, wrote his last novel about what the *Philadelphia Inquirer* calls "the brief life and mysterious, violent death of the Elizabethan poet, playwright and reluctant spy Christopher Marlowe," killed in a barroom brawl in 1580 after spying on Catholics in France for the British. On this subject you might want to try George Garrett's novel *Entered from the Sun: The Murder of Marlowe.*

272 pp.; 1995

4. *Black Cherry Blues*   **James Lee Burke**

Third in a series featuring ex–New Orleans cop Dave Robicheaux, Vietnam vet, widower whose wife was murdered in their bed, recovering alcoholic, father to an adopted Salvadoran child, and son of an illiterate Cajun who was killed on an oil rig. *Cimarron Rose* won the Edgar for Best Mystery in 1998. The newest is *Sunset Limited.*

290 pp.; 1989

5. *The Big Sleep*   **Raymond Chandler**

First of Chandler's novels starring his hero detective Philip Marlowe. The others are *Farewell, My Lovely; The High Window;* and *The Lady in the Lake.*

155 pp.; 1939

6. *The Chatham School Affair*   **Thomas H. Cook**

When a young woman gets off a bus in a Cape Cod village in 1926, she ignites the sparks that will become an inferno of scandal, suicide, and murder. Also *Breakheart Hill.*

292 pp.; 1996

7. *The Woman Who Walked*   Philip R. Craig
   into the Sea

If you can't get to Martha's Vineyard, read the Jeff Jackson mysteries for the details, correct down to the smoked bluefish pâté. Jackson, a former Boston cop and now a Vineyard fisherman, turns up in *Cliff Hanger* too.

215 pp.; 1991

8. *Voodoo River*   Robert Crais

This is the fifth in a series with Los Angeles P.I. Elvis Cole, who is hired to help a TV star find her birth parents. Most of the story takes place in Ville Platte, Louisiana.

256 pp.; 1995

9. *The Mexican Tree Duck*   James Crumley

In his first novel in ten years, Crumley returns with P.I. C. W. Sughrue, last seen in *The Last Good Kiss*. Here he tries to find a beautiful kidnapped woman.

256 pp.; 1993

10. *The Riddle of the Third Mile*   Colin Dexter

In this one, British Detective Chief Inspector Morse must deal with a mutilated corpse found floating in the Oxford Canal, and the disappearance of Oliver Maximilian Alexander Browne-Smith, a cantankerous Oxford professor. Read *The Way Through the Woods* and, especially, *Death Is Now My Neighbor,* in which my favorite Latin proverb, *Initium est dimidium facti,* appears. Cranky though he is, I am in love with Inspector Morse.

224 pp.; 1983

11. *Longshot*   Dick Francis

A writer waiting for his novel to hit the bestseller list starts a biography of a racehorse trainer, which means danger in rural England. Also *Blood Sport*, about stolen stallions. *Came to Grief* won the 1996 Edgar.

320 pp.; 1990

12. *The 6 Messiahs*   Mark Frost

A thriller set in the nineteenth century and involving the *Book of Zohar,* Sherlock Holmes, Arthur Conan Doyle, his brother, the Arizona desert, and an eerie dream—for starters. In some ways it follows *The List of 7*.

404 pp.; 1995

13. *Book*   Robert Grudin

This is even better if you've taught in a college English department where you spent the dull hours at obligatory faculty meetings fantasizing about ways to kill the critical theory people, among others. This novel has a sexually dazed chairwoman. *Right. Sure.* (It's fiction, remember?)

251 pp.; 1992

14. *The Glass Key*   Dashiell Hammett

The film *Miller's Crossing* used this plot. A gangster named Ned Beaumont turns into a detective in order to save his own life. *Red Harvest* is as much a western as a mystery. Hammett invented Sam Spade.

285 pp.; 1931

15. *Strip Tease*   Carl Hiassen

As Congressman David Dilbeck says, "I should never be around naked women." This time, between the strippers and the sugar growers in Florida, he gets into plenty of trouble. Hiassen, a newspaper reporter in Miami, my hometown, can really write. Also *Skin Tight, Native Tongue,* and a new one, the particularly hilarious *Lucky You*.

354 pp.; 1993

16. *Coyote Waits*   Tony Hillerman
The murder of a Navajo tribal policeman and an ancient artifact are connected. *Skinwalkers* followed. (In Navajo legend, a skin-walker is a Navajo who does not follow the path of beauty.)

292 pp.; 1990

17. *Lieberman's Folly*   Stuart M. Kaminsky
Kaminsky is famous for the Edgar-winning *A Cold Red Sunrise*, his fifth novel about a Moscow policeman, Porfiry Petrovich Rost-nikov. This novel is from his third series, which features Chicago cop Abe Lieberman and his partner, William Hanrahan, known to-gether as "the rabbi and the priest."

216 pp.; 1991

18. *Private Eyes*   Jonathan Kellerman
The detective here, Alex Delaware, is also a psychologist. Now he comes to the rescue of an actress menaced by someone recently released from prison. *Time Bomb* is good too. *Blood Test* is a serial-killer story and ultraviolent. *When the Bough Breaks* deals with child molestation.

475 pp.; 1992

19. *The Spy Who Came In from the Cold*   John le Carré
This was a runaway bestseller thirty years ago and it still works. The spy wants to quit the business, but somehow he can't get out.

256 pp.; 1964

20. *Maximum Bob*   Elmore Leonard
This time the crackpot judge (see title) in Palm Beach County, Florida, tries to get rid of his wife by introducing an alligator into their happy home. *Rum Punch* is good too, as is *Pronto*.

304 pp.; 1991

21. *The Summons*   **Peter Lovesey**

Third in a series, followed by *Bloodhounds*, preceded by *The Last Detective* and *Diamond Solitaire*, these feature Bath detective Peter Diamond. Can he discover the identity of the mute Japanese child who is hiding in the furniture department at Harrods?

359 pp.; 1995

22. *The Road to Omaha*   **Robert Ludlum**

In this funny thriller a master of suspense resurrects his two most outrageous characters, General MacKensie Lochinvar Hawkins— the Hawk—and Harvard-educated legal wizard Sam Devereaux. Yale-educated Bill Clinton reads Ludlum. Also *The Road to Gandolpho*, *The Scorpio Illusion*.

487 pp.; 1992

23. *Eight Black Horses*   **Ed McBain**

McBain (who is the author Evan Hunter) writes the "87th Precinct Mysteries" and in this one a very naked dead woman is somehow connected to the odd messages being received at the stationhouse. (Remember the Dead Man from previous McBain novels? He's back!) Also *Mischief*.

250 pp.; 1985

24. *The Song Dog*   **James McClure**

This is a prequel, harking back to 1962, where we learn how McClure's ratchet-tongued South African detective, Lieutenant Tromp Kramer, met his Zulu partner, Sergeant Mickey Zondi. *The Artful Egg* is great too. *Mary, Mary* features the Florida criminal attorney Matthew Hope.

274 pp.; 1991

25. *The Blue Hammer*   **Ross MacDonald**

One of the best Lew Archer mysteries. MacDonald, Richard Hugo, Charles Willeford, James Crumley, and James Lee Burke are all considered third-wave naturalistic writers; they are famous for gritty realism and strong characters.

270 pp.; 1976

26. *Rumpole à la Carte*   **John Mortimer**

Eighth collection of stories about this rumpled barrister who became famous on PBS.

246 pp.; 1990

27. *Devil with a Blue Dress On*   **Walter Mosley**

Easy Rawlins, Mosley's detective, is an African American who fights crime and prejudice in the 1950s. I like Mosley's angle of vision.

215 pp.; 1990

28. *Pastime*   **Robert B. Parker**

In the eighteenth of Parker's Spenser novels, we get a sense of this Boston detective's childhood and his initiation into manhood. *Promised Land* and *Paper Doll,* set in the South, are recommended as well.

342 pp.; 1991

29. *Kiss the Girls*   **James Patterson**

Patterson writes a series of books about Alex Cross, an African-American homicide detective in Washington, D.C., who is also a psychologist. Here he is dealing with a serial killer who actually thinks he loves the women he murders.

451 pp.; 1995

30. *Maigret in Holland*   George Simenon

The French Inspector Maigret arrives in Delfzijl to find out who murdered Conrad Popinga, a teacher. Watch that Manila cigar butt on the dining room carpet!

165 pp.; 1993

31. *The League of Frightened Men*   Rex Stout

Mysteries and Nero Wolfe are synonymous. The detective weighs one seventh of a ton, has a collection of ten thousand orchids, and obviously loves food. Read *The Black Echo* too.

217 pp.; 1982

32. *Pop. 1280*   Jim Thompson

Thompson is a hard-boiled crime writer but his small-town sheriff, Nick Corey, gets the job done here. *The Grifters* became the movie with Anjelica Huston.

217 pp.; 1990

33. *Brothers Keeper*   Donald E. Westlake

Great title for a comic thriller about Brother Benedict and his fight to save the Manhattan Crispite Monastery from someone who seems familiar . . . if you've heard of Donald Trump. *The Ax*, complete with antihero, has a new definition of justifiable homicide, and his career criminal, Parker, is back after twenty-three years in *Comeback*.

254 pp.; 1975

One to Beam Up, Mr. Scott

Science fiction as a commercial genre originated in 1926 with the publication of a magazine called Amazing Stories. *There are now so many science fiction writers, male and female, and so many books, that this list could never have been completed without the inestimable help of Dr. Chip Sullivan in North Carolina and two eager readers in New Jersey, John C. Goodwin and his son, David S. Goodwin.*

SCIENCE FICTION BY MEN

1. ***The Hitchhiker's Guide to the Galaxy***   **Douglas Adams**

This trilogy in five books is reputed to be the funniest science fiction story ever told. *Douglas Adams's Starship Titanic: A Novel* by Terry Jones is NOT a sequel.

215 pp.; 1980

2. ***Helliconia Summer***   **Brian W. Aldiss**

Second book in a trilogy (*Helliconia Winter, Helliconia Spring*) about the planet of Helliconia, where one Earth year lasts two and a half thousand years, and winter is seven centuries long. *Somewhere East of Life* is set in the twenty-first century.

398 pp.; 1983

3. *The Foundation Trilogy*   Isaac Asimov

Foundation is the colony founded by Hari Seldon and his band of Encyclopedists. This Hugo Award–winning trilogy—*Foundation*, *Foundation and Empire*, and *Second Foundation*, covers nearly four centuries of the rise of civilization from barbarism. *I, Robot* contains his best-known short stories and characters.

225 pp.; 1951

4. *The Drowned World*   J. G. Ballard

Idiosyncratic author of the autobiographical novel of wartime Shanghai, *Empire of the Sun*. His is a world of disaster, an interplay between man and the environment, written in a very polished style.

316 pp.; 1986

5. *Slant*   Greg Bear

Nanotechnology, which gives humans the ability to change their environment and themselves down to the cellular level, is Bear's subject. He wrote *Queen of Angels* and *Blood Music*.

349 pp.; 1997

6. *The Demolished Man*   Alfred Bester

Lincoln Powell is a telepathic cop in A.D. 2301 where the police stop murder before it happens. But not this time. The D.A., by the way, is a crusty but fair-minded computer. Also *The Stars My Destination*.

183 pp.; 1953

7. *A Case of Conscience*   James Blish

Blish builds the stories of four extraordinary men in two separate and complete worlds, idyllic Lithia and a culture on Earth that has gone below ground into a world of sub-cities.

188 pp.; 1987

8. *The Martian Chronicles*   Ray Bradbury

Considered the masterpiece of his twenty-four books, this is about the men of Earth who arrived on Mars in glittering rockets to find masked men who spoke their minds. Also *Fahrenheit 451,* about fascism and book burning.

204 pp.; 1950

9. *The Postman*   David Brin

Many readers mentioned this classic sci-fi writer. He wrote *Sundiver,* and the Uplift War series.

294 pp.; 1985

10. *Stand on Zanzibar*   John Brunner

Takes place in 2010 when seven billion plus earthlings live in an age of acceleratubes and Moonbase Zero. Featuring a riot-torn New York City, an Asian island threatened by a volcano, and the plague-ridden African Beninia, the future in Brunner's novels is dark, over-populated, and polluted. Also *Shockwave Rider.*

505 pp.; 1968

11. *Lost Boys*   Orson Scott Card

Enlarged version of Card's autobiographical short story by the same name. The Fletchers, devout Mormons, have a depressed son, Stevie, who has imaginary friends. Their problems start when real boys with the names of those friends start disappearing. In *Ender's Game,* another short story transformed into a novel, Ender is one of many children being trained by Earth as warriors and pilots to fight an intersteller war, Earth's last and only line of defense.

447 pp.; 1992

12. *Childhood's End*   Arthur C. Clarke

Clarke has written thirty books, which have sold two million copies in fifteen languages. This classic is the story of the last generation of mankind on earth. He wrote *2001: A Space Odyssey* from which came the film, and won the 1979 Nebula for *Fountains of Paradise*. Also *Imperial Earth*.

216 pp.; 1953

13. *Mission of Gravity*   Hal Clement

This novel reveals the demands of the Mesklinites and one of their sea captains (named Barlennan) when they recover a rocket for the earthmen. He is the exotic environment king.

224 pp.; 1953

14. *Nova*   Samuel R. Delany

A fantasy series about Neveryon and a philosophical journey too. Delany writes what are known as space operas and has won the Hugo and Nebula Awards for his speculative novels, where psychology, mythology, and imagery play a big part.

279 pp.; 1968

15. *The Man in the High Castle*   Philip K. Dick

A fine alternative world novel where Dick's typically complex, believable (and often schizophrenic) characters are on display. Because of the movie *Blade Runner,* made from his novel *Do Androids Dream of Electric Sheep?*, he is now a cult figure.

239 pp.; 1962

16. *Deathbird Stories*   Harlan Ellison

Here are nineteen stories, fantasies, and allegories written over a period of ten years, including "Pretty Maggie Money Eyes" and "The Whimper of Whipped Dogs." Ellison has won five Hugo Awards.

334 pp.; 1975

17. *Alas, Babylon!*   **Pat Frank**

This is a novel about the end of the world (courtesy of an H-bomb attack) and the day after that. How would you survive on a planet poisoned with radiation?

279 pp.; 1959

18. *Neuromancer*   **William Gibson**

This postmodern work won the Hugo, Nebula, and Philip K. Dick Awards. Case was the best interface who ever ran in Earth's computer matrix but he got caught in a double cross. Gibson founded the cyberpunk movement. His new futuristic novel, *Virtual Light,* is a tale about the consequences of virtual reality.

271 pp.; 1984

19. *The Moon Is a Harsh Mistress*   **Robert A. Heinlein**

Heinlein is an authorial descendant of Chandler and Hammett. His novels are often funny (even sentimental) and unusually bright compared to the traditional dark vision, and in this one there is a lunar rebellion against Earth. Also *Beyond This Horizon, Double Star,* and especially *Stranger in a Strange Land.*

383 pp.; 1966

20. *New News from Outerspace*   **John Kessel**

Kessel won the 1982 Nebula for Best Novella for *Another Orphan.* "Buffalo" describes an encounter between Kessel's immigrant father and his idol H. G. Wells.

402 pp.; 1989

21. *The Cyberiad*   **Stanislaw Lem**

Lem uses hard science and has a pessimistic twist. Here Trurl and Klapacius are constructor robots who try to out-invent each other and they almost destroy the universe in the process.

295 pp.; 1974

22. *A Canticle for Leibowitz*   Walter M. Miller, Jr.

Miller (like Leibowitz) was a convert to Catholicism. The setting here is a monastery in the American Southwest after a nuclear war; Miller was perhaps influenced by the American bombing of the Monte Casino monastery in Italy during World War II. Two years after Miller's death at seventy-three, we have *Saint Leibowitz and the Wild Horse*, which centers on the relationship between Brother Blacktooth St. George, a monk of the Abbey of St. Leibowitz and the ambitious Cardinal Brownpenny.

320 pp.; 1959

23. *The Ringworld Throne*   Larry Niven

Ringworld is a ribbon around a distant sun in what he calls Known Space; its inner edge has the surface area of a million earths—a million miles wide and six hundred million miles around—and is home to some thirty trillion sentient beings. Also *The Ringworld* and *The Ringworld Engineers*.

355 pp.; 1966

24. *Space Merchants*   Frederick Pohl

A classic story of interplanetary commerce.

158 pp.; 1953

25. *Red Mars*   Kim Stanley Robinson

In Robinson a more humanistic, literary, and softer science fiction is on display. *The Wild Shore* and *Pacific Edge* are by him too.

519 pp.; 1993

26. *Dying Inside*   Robert Silverberg

Silverberg started as a writer of pulp novels but is now greatly respected as an accomplished artist in this genre. As the *New York Times* said, "[*Kingdoms of the Wall*] is a parable about the danger of seeking more intimate contact with the powers that control the universe."

245 pp.; 1972

27. *Way Station*   Clifford Simak
This story of the solitary Enoch Wallace, who manages the Way Station and is earth's sole representative to the Inter-Galactic Council, still holds up wonderfully. Simak won the International Fantasy Award for *City*.

210 pp.; 1963

28. *Bug Jack Barron*   Norman Spinrad
An unusual novel in this genre because it is really about television, power, business, and more power. Spinrad's latest is *Deux X*, in which he wonders when a computer replica of a personality becomes the equivalent of a living person. *Stations of the Tide* is about a functionary caught between a humdrum bureaucracy and what James Morrow calls "the alluring Ur-reality fashioned by the protean wizard Gregorian."

327 pp.; 1969

29. *The Diamond Age*   Neal Stephenson
Nanotechnologist John Percival Hackworth of the neo-Victorians steals a copy of *A Young Lady's Illustrated Primer* for his daughter Fiona. Here comes BIG trouble.

512 pp.; 1995

30. *Resurrection Man*   Sean Stewart
David Goodwin is especially fond of this new writer. This novel is about angels, magic, mirrors, being possessed, autopsies, and family secrets.

248 pp.; 1995

31. *More Than Human*   Theodore Sturgeon

Five extraordinary individuals "blesh" in this one, thereby losing their separate identities. Unfortunately, only one of them is aware that some very important part of this new Self is missing.

186 pp.; 1953

32. *Genetic Soldier*   George Turner

Author of the 1991 *Brain Child,* this Australian crosses genres. Earth is polluted and the crew of a spaceship looks for a new home.

403 pp.; 1994

33. *The War of the Worlds*   H. G. Wells

Many of science fiction's most familiar concepts—the time machine, the invading alien, and the atomic bomb come from Wells. Also, of course, *The Time Machine.*

149 pp.; 1938

SCIENCE FICTION BY WOMEN

1. *Preternatural*   Margaret Wander Bonanno

Aliens intervene in human affairs; a funny parody of the *Star Trek* industry is included.

320 pp.; 1996

2. The Darkover Novels   Marian Zimmer Bradley

This is a trilogy composed of *Landfall, Sword of Chaos,* and *Leroni of Darkover* by the extremely popular writer of science fiction. Also *The Shattered Chain.*
Sword of Chaos: 240 pp.; 1982

3. *Xenogenesis* (trilogy)   Octavia E. Butler

All of Butler's novels feature black women struggling against racism and sexism: *Kindred* (1979), *Patternmaster* (1976), *Mind of*

My Mind (1977), and *Wild Seed* (1980). More walled communities in *Parable of the Sower;* alien invaders to Earth in *Clay's Ark.*

726 pp.; 1987–89

4. *Synners*   Pat Cadigan

Her women, like those males in the usual cyberpunk, are at the center of a high-tech, low-life adventure story.

435 pp.; 1991

5. *Walk to the End of the World*   Suzy McKee Charnas

Like Tepper, Charnas tries to dissuade the reader from accepting the obligation of men to act as macho maniacs after a nuclear world war. *The Unicorn Tapestry* won the 1980 Nebula for Best Novella.

214 pp.; 1974

6. *Cyteen*   C. J. Cherryh

Cherryh writes good, sexy space romps, and this one has a world where genetics and psychiatric intervention have been perfected. Others in the series are *Heavy Time, Hellburner, Rimrunners,* and *Downbelow Station.* In her novels women are in positions of absolute power. The most recent series includes *Rider at the Gate.*

680 pp.; 1988

7. *Carpathians*   Janet Frame

As the *New York Times* noted, "the inhabitants of a New Zealand town must come to grips with a frightening new reality: the gravitational effects of a quasar have distorted all perception of time and space."

196 pp.; 1988

8. *Herland*   Charlotte Perkins Gilman

An early twentieth-century story included here for historical interest. This describes a land without men, and if you read her novella *The Yellow Wallpaper* you'll understand why Gilman wrote this.

147 pp.; 1979 (reprint)

9. *Dream Years*   Lisa Goldstein

Bizarre characters and fable: a good mix. Also *The Red Magician*.

181 pp.; 1985

10. *Flesh and Gold*   Phyllis Gotlieb

In a brothel where they cater to the desires of "fifteen kinds of humanity," this novel by a poet affirms the universality of human lust and greed.

288 pp.; 1998

11. *Beggars in Spain*   Nancy Kress

Her novella with the same title won the 1991 Nebula. This is a brave new world of genetically engineered prodigies who are so smart they don't have to sleep. A good look at new hierarchies and corruption among an elite. Also *Brain Rose*.

448 pp.; 1993

12. *The Left Hand of Darkness*   Ursula K. Le Guin

This one, a Nebula winner, is on everyone's list and promotes great discussions. Le Guin creates Winter, a backward world, where all humans are genderless. Also *Planet of Exile*, *The Dispossessed*, and *City of Illusions*. Earthsea is her fantasy series.

286 pp.; 1969

13. *Dreamsnake*   Vonda N. McIntyre

The plots are complex and tightly written here, perhaps because of her work in movies. She has a humanistic side that is refreshing in this genre. Many readers like the four-volume Starfarer series.

313 pp.; 1978

14. *Daughters of Earth*   Judith Merril

Three novelettes: *Project Nursemaid, Daughters of Earth,* and *Home-calling.* The first two involve women's sacrifices and obstacles in space exploration and the third is about two children stranded on a strange planet.

255 pp.; 1969

15. *The Ragged World*   Judith Moffett

Furry aliens, time travel, and cosmic events reign here.

341 pp.; 1991

16. *Doorway into Time*   C. L. Moore

Really a tale first published in a September 1943 issue of *Famous Fantastic Mysteries.* Cloaked in the alias of Lawrence O'Donnell, Moore was hailed as an extraordinary discovery, then as a writer of the supernatural and the horrifying, and was published by *Weird Tales* magazine. Now she is the most outstanding woman writing in this field.

1943

17. *The Falling Woman*   Pat Murphy

Won the 1987 Nebula for Best Novel. Also *Rachel in Love.*

287 pp.; 1986

18. *Woman on the Edge of Time*   Marge Piercy

Consuelo Ramos, a Chicana in New York, is the woman in question, and through her we see how one person, perceived as faceless and invisible, becomes a potential subject for a neuroelectric experiment. Her future is in Mattapoisett, a playful, androgynous society. Piercy wrote *Small Changes,* many books of poetry, and *Gone to Soldiers.*

369 pp.; 1976

19. *The Female Man*   **Joanna Russ**

This is a novel about polarities—the individual and society; the actual and the possible; women and men—by one of the very best writers in this genre. Find a copy of her 1972 short story "When It Changed."

287 pp.; 1975

20. *Venus of Shadows*   **Pamela Sargent**

In *Venus of Dreams* Iris Angharads works on the Venus Project, an effort to carve a green and growing world out of the hellish wilderness of that planet. A generation later her children must find their way in that world. Sargent is famous for *The Shore of Women*.

544 pp.; 1988

21. *Mess-Mend: The Yankees in Petrograd*   **Marietta Shaginian**

Written by a Muscovite under the pseudonym Jim Dollar, this was published in biweekly installments in the Soviet Union seventy years ago. The hero is named Thingmaster.

375 pp.; 1923

22. *The Gate to Women's Country*   **Sheri Tepper**

In the walled towns of Women's Country, women and nonviolent men nurture what is left of the past after the world all but burned to ash three hundred years ago in the flames of a nuclear holocaust. Tepper wrote *After Long Silence* and *The Awakeners*.

278 pp.; 1988

23. *Brightness Falls from the Air*   **James Tiptree, Jr.**

Born Alice Sheldon, the author had the last laugh when male critics claimed that her sharp, pointed novels could only have been written by a man.

382 pp.; 1985

24. *The Snow Queen*   Joan Vinge

A Hugo winner featuring complex characters and mythic resonances. *The Summer Queen* is its sequel.

536 pp.; 1980

25. *The Dark Door*   Kate Wilhelm

Combination sci-fi and mystery novel stars the husband and wife team of Charlie Meiklejohn and Constance Leid.

352 pp.; 1988

26. *The Doomsday Book*   Connie Willis

Set in the English countryside during the Black Plague. Willis writes great time-travel tales that include *Fire Watch,* set in London during the Blitz and her latest, *To Say Nothing of the Dog,* which takes place in Victorian England. With a device known as "the net," you can travel backward in time and return, as long as you don't bring anything back with you.

445 pp.; 1992

Who's on First?

These are novels and nonfiction books about the most wonderful sport: baseball. (And I am too objective!) It should keep a sports-minded book club busy for an entire year. Go, Mets.

1. *Five Seasons: A Baseball Companion*   Roger Angell
Jonathan Yardley said many years ago that "this is the one absolutely essential book on baseball." It's the story of a love affair between the fans and the game.

413 pp.; 1977

2. *Balls*   Gorman Bechard
In the year 2000 the Supreme Court rules that twenty-four-year-old Louise Kathleen Gehrig, a Yale graduate called "Balls," can play in the major leagues for the Manhattan Meteorites. As my Aunt Bessie used to say, I should only live to see it.

369 pp.; 1995

3. *Ball Four*   Jim Bouton
Twenty years ago Bouton blew the whistle on baseball as a clean, all-American sport. Still a great read.

400 pp.; 1970

4. *Blue Ruin*   Brendan Boyd

Want to know what really happened during the notorious 1919 Chicago White Sox–Cincinnati Reds World Series?

352 pp.; 1991

5. *When the Game Was*   Bruce Chadwick
Black and White

Subtitled *The Illustrated History of Baseball's Negro Leagues*, this impressive collection of photographs with text is by the New York *Daily News* sportswriter.

204 pp.; 1992

6. *Ballpark*   Elisha Cooper

This story, about what happens all day at an old-fashioned, no-dome ballpark (without luxury boxes and catered meals; George Steinbrenner take note!) when the clouds burst and the rain starts, is written and illustrated for the age-five-and-up set. So if you are lucky enough to have a kid in the house, you'll both love it.

unpaged; 1998

7. *The Sweetheart Season*   Karen Joy Fowler

My mother would have loved this one. Irini Doyle, a worker in a Midwestern cereal factory, joins a baseball team called the Sweetheart Sweethearts in 1947. Her earlier novel, *Sarah Canary,* is a quirky, bizarre, and wonderful American quest tale, set in the Washington Territory in 1873.

352 pp.; 1996

8. *Wait Till Next Year*   Doris Kearns Goodwin

Tender, funny, endearing memoir by the Pulitzer Prize–winning author of *No Ordinary Time.* We hear the voice of the young girl on Long Island in the 1950s who loved the Brooklyn Dodgers, loved her father, and still understands that *Baseball Is Life!*

257 pp.; 1997

9. *Dock Ellis in the*   **Donald Hall/Dock Ellis**
   Country of Baseball

Profile of the gifted pitcher by the noted essayist, poet, and baseball fanatic.

254 pp.; 1976

10. *Bang the Drum Slowly*   **Mark Harris**

Fantastic baseball novel from the 1950s, and made into the best baseball movie ever (except for *Bull Durham*). *The Southpaw* is the sequel.

243 pp.; 1956

11. *The Annotated Baseball*   **ed. George W. Hilton**
    Stories of Ring W. Lardner, 1914–1919

A volume of twenty-four tales about the national pastime, rooted in actual events.

631 pp.; 1995

12. *The Boys of Summer*   **Roger Kahn**

A 1972 celebration of that golden time when the Brooklyn Dodgers reigned at Ebbets Field and Jackie Robinson made our hearts sing. Reissued recently with a new epilogue.

480 pp.; reissue 1998

13. *Shoeless Joe*   **W. P. Kinsella**

Kinsella's novel was later reissued as *Field of Dreams* after the baseball movie of that name was made. "Build it and they will come" has entered the vocabulary.

265 pp.; 1982

14. *Water from the Well*   **Myra McLarey**

A baseball game takes place in an Arkansas pasture in 1919. The remarkable part is that one team was black and one was white. A complex tale evolves from this event.

232 pp.; 1995

15. *The Natural*   **Bernard Malamud**

Much sadder than the movie with Robert Redford, and in all ways a truer story about baseball.

237 pp.; 1952

16. *Mortal Stakes*   **Robert Parker**

Parker writes the Spenser mysteries about the Boston detective and this one is about baseball, women with "pasts," and the Mob.

172 pp.; 1975

17. *Only the Ball Was White*   **Robert Peterson**

Here's a good read about the Negro Leagues of baseball in the 1920s and 1930s.

406 pp.; 1970

18. *Jackie Robinson*   **Arnold Rampersad**

One critic said correctly that the story of Jackie Robinson, like the history of the Holocaust, must be told to every new generation so that it will never be forgotten. The name of this Brooklyn Dodger has become a synonym for courage.

448 pp.; 1997

19. *The Glory of Their Times*   **Larry Ritter**

This is a classic, subtitled *The Story of the Early Days of Baseball Told by the Men Who Played It.* Good read on baseball players of the 1920s and 1930s.

360 pp.; 1966

20. *A Great and Glorious*   Kenneth S. Robson
Game: Baseball Writings of
A. Bartlett Giamatti

Eloquent essays by the former president of Yale University who was also the National League president and baseball commissioner. Before his sudden death in 1989 he said that "baseball is about going home, and how hard it is to get there." Amen.

121 pp.; 1998

21. *Almost Famous*   David Small

This is a small, dark novel about baseball and frustration.

416 pp.; 1982

22. *Murder at Ebbets Field*   Troy Soos

One of a series of mystery novels where murder happens on the historic ballfields of the early twentieth century. Real baseball players—Ty Cobb, Casey Stengel, et al.—are inserted as characters. The hero is Mickey Ramlings, a utility player in the early 1900s. Here Mickey is playing for the New York Giants in 1914.

280 pp.; 1995

23. *Hoopla*   Harry Stein

This is a Chicago White Sox story.

366 pp.; 1983

24. *Bunts: Curt Flood,*   George F. Will
Camden Yards, Pete Rose and
Other Reflections on Baseball

Several witty critics have observed that Will is a better writer and better thinker on baseball than on politics. I'll vote for that.

352 pp.; 1998

Be a Sport

Excluding baseball, which, because it is (of course) the best sport, has its own list: "Who's on First?" Here we have boxing, cricket, football, girls' basketball, women's pro basketball, fly-fishing, golf, men's college basketball, men's pro basketball, men's playground basketball, tennis, ice hockey, and crew.

1. *Punch Lines*   **Phil Berger**
Berger formerly wrote about boxing for the *New York Times,* and these are magazine and newspaper articles published over the last twenty-five years.

328 pp.; 1993

2. *Friday Night Lights*   **H. G. Bissinger**
This one is as much about small-town life in Odessa, Texas, and the struggle between sports and education as it is about football.

364 pp.; 1990

3. *In These Girls, Hope Is a Muscle*   **Madeleine Blais**
Nonfiction account written by a Pulitzer Prize–winning reporter about a Springfield, Massachusetts, high school basketball team— the Amherst Lady Hurricanes. Don't miss it.

272 pp.; 1995

4. *Dogleg Madness*   **Mike Bryan**

Believe it or not, a good book on golf! Herbert Warren Wind writes well about this sport too. And there is *Jack Nicklaus: My Story* by Jack Nicklaus with Ken Bowden.

228 pp.; 1988

5. *Venus to the Hoop: A*   **Sara Corbett**
Gold-Medal Year in Women's Basketball

After the United States lost to Russia and China at the 1992 Olympics, USA Basketball held a team trial fourteen months before the 1996 Olympics began. This team went undefeated for sixty games and won the gold medal. Corbett also chronicles the development of the two rival professional leagues for women, the American Basketball League and the Women's National Basketball Association.

342 pp.; 1997

6. *Final Rounds*   **James Dodson**

A father-son love story and the golf journey of a lifetime. You don't even have to like sports for this one.

257 pp.; 1996

7. *A Season on the Brink*   **John Feinstein**

There's plenty to say about the notorious Indiana University coach Bobby Knight. For those who are still mystified, Feinstein explains how he wins and why his players are loyal.

311 pp.; 1986

8. *What the River Knows*   **Wayne Fields**

He fly-fishes a single stream in Michigan's Upper Peninsula and compares it to writing: "an awkward fumbling after grace."

252 pp.; 1990

9. *Handful of Summers*   **Gordon Forbes**
A good book about tennis players, South Africa, and one man's life.

238 pp.; 1979

10. *The Breaks of the Game*   **David Halberstam**
The writer spends a year with the Portland NBA team and the famed Bill Walton.

362 pp.; 1981

11. *Muhammed Ali*   **Thomas Hauser**
A moving and probing oral history–type portrait of the most popular man in the world.

544 pp.; 1991

12. *Beyond a Boundary*   **C. L. R. James**
Good read on the West Indies, black-white relations, the legacies of the British Empire, and cricket. Some beautiful writing here by the famous Marxist historian and critic.

255 pp.; 1963

13. *Sportsworld*   **Robert Lipsyte**
Unsurpassed if cynical essays about America's obsession with pro sports from the seasoned *New York Times* reporter. Especially brilliant on Muhammed Ali. Also recommended is his bestselling Young Adult novel, *The Contender*, about a young black boxer.

292 pp.; 1975

14. *A Different Angle*   **Holly Morris**
A collection of fly-fishing stories by women.

270 pp.; 1995

15. *Jim Murray: An Autobiography*   **Jim Murray**

Pulitzer Prize–winning columnist for the *Los Angeles Times* writes about Michael Jordan and many others, but the parts about his own childhood and family in Hartford are sweetest.

268 pp.; 1993

16. *On Boxing*   **Joyce Carol Oates**

Evolved from a philosophical essay on the sport of boxing for the *New York Times*. Boxing also dominates her novel *You Must Remember This.*

118 pp.; 1987

17. *My Usual Game: Adventures in Golf*   **David Owen**

Okay, I admit it. Even though I love sports and I love walking, I just don't get golf. But Owen's account of his obsession with this sport, and of how he devoted every waking moment to improving his game, is funny.

271 pp.; 1995

18. *Joe and Me: An Education in Fishing and Friendship*   **James Prosek**

FISHING, I understand. By the author of *Trout: An Illustrated History,* this lovely illustrated journal describes the relationship between a young man and a mentor who opens his heart to nature. I wish I could have gone along.

190 pp.; 1997

19. *Papa Jack*   **Randy Roberts**

You can rent *Great White Hope* after you've read this book about the boxer Jack Johnson.

274 pp.; 1983

20. *Second Wind*   **Bill Russell/Taylor Branch**
Opinionated, sometimes scary memoir by basketball's big man.
Taylor Branch is the author of *Parting the Water*s.

265 pp.; 1979

21. *Heaven Is a Playground*   **Dick Telander**
Telander writes about inner-city kids on the basketball courts,
aiming for the NBA.

282 pp.; 1976

22. *The Appearance of Impropriety*   **Walter Walker**
A murder mystery about basketball, blackmail, and murder.
Colin Cromwell, a Bay Area sportswriter, attempts to document
the goings-on in the NBA's latest expansion team, the Golden
Gaters. Greedy owners, out-of-control managers and agents; in
other words, pro ball today.

336 pp.; 1993

37

Stop Kidding Around

Children's and Young Adult Books

I could spend the rest of my life reading and listing books for children and young adults because so many good ones exist. So I called on some of the "children" I know (some of them now college graduates, parents, and/or grandparents) and their names are listed where possible in parentheses. Thanks to all.

BOOKS FOR YOUNGER CHILDREN

1. *Aesop's Fables*
"The Ant and the Grasshopper," "The Hare and the Hound," and "The Goose with the Golden Egg" have already lasted about three thousand years and have been translated into almost every language on planet Earth. Your kids will love them too.
(Rob Mank and Michael Ben David)

2. *Best Friends, Together Again*   Aliki
A charming book for very young children. Another good book on this subject is Leo Lionni's *Frederick.*   (Jasper Anderson)
unpaged; 1995

3. *On My Honor*   Marion Dane Bauer

Joel is overcome with guilt when his best friend, Tony, drowns while they are swimming in the forbidden and treacherous waters of the Vermilion River.   (Sandy Benítez)

90 pp.; 1987

4. *Madeline*   Ludwig Bemelmans

"In an old house in Paris that was covered with vines lived twelve little girls in two straight lines." What a Parisian treat! (Brooke Hirschfelder)

46 pp.; 1939

5. *Goodnight Moon*   Margaret Wise Brown

If you can get someone to come over here and read this one to me every night I would certainly appreciate it. The *New York Times* calls it the original bedtime book for boomers. By the author of everybody's favorite, *The Runaway Bunny.*   (Sally Coventry Holzapfel and Lizzie Coventry Holzapfel)

unpaged; 1942

6. *Shoeshine Girl*   Clyde Robert Bulla

Troubled Sarah Ida, ten, is sent to live with Aunt Claudia for the summer. She gets a job with Al, the shoeshine man, and learns to respect hard work. And when Al gets hurt she saves the day. (Bonnie Benowitz)

84 pp.; 1975

7. *The Secret Garden*   Frances H. Burnett

When the young orphan Mary Lennox arrives on the Yorkshire moors from India, she makes discoveries about what illness means and how sad some secrets can be. A classic for all ages. (In this house we've worn out at least eight copies!)

375 pp.; 1911

8. *The Pinballs*   **Betsy Byars**

Although this engaging novel about kids sent to a foster home was an ALA Notable Children's Book many years ago, the subject of young people without viable parents is still prevalent today. Also *Summer of the Swans* and *The Seven Treasure Hunts.*

136 pp.; 1977

9. *Ramona the Pest*   **Beverly Cleary**

First of five Ramona titles about a girl who is not "a slow poke grownup." She has been charming young readers for thirty years.

192 pp.; 1968

10. *Walk Two Moons*   **Sharon Creech**

Won the Newbery Medal for 1994. Her new book, *Absolutely Normal Chaos,* less serious and complex, concerns thirteen-year-old Mary Lou Finney's visit from her cousin, Carl Ray, who arrives from West Virginia.

280 pp.; 1994

11. *The Cat Ate My Gymsuit*   **Paula Danziger**

An all-time favorite about the bored Marcy Lewis, her tyrannical father, the usual anxieties about weight and acne, and the good English teacher, Ms. Finney, who creates an uproar over her refusal to pledge allegiance to the flag. Danziger wrote *The Pistachio Prescription* and *Can You Sue Your Parents for Malpractice?*

147 pp.; 1974

12. *Are You My Mother?*   **P. D. Eastman**

This was a great favorite of my godson, the one with the Ph.D. in math from Berkeley in fractals and chaos theory. I guess you have to be careful what you read to these kids.   (Rafi Laufer)

64 pp.; 1960

13. *Asterix and Caesar's Gift*   Rene de Goscinny
drawings by M. Uderzo

My daughter took her *Asterix* books with her when she left for college. These sophisticated picture books with text (they look something like cartoons) are often full of puns, word play, and information about culture, history, and language. Since they are imported they are a bit more expensive than the usual books for kids but worth it in every sense; several volumes come in Latin (*Asterix Apud Brittannos*), French, and so on. Try *Asterix and Cleopatra*, *Asterix and the Golden Sickle*, *Asterix in Belgium*, etc.   (Mia Pearlman and Will Levine)

48 pp.; 1977

14. *Seven Brave Women*   Betsy Hearne

Hearne writes "about the generations of women who did the sort of great and heroic things that we have ignored throughout history. . . . Grandmother Margaret did not become a doctor or an architect; she became a widow. Her husband died when her two children were babies. She got a job as a secretary and took care of her sick father, her old mother, her six younger brothers and sisters, and her two children." And "at the end of that sentence, if you're human, you want to stand up and applaud." Exactly.

unpaged; 1997

15. *Robert the Rose Horse*   Joan Heilbroner

My son the jazz musician thought this was the funniest book in the house. I thought so too. And every time I sneeze I think about it. He also wore out several copies of Gyo Fujikawa's *Oh, What a Busy Day!*   (Ted Pearlman)

64 pp.; 1962

16. *Amazing Grace*   **Mary Hoffman**

A little girl wants to be Peter Pan in the school play. But Peter Pan wasn't an African American and he wasn't a girl. Here comes Grandmother to the rescue.

unpaged; 1991

17. *Minn of the Mississippi*   **Holling C. Holling**

It's never too early to talk about the importance of rivers. This one has illustrations of flora and fauna in the margins.

85 pp.; 1951

18. *Harold and the Purple Crayon*   **Crockett Johnson**

Published over forty years ago and still wonderful, and it doesn't even mention words like "gouache" or "chiaroscuro," which is in itself a blessing.

60 pp.; 1955

19. *Ooh-La-La (Max in Love)*   **Maira Kalman**

Thousands of adults have been caught sneaking into the kids' section of bookstores nationwide for the Parisian adventures of Max Stravinsky, Kalman's dog poet. The illustrations are marvelous. Don't miss *Sayonara, Mrs. Kackelman* or *Max in Hollywood, Baby,* where Max Stravinsky is hanging with the West Coast crowd. His limo is, thankfully, chauffered by Ferrrnando Extra Debonnaire.

unpaged; 1991

20. *From the Mixed-Up*   **E. L. Konigsburg**
    Files of Mrs. Basil E. Frankweiler

My daughter the artist (who now lives in a loft in Brooklyn) was no doubt influenced by this one, in which Claudia and Jamie escape from the suburbs into the Metropolitan Museum of Art.

162 pp.; 1967

21. *Boom Town*   Sonia Levitin

Social history expressed through the lives of ordinary people of the past is always welcome. A California gold rush town is transformed through the energies of a little girl named Amanda. Everybody WORKS, nobody is beautiful, and everyone is welcome.

32 pp.; 1997

22. *Pippi Longstocking*   Astrid Lindgren

Hooray, a book with no disease, divorce, child abuse, or pollution. Lindgren created this red-haired delight—who lives alone in Sweden without parents but with a horse on the porch, a pet monkey, and a treasure of gold pieces—for her sick daughter. *Pippi Goes on Board* and *Pippi in the South Seas* followed.   (Sanda Cohen)

160 pp.; 1950

23. *Anne of Green Gables*   Lucy Maude Montgomery

The skinny, freckled redhead named Anne Shirley who arrives on Prince Edward Island first appeared more than eighty years ago. By 1943 it had gone through forty-four printings and was followed by *Anne of Avonlea, Chronicles of Avonlea, Anne of the Island, Anne of Windy Poplars, Anne's House of Dreams,* and *Anne of Ingleside.* Even today, Montgomery's farmhouse is treated like a shrine, particularly by the Japanese.

309 pp.; 1908

24. *My Friend Gorilla*   Atsuko Morozumi

If there are no kids around I might be tempted to read this one to myself. In this book about friendship and tolerance the zookeeper's son sleeps on the top bunk, and the gorilla who lives with the family sleeps on the bottom. Wonderful.

unpaged; 1998

25. *The Seedlings Journey*   Janet Pfeiffer
Written for young children, but this parable about growth and possibility has meaning for adults as well.

unpaged; 1994

26. *Fairy Tales of*   collected by Neil Philip
Hans Christian Andersen
A dozen favorite stories from the Danish master. I loved these as a kid and I still do. And "The Emperor's New Clothes" and "Thumbalina" never go out of style.

139 pp.; 1995

27. *Tar Beach*   Faith Ringgold
Cassie Louise Lightfoot dreams of floating over a 1930s New York City and wearing the George Washington Bridge for a necklace. Based on the author's quilt painting of the same name.

32 pp.; 1991

28. *The Absolutely True Story . . .*   Willo Davis Roberts
How I Visited Yellowstone
Park with the Terrible Rupes
And boy, the Rupes *are* terrible. They eat junk food, the father can't drive their motor home, their three children are unsupervised—as twelve-year-old Lewis Dodge and his sister find out—when all five children are kidnapped.

144 pp.; 1994

29. *Where the Wild Things Are*   Maurice Sendak
This one and *Mickey in the Night Kitchen* always scared me more than they did my children. But a little fear is healthy, I think.

40 pp.; 1963

30. *The Gardener*   Sarah Stewart

This charming story concerns a country girl who is sent in 1935 to live with her Uncle Jim in a large dark city during the Depression. Flowers become the vehicle of transformation. I love this book.

unpaged; 1997

31. *There Was an Old Lady*   retold by Simms Taback
    Who Swallowed a Fly

"I don't know why she swallowed the fly./Perhaps she'll die." Gross, as we used to say. And terrific.

32 pp.; 1997

32. *Eloise*   Kay Thompson

I read this tale of irrepressible, never-bored Eloise having fun and raising Cain at the Plaza Hotel when I lived in hot, and (then) un-air-conditioned Miami. Could that be why I moved to New York City a few years later? Stranger things have happened.

65 pp.; 1955

33. *The Hobbit*   J. R. R. Tolkien

The doyen of the fantastic, the creator of Middle Earth, where the language spoken is Elvish. *Lord of the Rings* is the meal; *Hobbit* is dessert. Both of my nephews loved this one.   (Gary Heiman and Bill Glaser)

335 pp.; 1974

34. *Alexander and the Terrible,*   Judith Viorst
    Horrible, No Good, Very Bad Day

My goddaughter, now a teacher, remembers this one as her favorite. And her own students love it.   (Simone Laufer)

unpaged; 1972

35. *Little House in the Big Woods* Laura Ingalls Wilder

First in a series of nine volumes where the narrator, based on the author, emerges as a five-year-old in Wisconsin and grows up to be a bride in South Dakota. A new biography, *Becoming Laura Ingalls Wilder,* by John E. Miller, alludes to the complicated relationship between Wilder and her daughter, the writer Rose Wilder Lane. (Jessica Appleman)

237 pp.; 1932

36. *Owl Moon* Jane Yolen

I think we need more stories of loving relationships between fathers and daughters, don't you? This is a good one.

32 pp.; 1987

37. *Rapunzel* retold by Paul O. Zelinsky

The Grimm brothers included this one in their nineteenth-century collection of fairy tales but it has existed in one form or another since an Italian version in 1634. The tower, the prince, their twins, the sorceress, the long hair—it all captivated me as a child. (And still does.)

unpaged; 1997

BOOKS FOR OLDER CHILDER

1. *Sounder* William. H. Armstrong

Courage and love bind a black family together despite prejudice and inhumanity in the Deep South.

136 pp.; 1969

2. *Cherokee Bat and the Goat Guys* Francesca Lia Block

As she did in *Weetzie Bat* and *Witch Baby,* Block creates an idiosyncratic version of Los Angeles. Cherokee, her "almost-sister"

Witch Baby, Raphael, and Angel Juan, two other members of The Goat Guys, a rock band, all get magical costumes that have a very bad influence on them. Five dreamlike fables appear in *Dangerous Angels: The Weetzie Bat Books*.

128 pp.; 1992

3. *Blubber*   Judy Blume

The *New York Times* called it an Outstanding Book of the Year more than twenty years ago and it remains so today. Linda's weight problems inspire the cruel instincts of the mob in her fellow fifth graders, and any child who feels victimized will appreciate this one. Blume is famous for *Are You There God? It's Me, Margaret; Then Again, Maybe I Won't; Otherwise Known as Sheila the Great; Tales of a Fourth Grade Nothing;* and *Iggie's House*.

153 pp.; 1974

4. *Caddie Woodlawn*   Carol R. Brink

Another golden oldie, based on stories told by Brink's grandmother, this is a tale of a redheaded tomboy in 1860s Wisconsin. The sequel is *Magical Melons*.

270 pp.; 1935

5. *A Hero Ain't Nothin'*   Alice Childress
but a Sandwich

Benjie is a thirteen-year-old with a monkey on his back—in this case heroin. But he is also a funny, courageous kid about whom the reader cares.

126 pp.; 1973

6. *The Chocolate War*   Robert Cormier

A classic in which a high school freshman discovers what happens when he arouses the wrath of the school bullies. Cormier is most famous for *I Am the Cheese*.

253 pp.; 1974

7. *The Midwife's Apprentice*   Karen Cushman

This story of a homeless young woman in medieval England who becomes the midwife's apprentice won the Newbery.

122 pp.; 1996

8. *The Witches*   Roald Dahl

Modern classic about a young boy and his Norwegian grandmother, an expert on witches, who together foil a witches' plot to destroy the world's children by turning them into mice. In *Charlie and the Chocolate Factory* a good boy visits Willie Wonka's amazing candy works.   (Sam McFarland)

201 pp.; 1985

9. *Hardy Boys Casefiles,*   Franklin Dixon
Case 75: No Way Out

See comments on Nancy Drew. Rob Niles is a master of the wilderness sport of orienteering. But he's in trouble on this trip and the Hardy boys, Frank and Joe, have to use their survival skills to avoid the rattlesnakes, rock slides, and sniper fire. All the stories have been updated.   (Marv Rayfield)

154 pp.; reprint 1993

10. *Morning Girl*   Michael Dorris

Columbus's arrival as seen through the eyes of Morning Girl, and her younger brother, Star Boy, both growing up in 1492 on a Bahamian island.

74 pp.; 1992

11. *Nobody's Family Is*   Louise Fitzhugh
Going to Change

Eleven-year-old Emma wants to become a lawyer; her seven-year-old brother wants to be a dancer. The message here is that children must take the initiative for their own lives since parents are often stuck in old ideas.   (Mia Pearlman)

221 pp.; 1974

12. *Mister God, This Is Anna*   Fynn

My informally adopted daughter, now a professional newspaper photographer, recommended this story of an extraordinary four-year-old waif in the East End of London, who is found and informally adopted by a kindhearted family. It ends unhappily when Anna dies from a fall at age eight. This tale is in the tradition of Antoine de Saint Exupéry's *The Little Prince* and Paul Gallico's *Snow Goose.*   (Gayle Shomer)

180 pp.; 1976

13. *Your Old Pal, Al*   Constance C. Greene

Al is a twelve-year-old girl whose father has just remarried. On top of that, her best friend has just invited sophisticated Polly to stay with her for two weeks. Also *A Girl Called Al; I Know You, Al;* and *Al(exandra) the Great.*

149 pp.; 1979

14. *Dustland*   Virginia Hamilton

Part of a trilogy: volume one is *Justice,* two is *Dustland,* and three is *The Gathering.* Four children, all possessing extraordinary mental powers, are projected far into the future to a bleak region called Dustland. *A Ring of Tricksters: Animal Tales from America, the West Indies, and Africa* should be in every child's library.

80 pp.; 1980

15. *Words of Stone*   Kevin Henkes

Two lonely children in rural Wisconsin become friends one summer. This is a book about kinship and betrayal by the author of *Chrysanthemum* and *The Zebra Wall.*

160 pp.; 1992

16. *Tintin in the New World*   Hergé

No child who likes to read and loves mysteries should grow up without Tintin; hold on to them because they will no doubt be collector's items. Most editions are also available in French. *Tintin's Moon Adventures*, *Land of Black Gold*, *Destination Moon*, *Tintin in Tibet*, *The Castafiore Emerald*, *Valley of the Cobras*, and many more. (Craig and Max Castleman)

62 pp.; 1975

17. *The Outsiders*   S. E. Hinton

Three brothers struggle to stay together after their parents' death. Great book about establishing identity among the conflicting values of adolescent society.

188 pp.; 1967

18. *Nancy Drew Files,*   Carolyn Keene
Case 82: Dangerous Relations

No list for kids can be complete without *Nancy Drew,* now more than fifty years in print. All of them have been updated and even the most reluctant reader will get hooked on these. And guess what? A single parent, a father (!) is raising her, and the family is not dysfunctional or on welfare.   (Abby Werlock, Ph.D.)

154 pp.; reprint 1993

19. *Eli's Songs*   Monte Killingsworth

A twelve-year-old boy from Los Angeles is sent to live with relatives in rural Oregon and takes solace in a nearby forest that is eventually threatened by loggers. Unbelievable as this may sound, the citizens of Molalla, Oregon, where Killingsworth lives, have tried to ban this book from the school library for what they see as "logger bashing," so great apparently is their love affair with tree stumps, ugliness, and the chain saw.

144 pp.; 1993

20. *A Separate Peace*   John Knowles
Two sixteen-year-olds, intellectual Gene and athletic Finny, attend a New England boarding school during World War II. A classic story of adolescence.

186 pp.; 1959

21. *A Wrinkle in Time*   Madeleine L'Engle
Won the Newbery Award thirty years ago and still going strong. The first in a quartet about the Murray family, this timeless story tells the adventures in space and time of Meg, Charles, and Calvin, as they search for Meg's father, a scientist who has disappeared. In *A Ring of Endless Light,* fifteen-year-old Vicky, whose grandfather is dying of leukemia, finds comfort with the pod of dolphins on whom she has been doing research.

211 pp.; 1962

22. *The Brave*   Robert Lipsyte
Seventeen-year-old Sonny Bear comes from the reservation of the Moscondaga Nation, but when he lands in New York City, Alfred Brooks, a cop and the hero of *The Contender*, is the one who protects him. In *The Chief*, the finale in this trilogy, it is Sonny Bear's Harlem sidekick, Martin Witherspoon, who saves the day.

208 pp.; 1991

23. *Anastasia Krupnik*   Lois Lowry
All of Lowry's award-winning books about this delightful young girl are highly recommended. Anastasia faces the issues of the day without drenching the reader in sorrow and helplessness, since she is surrounded by a loving if slightly eccentric family. Lowry's books about Anastasia's brother, Sam, are equally wonderful. Try *Anastasia Again!; Anastasia at Your Service; Anastasia, Ask Your Analyst; Anastasia on Her Own; Anastasia Has the Answers; Anastasia's Chosen Career;* and *All About Sam.*

113 pp.; 1979

24. *Sarah, Plain and Tall*   Patricia MacLachlan
Many kids know about Sarah from the TV production. The father of Caleb and Anna invites a mail-order bride from Maine to come live with them on the prairie. She turns out—in a twist on the usual story—to be the perfect stepmother. Also *Seven Kisses in a Row.*

58 pp.; 1987

25. *Shizuko's Daughter*   Kyoko Mori
Yuki, a twelve-year-old Japanese girl, finds a way to live with her gentle mother's suicide, her distant father, her antagonistic step-mother, and a traditional and repressive society. A bitterly painful coming-of-age story.

227 pp.; 1994

26. *Now Is Your Time*   William Dean Myers
Subtitled *The African-American Struggle for Freedom,* this choice for both the ALA 1991 Notable Children's Book and ALA 1992 Best Books for Young Adults focuses on nearly three centuries of African-American experience.

292 pp.; 1991

27. *Shiloh*   Phyllis Reynolds Naylor
Marty finds a lost beagle in the hills behind his West Virginia home. He tries to hide it from his family and the dog's mean-spir-ited owner who shoots deer out of season and mistreats animals.

144 pp.; 1991

28. *Lyddie*   Katherine Paterson
The Industrial Revolution in America, specifically the mills of Lowell, Massachusetts, in the mid-1840s, provide the setting for the endurance of Lydia Worthen. *Bridge to Terabithia* is about a ten-year-old boy in rural Virginia whose friend meets an untimely death. Also *Jacob Have I Loved.*

182 pp.; 1991

29. *Hatchet*   Gary Paulson

A plane crash causes thirteen-year-old Brian to spend fifty-four days in the wilderness, learning to survive initially with only the hatchet given to him by his mother. In *Dogsong*, a fourteen-year-old Eskimo boy takes a 1,400-mile journey by dog sled, seeking his own "song."

195 pp.; 1987

30. *Shabanu: Daughter*   Suzanne Fisher Staples
   of the Wind

Takes place in the Cholistani desert in Pakistan, where Shabanu finds out that she is not any freer than the camels. Followed by *Haveli.* (Katharine McFarland)

240 pp.; 1989

31. *The Weirdo*   Theodore Taylor

Samantha finally meets the Weirdo and together they search for the killer who stalks innocent victims in the swamp. Taylor wrote *The Cay*, the story of a white boy blinded by a blow to the head and an old black man from whom he acquires a new kind of vision.

224 pp.; 1991

32. *Dicey's Song*   Cynthia Voigt

Dicey Tillerman manages to reach her grandmother's rundown farm on Chesapeake Bay with her three younger siblings in tow. In *Homecoming,* the four of them, with eleven dollars to their names, walk to their aunt's house in Connecticut. *A Solitary Blue* is about the return of Jeff's mother, who deserted the family years ago, and the boy's relationship with his father.

196 pp.; 1982

33. *The Star Fisher*   Lawrence Yep

Yep won the Newbery for *Dragonwings*, a wonderful book about a Chinese-American boy and his father in San Francisco. Yep's own grandparents, mother, aunts, and uncles were the first Chinese family to settle in Clarksburg, Virginia. The star fisher bird, a magical creature who is half bird and half woman, is a symbol for the stress immigrants feel when their children turn into Americans.

150 pp.; 1991

34. *The Pigman & Me*   Paul Zindel

This recalls Zindel's teenage years on Staten Island when his life is enriched by finding his own personal pigman, or mentor. Also *The Pigman*.

178 pp.; 1992

On the Beach

Or even in the backyard hammock!

1. *Municipal Bondage*   Henry Alford

In this hilarious send-up of life in the postmodern Big Apple, Alford describes his stint as unpaid chauffeur to the governor of Colorado during the 1992 Democratic Convention, the invention of his "yummy" snack food, Nubbins, and his life as a high-ranked earlobe model. Think of it as a treat after you read *Anna Karenina*.

231 pp.; 1993

2. *Midnight in the Garden of Good and Evil*   John Berendt

Nonfiction account of a murder in Savannah's grandest mansion on the morning of May 2, 1981. This reads like fiction but you couldn't make this stuff up—as those of us from the South already know. And it holds the record for most weeks on the *New York Times* bestseller list.

388 pp.; 1994

3. *In the Slammer with Carol Smith*   Hortense Calisher

Carol Smith spends twenty years in jail for being an accessory, as an undergraduate, to a bomb plot in the 1970s. She ends up back in Manhattan—in a shabby room in Spanish Harlem—but all is not lost.

204 pp.; 1997

4. *Snagged*   Carol Higgins Clark

Her second Regan Reilly mystery, this one takes place in South Miami Beach where two conventions—one for panty hose manufacturers, one for representatives of the funeral industry—are meeting at the same hotel. Very funny book with a great title!

227 pp.; 1993

5. *Jurassic Park*   Michael Crichton

Gives all of us past the dinosaur stage of childhood a chance to indulge our continuing fascination with them and serves our more grown-up interest in genetics, DNA, and the rest.

399 pp.; 1990

6. *Pillars of the Earth*   Ken Follett

The twelfth century, feudal England, forests, walled towns, monasteries, and cathedrals. Enter Tom, the master builder; Aliena, the noblewoman; Jack the artist; and Ellen, the woman from the forest. And more. And no more letters about having left this book out the last time around. Mea culpa!

973 pp.; 1989

7. *The Pelican Brief*   John Grisham

A good read about a law student who looks into the murder of two Supreme Court justices. And I want to thank Grisham for using some of his megabucks to help other writers. Also *The Firm*, my favorite.

436 pp.; 1992

8. *Ruby*   Ann Hood

By the author of *Somewhere Off the Coast of Maine.* Oy, something else to worry about: the perfect husband gets killed while out jogging; a pregnant, unwed fifteen-year-old breaks into the beach house; etc. I loved it.

225 pp.; 1998

9. *A Prayer for Owen Meany*   John Irving

Mark Steven Johnson, who adapted a part of this novel for a movie, says, "It's kind of about a tiny boy who believes he's an instrument of God and accidentally kills someone he loves with a foul ball and then realizes everything happens for a reason." That's about it. And I know from the mail: a lot of people love this book!

543 pp.; 1989

10. *After All These Years*   Susan Isaacs

The now very rich Rosie Myers, dumped by husband Richie the morning after their twenty-fifth wedding anniversary, is busy stuffing her face in her mansion on Long Island. On the way to the kitchen she trips over a dead body. One guess as to whose it is?

343 pp.; 1993

11. *The Underground Man*   Mick Jackson

Finalist for the 1997 Whitbread Prize for Best First Novel, it is based on the life of the Fifth Duke of Portland—the famous Victorian whose obsessive passion for digging tunnels was only one of his many bizarre eccentricities.

262 pp.; 1997

12. *Le Divorce*   Diane Johnson

Johnson, a two-time finalist for both the Pulitzer Prize and the National Book Award, tells the story of Isabel, a film school dropout, who goes to Paris to help her very pregnant stepsister, Roxy, who has recently been deserted by her French husband. All this is complicated by a contretemps over a valuable painting now claimed both by the American Walker family and the French de Persands. *La situation; elle est complexe et animée.*

309 pp.; 1997

13. *Misery*   Stephen King

Sometimes those fans just turn ugly, and the writer Paul Sheldon is in big trouble when he runs into one of them: Annie Wilkes. For my money, this is King's best book.

310 pp.; 1987

14. *Living Other Lives*   Caroline Leavitt

A good study of human character, especially of three women, each from a different generation, and what happens when they lose the man they all love. Leavitt is a beautiful writer.

327 pp.; 1995

15. *How Stella Got Her Groove Back*   Terry McMillan

Stella Payne, a forty-two-year-old woman with a great body, a BMW, designer clothes, a loving son, good friends, and reasonably decent sisters, goes on vacation to Jamaica and acquires a sexy boyfriend who is half her age. Should I have listed this one under fairy tales?

368 pp.; 1996

16. *Salaryman*   **Meg Pei**

Jun Shimada is a "salaryman," a Japanese corporate climber with a self-effacing dedication to his company. When he gets to America, however, he falls off the ladder.

296 pp.; 1992

17. *Freedomland*   **Richard Price**

From the man who wrote *Clockers,* this novel has a carnapping/kidnapping, a racial firestorm, and a detective who grew up on the streets of New Jersey. Plenty of action.

546 pp.; 1998

18. *Belinda*   **Anne Rampling (Anne Rice)**

Great read about dolls, attics, and a not quite kosher love affair.

439 pp.; 1988

19. *I'll Take It*   **Paul Rudman**

Three elderly women and a young man—all shopaholics—take a trip through New England with the goal of robbing L.L. Bean.

292 pp.; 1989

20. *On Gold Mountain*   **Lisa See**

See, the daughter of the novelist Carolyn See and great-granddaughter of Fong See, writes about a shrewd immigrant who prospered in nineteenth-century California.

394 pp.; 1995

21. *Dreams Like Thunder*   **Diane Simmons**

Ten-year-old Alberta tells this 1959 story of life on a small eastern Oregon farm between Baker and Hells Canyon. An endearing, touching story.

189 pp.; 1992

22. *Cape Cod*   Henry David Thoreau

Listen, you're already lying on the sand, so why not start the summer with the original beach book?

148 pp.; 1951 (1st ed.)

23. *Presumed Innocent*   Scott Turow

Rusty Sabich, a chief deputy prosecutor, investigates the rape and murder of Carolyn Polhemus, his colleague and former lover. Suddenly he becomes the accused.

431 pp.; 1987

24. *Divine Secrets of the*   Rebecca Wells
Ya-Ya Sisterhood

This would be my candidate for the book found in most sandy hands on the beaches in the summer of '98. Marriage, motherhood, and aggravation in three generations of Southern women.

356 pp.; 1996

25. *Island Justice*   Elizabeth Winthrop

Winthrop's sensitivity to relationships emerges in her new book about a woman, her inherited Victorian seaside house, and the tight-knit island community in which she finds herself.

356 pp.; 1998

Author Index

Title Index

Note

Dear Reader:

Please let me know if I missed any of your favorite books!

1.

2.

3.

4.

5.

(your name)

(your address)

Send to:

Mickey Pearlman, Ph.D., author of *What to Read*

c/o HarperCollins Publishers

10 East 53rd Street

New York, New York 10022

or E-mail me at

drmlp@hotmail.com

If you E-mail, please include your snail-mail address.

Thanks.